MEMORIES
Of a Fighter Pilot

MEMORIES
Of a Fighter Pilot

By

Col Jay E. Riedel, USAF (Ret)

Dedication

This book is dedicated to all my friends and family who have encouraged me to jot down the many stories I have been telling throughout the years. I thank them very much for their support.

I would also like to dedicate this work to my parents, who supported me one hundred percent in every decision I made in my life, for without them, I would not be here. Thanks Mom & Dad.

Mom & Dad circa 1970

Walter Christian Riedel
23 Nov 1902 – 28 Oct 1973

Elsie Dahlstrom Riedel
4 May 1904 – 24 Nov 1996

The ultimate responsibility of the pilot is to fulfill the dreams of the countless millions of earthbound ancestors who could only stare skyward and dream.

Contents

Foreword

Fighter pilots are rare creatures in number and in makeup. There are more Doctors in New York City than fighter pilots in the United States Services on any given day. Given their behavior, most fighter pilots are thought to have a screw loose from time to time, and they do. Jay Riedel recalls his life and times because it is a story worth telling and a memory to be treasured by his family.

No fighter pilot is ordinary, but Jay's story is extraordinary. He flew three different aircraft in South East Asia over a span of nine years, first in KC-135s, then a full tour in F-100s, where fighter pilots who were smokers and thought they were going to die of cancer were considered optimists, before going back to the well once again in the A-7, a jet some thought too slow to survive in North Vietnam. He survived where many did not and excelled where most were unwilling to return for a second tour. You could conclude that he was either courageous or stupid to a fault, but you would be wrong on both counts. Jay is just enthusiastic, and he loves the challenge of flying and the sting of battle. He is simply a warrior. His service to our country was not without cost.

Living with a fighter pilot is not easy. As the saying goes, "Fighter pilots are full of confidence, often wrong, but never in doubt!" That alone makes them hard to live with. Then add in the demands of leaving home frequently for long periods of time and the already huge challenges of being married and a parent are magnified. Jay's private life was imperfect he will be the first to admit, but then the last perfect person was nailed to a cross a number of years ago.

i

Jay's life can be summed up as one well lived. It is a life of a man who embraces challenges, danger and uncertainty. It is a testament to courage and intensity. It is a life of service to his country and fellow man. Best of all, it is a life of one whom never looks back with regret and welcomes each new day with thanks to God.

Chuck Horner

General (Ret.), USAF

Gen. Charles A. Horner is an Iowa native, and entered the Air Force through the Reserve Officer Training Corps program from the University of Iowa.

He was awarded pilot wings in November 1959 from Laredo Air Force Base, Texas. During his Air Force career, he commanded a tactical training wing, a fighter wing, two air divisions and a numbered Air Force.

While commander of 9th Air Force, he also commanded U.S. Central Command Air Forces, and he was the architect of the air campaign against Iraq in Operation Desert Storm as the Joint Force Air Component Commander. He commanded U.S. and allied air operations for Operation Desert Shield and Desert Storm in Saudi Arabia from August 1990 until his return to Shaw AFB in April 1991. The lessons from the past of conflicting responsibilities and command and control were learned well, and the diverse coalition air forces were carefully directed into a single statement of air superiority. Gen. Horner had the responsibility of coordinating 2,000 - 3,000 sorties required per day with control of all aircraft in the theater except those of the Navy in sorties over water, Marines supporting their ground units and helicopters flying below 500 feet.

He is a command pilot with more than 5,300 flying hours in a variety of fighter aircraft. During the Vietnam War, he flew

41 combat missions over North Vietnam in the F-105 in his first tour. He later flew more than 70 combat missions as an F-105 Wild Weasel pilot, deliberately drawing anti-aircraft fire to identify and destroy North Vietnamese defenses.

In his last assignment, Gen. Horner commanded the North American Aerospace Defense Command and the U.S. Space Command; and Air Force Space Command, Peterson Air Force Base, Colorado.

He retired from active duty 30 September 1994. He has written a book with Tom Clancy, *Every Man A Tiger* (Putnam 1999).

His major awards and decorations include the Distinguished Service Medal with oak leaf cluster, Silver Star with oak leaf cluster, Legion of Merit, Distinguished Flying Cross, Meritorious Service Medal with three oak leaf clusters, Air Medal with 10 oak leaf clusters, Air Force Commendation Medal with three oak leaf clusters, Combat Readiness Medal, National Defense Service Medal with bronze star, Armed Forces Expeditionary Medal with bronze star, Vietnam Service Medal with bronze star, and the Republic of Vietnam Campaign Medal.

General Horner has also been decorated with Canada's Meritorious Service Cross, and he has been honored by France, Pakistan and the sovereign states of Bahrain, Kuwait, Saudi Arabia and the United Arab Emirates. He has received numerous other awards and is an honorary LifeTime Member of the 80th Fighter Squadron Headhunters' Association.

(Information and photo from multiple Internet sources)

Preface

*I*t gives me great pleasure to finally sit down today, 20 December 2001, and begin to jot down my memories over my 62-plus years. Unfortunately, almost all of my photos, records, diaries, maps, and other personal memorabilia have been lost. However, the few I have left have been included, as well as many others I have recently found in my parents' photo albums. I have also gleaned some photos from friends I was stationed with in the different squadrons. Other information came from the Internet, and detailed information from the 1972 period came from the Official USAF History of the 354th Tactical Fighter Wing.

This project will not win the Pulitzer Prize for literature, nor will it be a fast-moving bestseller action-drama with movie producers scrambling for first rights to a movie contract; however, I have had a few life-altering experiences that I would like to jot down for my children, grandchildren, and great-grandchildren. I hope someday they will enjoy reading this and seeing how it was "in the good old days" of Granpa Jay's life.

I also believe others who read this book will enjoy it and, hopefully, gain some useful information to use in their own lives.

Before we begin, I would like to thank Belinda D'Alessandro for her outstanding support and unselfish assistance to me while I was preparing this book for print. Her knowledge of book structure and the publishing process was an enormous help to me. It is greatly appreciated. Ms. D'Alessandro is the Director, BDA Books Pty Ltd and the Author of *Discovering Wounded Justice: Cruel Menace.* She can be reached at email: belinda@bdabooks.com.au or through her web site: www.bdabooks.com.au

Finally, this book is rated PG-13 for three or four medium cuss words—the warrior's vernacular. Let us begin.

My mother, Elsie Dahlstrom Riedel, told me I was born at five o'clock on the rainy Sunday afternoon of 19 November 1939 in Freeport, Long Island, New York. She worked in the hospital there as a registered nurse. My father, Walter Christian Riedel, was a tool and die maker. My only sibling is my brother, Paul, who is eight years my senior. Although born in Freeport, we lived in Bellmore just a few miles away.

The stage has been set. Raise the curtain!

Capt. Jay E. Riedel
F-100 *Super Sabre* pilot
510th Tactical Fighter Squadron
Bien Hoa Air Base, South Vietnam
13 October 1969

Chapter 1
My Earliest Memories

My earliest childhood memory is hanging upside down from our second floor balcony in our home in Bellmore, Long Island, New York, when I was three years old. I had dropped a toy over the side, and had looked through the wooden railing to see where it had gone. Dad was working, Mom was outside for a minute, and my older brother Paul was in school. As I looked through the railing, I must have lost my balance and fell. However, somehow my foot and ankle became wedged between two of the spindles suspending me upside down by one foot. I distinctly remember not being afraid, because I knew, as any three-year old knows, that I was perfectly safe, and my foot felt perfectly secure. I also remember feeling that this was pretty neat—being upside down so high up!

I also remember that I could not do much about my predicament, so I resorted to doing what every other three-year old does in a similar situation—call to Mom. Again, I distinctly remember calling to her in a calm voice so as not to scare her, but when she came in and saw me hanging above her by one foot, my calmness didn't matter—she almost had a heart attack! As she started running up the stairs to get to me, I tried to reassure her in my proficient eloquent three-year old speech that I was perfectly safe, and my foot was securely jammed—with no possibility of falling. It didn't work. She kept running up the stars to me— "Don't move, DON'T MOVE!" As she pulled me back up to safety, I did notice my foot came dislodged fairly easily.

1

I also found out fifty-five years later as Mom and I talked about that episode so long ago, that I was not only hanging upside down from the second floor, but I was directly over the furnace steel floor grating in the living room—a not-so-good landing area! Shortly thereafter, Mom, Dad, Paul, and I moved from Bellmore to a 128-acre farm outside Montrose, Pennsylvania. This took place in the summer of 1943, and we were at war, so I was told—whatever that was.

My only brother Paul was eleven at the time and very interested in flying and airplanes. I remember he had a pack of playing cards that were aircraft identification spotter cards as well. The four card suits had aircraft from the U.S., Japan, Germany, and England. I can remember studying them when Paul was in school. By the time I was four, I had most of them memorized—all the major aircraft of World War II. As a side note, Bonnie's youngest daughter, Donna, gave me an exact replica of this deck as a gift in 1997. On the outside of the pack, it says, *"Airplane Spotter Playing Cards WWII, Facsimile of a deck first issued in 1943"*—what memories it brings back! Thank you, Donna!

Our Farm was a fun place for young boys. The large two-story farmhouse was on a dirt road with the nearest neighbor almost a mile away. It had no indoor plumbing. An outhouse in the rear and a pump on a well out front was our plumbing. I was now four, and Paul was twelve. He had a horse named Gypsy, and we also had chickens, a large garden and apple orchard. I can remember Mom giving me a basket and letting me go gather eggs from the chicken coop—great fun! I was also allowed to take feed out and throw it on the ground for the chickens. They would all come running as soon as they saw me, and would surround me as they frantically waited for my little hands to scatter the feed. It made me feel good that little me was doing something helpful for those chickens.

We also had our family dog, a German Shepherd named Cappy. He was a great friend and pet to all of us. He would go with me every time I'd run away from home—all the way to the end of our 100-yard long driveway, before returning from my adventure because I was hungry. I can't remember to this day why I would run away, as our family life was great. It must have been for the adventure and thrill of being on my own. Paul and I also had the

At the Farm in winter of 1943 with Cappy—almost to the end of our long driveway that connected to a dirt road.

freedom to go wherever we wanted on our 128 acres—as long as we had Cappy with us. We had a great time.

Paul went to school at a small one-room schoolhouse about two miles on dirt roads from our farm. In good weather he would walk about half a mile to a bus. When it snowed heavily, the bus didn't come, so he usually stayed home.

At one time during the year we were at the farm, his school had a party, and the students could bring their brothers and sisters. Wow—I was going to school with my big brother! I don't remember exactly what kind of party it was, but it must have been a Christmas Party, as we walked to school in the snow. We left plenty early so we could play along the way—more fun!

In my old "Army" days at the farm with my constant companion, Cappy.

Probably the most traumatic episode of my young life had to do with my brother's bow and arrows and his Army pup tent. Paul had his tent set up on the front lawn, and I came up with a really neat idea to use it to play cowboys and Indians. I got his bow and arrows, my Indian headdress, and, in the best fashion I had ever watched from numerous cowboy movies, galloped around the pup tent with my best Indian war-whoops while shooting all dozen arrows into the circled covered wagons—the pup tent! The Indians had won! Unfortunately, when Paul got home from school and saw his twelve arrows sticking out of his tent like a porcupine, he immediately assumed it was I who was responsible. Not only was he quite disturbed, but he told me he was going to tell Dad when he got home from work.

Reality began to set in—I realized I was in deep trouble—but thought if I explained my actions to Dad, all would be forgiven. Sure enough, as soon as Dad got home, Paul told him what I had done—and took him outside to view the carnage first-hand. Dad called me over, knelt down to my level, and asked me why had I done this. I told him I didn't mean to ruin the tent and didn't do it on purpose—I was just playing cowboys and Indians. I was sorry. Dad explained to me that the tent, bow, and arrows were Paul's, and I shouldn't have been playing with them in the

4

first place. In the mind of a four-year old, I didn't fully comprehend this *"I can't play with your toys"* idea, but I said I was sorry again. That was the end of it.

The next day, Paul was at school again, and the tent was still there. I remember it was a very bright sunny day, and there were a couple of large horseflies buzzing around the tent and landing on it every once in a while. Again, in the mind of a four-year old, this made me quite angry! *"If I can't play with the tent, these darned flies*

The cowboy and his trusted friend

aren't going to, either!" I recall thinking to myself. I marched around to the woodshed, picked up Dad's sickle, and stomped back to the tent. Sure enough, there in plain sight and thumbing his nose at me was a big horsefly resting in the sun on the side of the tent! I will make Paul proud of me—I'll protect his tent from that pesky fly! With one mighty swing of my trusty sickle, and again in the best fashion I had ever seen in a Three Musketeers sword fight, I brought the curved blade down with all my might... *Rrriiipppp!* Uh-oh—a twelve-inch gash in the side of the tent. Right off, I knew I had messed up again. No one will ever believe what I was trying to do. But Mom will!

I ran to Mom and told her what had happened. She wasn't too responsive to the events of the day, and told me that Dad would take care of it when he got home from work. Oh no! I waited for Paul to come home from school and told him the story. He wasn't impressed, either—"Wait 'till Dad gets home!" he said.

I knew now I was in very bad trouble—the worst in my entire four years of life. I went back to Mom and asked her when Dad would be home. She said 5:30. I asked her what time it was (I hadn't mastered telling time perfectly, and wanted to get a professional time-teller's answer.) She said it was 4:00. Now what? The only way out of my predicament was to run away from home.

I gathered my teddy bear, and off Cappy and I went to the far end of our driveway. But now what? There's no place else to

Paul & me, a bushel of our apples, and Dad's 1932 Franklin

go, and no place to hide—no trees or shrubs in the area. I sat down and tried to come up with a plan. I was one scared four-year old. But wait a minute—there are plenty of neat places to hide in the house! I came slowly back to the house, and asked Mom again what time it was—4:45. I roamed around the house looking for the best hiding place I could find. Finally I decided to hide behind a large stuffed easy chair that was cater-cornered in the far left corner of the den—without a light nearby and with plenty of room. I tried it to make sure it would work, then got back out and waited with Mom for Dad to come home.

Sure enough, at about 5:30, Dad turned into the driveway in his 1932 four-door Franklin and started up to the house. That was my cue to make for the hiding place without being seen. I huddled behind the large chair in the dim light and waited. I

6

heard Dad come in, and I heard Paul telling him what I had done to his tent. They started calling me. I started to cry. Mom, Dad, and Paul were looking everywhere. I heard someone come into the den, but then leave again. I tried to be as quiet as possible, but my sobbing wouldn't quit. About ten minutes later, Paul came in calling my name. I called quietly to him and told him where I was. "DAD, HERE HE IS!" he yelled. I had been betrayed.

Mom and Dad came into the den as I was crawling out from behind the chair. I was sobbing uncontrollably. I was petrified. Once more Dad knelt down on one knee to my level and asked me what happened. Through a flood of tears, I stood there in front of him "on the carpet," and explained what happened and why I did it. He told me to tell Paul I was sorry for ruining his tent. I quickly did. He then told me, while shaking his finger at me, that I was never to play with Paul's tent or bow and arrows again. I quickly agreed. Then came the best part—they all gave each other and me a big hug, and we all went to eat dinner. I was glad it was over. However, I wasn't very hungry.

In hindsight, that was the closest I ever came in my life to getting spanked, slapped, or hit. There is a lot to be said about listening to your children and not overreacting to an event that, most probably, you both are now aware of and sorry it happened. In the minds of children, some behavior, which is obviously wrong and dangerous to adults, is often times quite logical to young children. It's our job as adults to explain why the behavior is wrong and why they shouldn't do it again. My parents were perfectionists at this, for which I'm eternally grateful.

Other vivid memories I have of these short times at our farm are both happy and shocking. The happy ones are sitting on the front porch helping Dad and Paul husk fresh corn from our large garden after we harvested the big, beautiful ears from corn stalks that, to me as a four-year-old, looked ten feet tall. When we had them all cleaned, we took them in to Mom, who had boiling water on the wood stove ready for them. I remember those Golden Bantam ears of corn as the best I've ever had in my life—from garden to dinner table in fifteen minutes.

Another happy memory I have is of Mom painstakingly picking wild blackberries from many great blackberry patches we had on our property, and of Gypsy, our horse, nonchalantly

walking up quietly behind her and eating them from Mom's pail as she was busy reaching way over the thorny bushes to get more! What could she do? The fat, juicy berries had already been munched on and were beyond saving, so Mom just stood there, holding the pail full of plump berries, which represented about two hours of picking, waiting for Gypsy to finish her mid-afternoon snack! What a picture in my mind! Mom was very quiet the rest of the day.

Paul (rear) with friend Richard Lutine on Gypsy as I look on in August 1944. Gypsy loved handpicked blackberries!

Remember Paul's bow and arrows? Well, Paul and I were out playing in our front yard one day with them, and, as always, Cappy was out playing with us. Paul decided to see how far he could shoot an arrow straight up in the air. He practiced a few times to make sure he knew how to get it straight up. With these preliminaries complete, he leaned back to the required angle, pulled the arrow back as far as possible, and shot. The arrow took off like a bullet—straight up almost out of sight. Just as we were about to lose sight of it, it turned back over and headed down, picking up speed as it came.

As we watched with delight the fruit of our experiment, horror gripped us as we noticed for the first time Cappy, who also was watching the arrow, running around barking at it to get it to come back! Well, it did just that—as Cappy was running to "fetch" it, the arrow, now at near terminal velocity of almost 70 miles per hour, hit and stuck in the ground mere inches in front of Cappy's nose! I can still see and hear the picture of the arrow striking the ground, the twang it made as it quivered in front of Cappy's nose, and the very surprised, simultaneous yelp and flinch from Cappy as he almost ran into it! Paul and I were terrified, as we had, within inches and a fraction of a second, almost pinned Cappy to the ground. That was the end of the bow and arrows for that day, and my last recollection of them forever.

One of my not-so-happy memories is swinging on a swing that Dad had made for us, and falling out of it and landing on an old rusty tin can cover. It cut my right knee quite badly, and I ran crying inside to Mom. Mom was a nurse, and it was a good thing. Not only did she take care of this until Dad came home from work, and had to cut a big flap of skin from the wound, but it would really pay off later. I still have that large scar today.

Paul giving Cappy a bath while I'm on the infamous swing.

One beautiful fall day, Paul, Cappy, and I were out playing in our apple orchard when Paul decided to get an apple for each of us. Of course, the best apples are still on the tree—not half-rotten on the ground. The trees were not easy to climb, so the next best way of getting them would be to throw something at them to knock them down. The only object around was a large rock. Paul threw the rock up many times aiming at those large, juicy apples, but they were hard and elusive targets. He decided he must be as close as possible to minimize errors—directly underneath. With a mighty throw, Paul fired his rock up, and sure enough, it hit a limb, which jarred a few apples loose. As we watched the apples fall, we forgot about the rock. It hit him in the head above the left eye, knocking him down and stunning him. As with all head wounds, blood was everywhere. Paul was quite dazed, but I was scared to death. He couldn't get up. He told me, "Jay, go get Mom!"

I took off like a jackrabbit running back to the house, which was almost a quarter-mile away. Cappy stayed with Paul and lay down next to him. When I got to the house, I told Mom what had happened. She grabbed some cold, wet towels, and we both ran back to where Paul was laying in the orchard. By this time, he had managed to get up, and he was walking slowly back towards the house with Cappy by his side. Mom inspected the damage, and said she could see the skull at the bottom of the gash. She put the washcloth on the wound, and we both helped Paul back to the house.

Again Mom's training as a nurse was crucial to caring for Paul's injury, but this episode was probably the main cause of Mom's decision to move from this place back to a city. Without a telephone, car,

Paul and me with our best friend, Cappy. We never had to lock our doors at night, and we weren't worried about getting kidnapped.

and not having the dirt road plowed in the winter, her fear of being alone and stranded during a crisis like this was too much. She let Dad know this as soon as he came home from work five hours later.

Probably the most influential occurrence in these early days of mine was the fact that Paul loved airplanes and enjoyed building very light rubber band-powered models from balsa wood covered with tissue paper, which was shrunk tight by sprinkling the very light paper with water spray. He would wind up the rubber band "engine" by holding the plane in his left hand and winding the propeller clockwise with his right index finger. When the rubber band was wound up as far as it was supposed to go, he would launch it from one of our second-story windows out over our front yard. What an incredible sight (and fun!) to see this beautiful model glide flawlessly out over our yard—propeller spinning and completely free! It was at this time in my life—only four years old—that I decided this was what I wanted to do in my life. Fly! I also remember we used to set his old, worn-out models on fire before we launched them and watched them crash.

Our farm in the summer of 1944. Our large garden is at the extreme left in the photo. Paul & I would fly his model airplanes from the upstairs windows out over the front lawn.

I remember noting this was not something I wanted to do. However, I was not swayed from my decision—I was going to be a fighter pilot when I grew up! This decision never left me, and my life's planning was based on that end.

We all loved our farm, but the reality of the situation of Mom, Paul, and I being stranded all day there while Dad was in town working dictated that we needed to move into the city. Dad was a tool and die maker, and he worked in Binghamton, New York. We left the farm and moved to 40 Water Street in the summer of 1944. I would be five that November, so it was time for me to start school—kindergarten.

Chapter 2
The Early School Years

*T*he four years we lived in Binghamton (1944-1948) were spent in an upstairs apartment at 40 Water Street over an older Italian couple—the Martones. He was an alcoholic, and his wife was not the cutest, nor the most soft-spoken individual you have ever met. With the four of us, along with Cappy, above them, there was constant friction between the two families. Paul and I would play on the linoleum-covered floor with Cappy joining in on the fun. Quite often, "Martone," as we knew him, would bang on his ceiling with a broom handle and yell up to us to quiet down. We would for a few minutes, until our youthful exuberance of a five- and thirteen-year old would again overtake us.

On one occasion, we noticed a small house mouse in our kitchen. Before Dad set the mousetrap to catch this little intruder, we came up with the idea that maybe Cappy could catch him for us. I can remember sitting in the kitchen with Dad, who was holding Cappy waiting for the mouse to reappear from under the stove. Sure enough—a few minutes later, out comes the little rodent completely oblivious to the fate that awaited him! Cappy's ears perked up as he saw his adversary, and Dad simultaneously released him as he said, "SIC 'EM!"

Well, none of us could imagine the uproar that followed—the mouse's eyes got as big as saucers as he watched this huge ninety-pound German Shepherd try to get up to full attack speed on the linoleum floor! The mouse panicked, and instead of running back to safety under the stove or refrigerator, took off for the living room—directly back through Cappy's legs and past us. By this time, Cappy was just under Mach 1, heading directly to where the mouse just was. To stay in hot pursuit required a 180-degree turn back toward the living room! With considerable back-pedaling and feverish scrambling on the very slick floor, Cappy managed to get turned around, but not before upsetting the kitchen table and three chairs. Dad tried to catch him and quiet him down, but Cappy was on a mission—he was told to get that mouse, and nothing was going to stop him from his assignment.

After a few minutes more of this commotion, Cappy emerged from behind a living room chair with his mouse—and a very proud look on his face! The apartment was a shambles! I remember Martone's banging on the ceiling this time was the loudest and longest—it set a new record. What fun we had, but then it was time to put the furniture back in its proper place.

The only other memory I have of the Martones is hearing him, in one of his drunken stupors, tell his wife to leave him alone, and that he wanted to sleep until Christmas. She yelled back at him loud enough for the entire city block to hear, "Get uppa NOW, you bum—Christmas-a three days ago!"

Another great memory I have of this time was listening to Dad's 78-rpm records. Many were classical, which I loved, but the ones I remember most were the famous marches of John Philip Sousa, who wrote the most famous American military marches of all time, including "Stars and Stripes Forever," earning him the nickname "the March King." Dad would pick me up and put me on his feet, facing forward, left on left and right on right, and as he held on to my hands over my head, off we'd go marching around the room to this unforgettable patriotic music. I'm sure this was the beginning of my deep patriotism and reinforced my desire to fly. Whenever I hear those marches today, I recall those trips around the living room on Dad's feet in perfect cadence to the music. What could be a better memory?

I started kindergarten in September 1944. Mom used to walk me to school, as Dad had the car, and she couldn't drive. There were no school buses, either, in the city. The school was probably a mile away, and we would look in the store windows both going and returning home. In one window, there was something I just had to have—a realistic-looking bright red metal cash register approximately ten inches cube. I thought this would really be neat to have for selling lemonade on the sidewalk in front of our house—a place to keep all my money, just like a real store. I don't remember the price, as most five-year olds, but Mom told me it was too expensive. Oh well, I could look at it every day, anyway. That Christmas the one main gift I received was the bright red cash register—I was so happy!

We were still in World War II at this time, and I remember having an ongoing assignment in kindergarten to gather milkweed pods. We picked them in the empty fields around town and brought them to school. They were packaged up and sent to the government, where they were used for flotation material. That was my contribution to the War effort, but it did make me feel I was doing something important.

My kindergarten teacher's name was Miss Donnelly. She was very pretty, and it came to pass that she was my first true love—I had a crush on her. I think she knew it, because she always let me stay after school to help her clean blackboards and take out the trash.

School grades one through three in Binghamton are a complete blank. I have no memories of those school years from 1945–1948. It was routine schoolwork with no significant events to remember.

However, I have great memories of the weekends. There was a large hardware store around the corner from our apartment. I liked to go over there and look around at all the interesting things that any store of this kind had to offer. There were large barrels of different size dog biscuits lined up along a counter. I thought the largest ones tasted the best! During my many trips there, I became friends with one of the workers—a guy named Joe who was about forty, as I remember. Joe not only worked in the store, but he was also their deliveryman. He asked if I wanted to go with him in the truck while he made deliveries. Wow—what fun that would be! He told me to go home and ask my parents.

I ran home and asked Mom and Dad if I could do that. Dad walked me back to the store so he could meet Joe. He must have made a good impression, because it was approved. From then on, I'd ride around with Joe on weekends "helping" him make deliveries. He'd pay me a quarter a day for helping him— my first job! What a great time and friendship we had. He even took me to his house to meet his wife and have lunch a few times. This went on for three years until Dad got a new job, and we moved away from Binghamton to North Lansing, New York.

In retrospect, this would be unheard of today. I was only five to seven years old during this time, but in those days, it was completely natural and innocent. It's sad, but how our environment has changed since then.

When I wasn't "working" with Joe making deliveries, I went by myself to Saturday matinees for twenty-five cents. This was great, because I'd stay sometimes to watch the movie at least twice. Tarzan and cowboy movies were about all I wanted to see—once in a while a great war movie—with flying! Again, looking back at these times of a seven-year old walking through a city to a movie about a mile away and back three or four hours later by himself is also unheard of today.

During this early time when I was six, I had a large tricycle. I had it for quite a while and had pretty well mastered it. I had also mastered the act of tipping it up on the front and one rear wheel and riding around the entire city block that I lived on. I found it quite easy and received many curious stares from pedestrians watching me as I zipped past them on two wheels. Unfortunately, the stress on the rear wheel was too much, and it eventually broke off. I was ready for a two-wheeler.

Tricycle that I could ride around a block on two wheels! Six years old.

I have other great memories of Binghamton—being allowed to go out with Paul on Halloween was one of them. Paul, and his best friend, Paul Moshure, loved to go out trick or treating on Halloween. What a thrill it was for me to go with them on their rounds! I hardly remember getting candy, but I vividly remember watching my big brother and his friend sneak up on the porches of large homes in well-to-do sections of town to tie black thread to the doorknockers. We would then tiptoe back to behind some shrubs in the front yards where we would pull on the thread three times to make the *clack-clack-clack* of the knocker. We would then wait while peeking through the shrubs to see the porch light come on, and the homeowner open the door and look around to see who was knocking. Seeing no one, he would close the door and turn off the porch light. A minute or two later we would repeat the procedure—*clack-clack-clack!* On came the porch light, out came the person, and after an obvious increased level of frustration, would slam the door and switch off the light. What fun!

However, after about four or five of these cycles, things changed. The light would come on; the guy would come out and immediately start feeling around for the nearly invisible black thread. As soon as he found it, he'd start following it off the porch and towards the shrubs to its clandestine source. That was the signal for the three of us to "get out of Dodge!"

We would spend a few minutes savoring the last event before moving on to another house on the next block. On the way, we would pass city bus stops. These were equally good targets. If no one were there, we would take more of the black thread and weave it back and forth over the sidewalk and around the bus stop sign like a giant spider web. What great fun it was to watch a young couple with their arms around each other walk into it while approaching the bus stop. The flailing arms and hands, along with screams from the young girl as they were convinced they had strayed into the world's largest spider web, made our night complete!

On another occasion, I remember riding on the crossbars of Paul's bike and getting my shoe caught in the front spokes. This was about five minutes after Paul briefed me to be careful and not let my shoe get caught in the spokes. It tore the heel off my left shoe and bent a couple of spokes. I had to walk after that.

While Paul and I were playing one day in a park, we decided to have a sword fight—just like in the movies! Of course, we didn't have swords, but the next best thing would be to make a couple out of sticks we found nearby. Sure enough, they worked great! *Click, clack—click-clack* as we dueled it out like the best of pirates. Just when I thought I had him, Paul gave a thrust and got me—right in the left side of my face below the mouth. I don't remember crying, but as a six-year old who was just defeated in combat and bleeding from a face wound, I probably did. We decided to head home. Paul and I never thought of the seriousness of the mishap, but Mom and Dad sure did when they found out what had happened. Their reasoning was that I, being only six, didn't know any better, but Paul, being fourteen, *did* know better—that he could have poked me in the eye. I don't remember his punishment, but I do remember he really got a talking-to. I still proudly wear my first combat scar!

Paul and I used to walk to Sunday school, which was about a mile away, I would guess. The route took us right past Paul's high school, and I remember thinking what a great place this must be. Someday I, too, would be in high school.

Last, but not least, the only other memory I have of this period was going on vacation by car with Mom and Dad. While on one of these vacations, we saw a small airport that advertised airplane rides for $5. Dad asked me if I wanted to go. Did I! *YES!* Dad and I went up with the pilot and flew around the area for about five minutes. That was my first airplane ride, and I loved it. My goal in life had just been reinforced. I still have that ticket today. What a keepsake.

In the summer of 1948, we left Binghamton and moved to North Lansing, New York, which is about twenty miles northeast of Ithaca. Dad had found a new job at Therm in Ithaca, so he no longer had to commute the sixty miles back and forth from Binghamton.

North Lansing was a very small crossroads of two two-lane highways. It had a gas station on one corner owned and op-erated by the parents of a boy who I played with. On another cor-ner was a small store—the only thing I remember about it was getting sodas from a machine there for five cents. Our little three-bedroom house that we rented was across the two-lane highway from the gas station, and on the other corner, across from the store, was a farm. All of this was at the top of a shallow hill from where the highway sloped down about a half-mile to the south before rising back up again for another half-mile. At the bottom

19

of this grade was a small one-room schoolhouse, with a pot-bellied wood stove, where I went to fourth grade.

Not only did this little schoolhouse have my grade, but it also had grades one, two, and three. There were only four of us in fourth grade—Howard Keller, twins Jean and Joan Katola, and me. We were the big kids—the "senior class." Therefore, the one teacher for all fifteen kids, Mrs. Croft, called upon us regularly to help with the younger kids. This was actually a lot of fun and a great way for us to learn. I loved the twins—especially Joan—and when the four of us would get together at their house (a farm across the highway from the school) to study multiplication tables, I was very happy, as it was an excuse to be with them.

Mrs. Croft and her Grades 1-4 of the one-room schoolhouse in North Lansing, NY taken in April 1949. Howard Keller (standing third from right), twins Jean & Joan Katola (Jean second from right, Joan on end standing), and I (back row with tie) were the "senior" forth grade. How did Howard get to stand next to the Twins? I loved them both!

Now that I was eight (and only two months away from being nine), my Schwinn bike served as my transportation to and from school. Cowboy movies were very popular during this time. Roy Rogers, Gene Autry, Hopalong Cassidy, and many others were our heroes. It was quite something to see them do tricks of jumping off and back on their horses at full gallop—wouldn't that be fun to do! Well, at this time, none of us had horses, but we did have our bikes. I suggested we all try this as we got up a full head of steam heading down the hill from our house toward the school. Since it was my idea, they let me go first…

After going as fast as I could down the hill, I stood up on my left pedal as I swung my right leg over to touch down and have it bounce back up and over to the starting position. In theory, it really is a neat idea; however, in reality it didn't work. At about thirty miles per hour, the bike became quite unstable while I tried to jump off and back on. The end result didn't look or feel anything like the movies. I ended up in a bloody pile with the bike in the middle of the very hard blacktop highway. The others decided not to try. That was the end of our cowboy adventures and horse tricks.

The most pleasant memory I have of North Lansing is

starting to collect stamps when I was eight. Dad got me interested in this great hobby, and we had a great time together with this. Every Saturday, Mom, Dad, Paul, and I would go to Ithaca, and while

Working on my stamp collection on my tenth birthday, 19 November 1949.

21

Mom was at the grocery store, Dad and I would go to see Paul Patten at Patten's Jewelers to buy, sell, or trade for new stamps. What a great hobby it was—many, many happy hours, months, and years that I had actively collecting until I graduated from college twelve years later.

My brother Paul taught me how to shoot and how to handle firearms safely. Being seventeen at the time, he had a beautiful .22 rifle with a 6-power scope. We would go out back and shoot at tin cans, or would drive around a few miles in all directions to help farmers rid their fields of pesky groundhogs— woodchucks we called them. What great sport, and Paul would even let me shoot once in a while.

That Christmas of 1948 after just turning nine, I got a BB gun, and loved to shoot at everything. One winter day soon after I got it, I shot at a little sparrow sitting in a tree about thirty feet away. I hit him and he fell to the snow-covered ground. I was so happy and proud of a great shot, and I ran over to where it fell. It was bleeding on the clean white snow, and to my surprise, it was still barely alive. It looked up at me with a very penetrating, *"What did I ever do to you to deserve this?"* look before it died. I cried. This had a very profound impact on me, and it has haunted me ever since. Although I still love to shoot at targets, I do *very* little hunting to this day—only if something is making trouble for others. This is most probably the beginning of my love for wildlife.

Paul & me on the way out to do some shooting with his .22 rifle

22

Of course, my love for animals began long before this, as we had our great German Shepherd, Cappy, before I was born. As long as I could remember, Cappy was there with me either inside or outdoors. But by this time, he was fourteen years old, and had gotten to the point that he couldn't walk anymore and was in constant pain. We had taken him to different vets, but there was nothing they could do for him. He had to be put down. We decided that we would do it ourselves. Dad bought some ether from the drugstore in Ithaca, and as I petted and consoled Cappy as he lay on the floor, Dad held a washcloth soaked with ether over his nose. Dad's fourteen-year and my life-long companion peacefully closed his eyes, and, after a few minutes, with a final sigh, passed from this world—hopefully to a better one. It was very hard on all of us, especially Dad and me. Cappy was truly one of our family.

Shortly after losing Cappy, I had an all-black cat named Blackjack. I got him as a kitten, and we were inseparable. Cats usually do what they want and when they want, but Blackjack was different. He acted almost like a dog. He would run over to me when I came home from school, and follow me around when I was playing outside. One day I was outside playing, and Black-jack, as usual, was following me around. For some reason I was on the other side of the road and decided to go back across to our house. I always looked before I crossed the two-lane, 50 mph highway, and seeing that I had plenty of time before an oncoming car got too close, I ran over to the other side.

However, I had forgotten about Blackjack. I turned around and saw him still on the other side looking at me. He hesitated, as he had seen the car coming as I had, but now that I had run and crossed, he decided to run across, too. Unfortunately, as I watched, the car hit him, but I thought he was okay, because he ran up the bank to me and lay down in my lap. It was then I noticed he had trouble breathing, and had blood coming out of his mouth. The car had crushed him. As I held him, he died about a minute later. Losing Cappy and now Blackjack made for a very sad period in my young life.

In our second and last year in North Lansing (1949), I went to fifth grade at Lansing Central School in Lansing—about ten miles from our house. That was the first time I rode a school bus, but not the last. I rode a school bus through my school years from fifth through eleventh grade. I enjoyed it, and it was a great way to relax before and after school.

While in the fifth grade I was a pitcher for the school baseball team, but I threw too hard and messed up my right shoulder. It's still not right to this day, and I can't throw well. The shoulder even looks different from my left.

Dad made some blocks for me out of Lucite for Christmas, 1949. He even made a bright red box to keep them in, which was about 20 inches long, 15 inches wide, and about 10 inches deep. When you removed the top of the box, there was a smoked glass top on which you would build. The front panel of the box could also be unhooked and removed to show two drawers that stored the blocks plus another top draw. The blocks were smoked Lucite, and all were near perfectly made—when you put some together, they fit so perfectly that they would stick together—no air could get between them. After you built something, like a church, the best

Unfortunately, a poor photo of my Lucite blocks — but the only one I have.

was yet to come! You could pull out that top draw to find small colored lights in small, metal open-topped boxes that you could move around on a pegboard under your church. When you turned them on and slid the draw back in, the colored lights shined up through the smoked glass box top and up into the Lucite church—absolutely beautiful at night—and a unique gift to me from Dad.

Another great memory of this period was riding on top of the neighbor's large tractor-towed farm wagon piled high with fresh harvested peas from their field. The entire pea plant is pulled up and put on the wagon. When it was full, a few of us kids would climb up, twelve to fifteen feet high, and ride to the next town about four miles away, where there was a large, belt-driven threshing machine for peas. On the way, we would gorge ourselves on all the fresh peas we could eat—delicious!

The last memory I have of North Lansing was playing hide-and-seek at night across the street at the gas station with most of the kids in the area. We all got along with each other quite well, and we all had a great time.

After two years of this long drive back and forth to work for Dad, all the way into town for shopping, and with Paul now in college at Cornell, we decided to move closer to where we all needed to be. In the summer of 1950, we moved to 104 Compton Road, about three miles south of Ithaca, New York. This would be my home for the next seven years from sixth grade until I graduated from high school and went off to college in 1957. I call this my home in my hometown.

Paul also went to graduate school in Wisconsin and left in 1952 after graduating from Cornell. Mom and Dad stayed there until Dad retired in 1972. It was a small two-bedroom house with about four acres, but Dad added on a one-car garage, which was connected to the house with an enclosed breezeway. The breezeway was a small entrance room for the new front door, and it was the home of a new large chest freezer. Dad also transformed an old entrance/woodshed area into a beautiful modern kitchen—including a large new picture window over the sink. This new kitchen was at the other end of the new breezeway.

Dad made a very small bedroom for Paul out of one end of the attic under the peaked roof. A steep, narrow wooden staircase, almost the same width as a wooden ladder, led up to it through a thin trapdoor from the back of the kitchen. As you went up the stairs and pushed open the quarter-inch thick trap door, you were facing the only small window of the small eight-by-six-foot room over a long six-foot tabletop desk, which ran from the left side to the right side of the room.

Ithaca home Christmas 1959 with snow melting off roof. Long window is over counter & sink in new kitchen. New front door in "freezer room" that was added on connects to new garage. Large apple tree can be seen in backyard directly behind kitchen window. Small bedroom of Paul's, then mine, under eaves above right of window.

On the left side of the room was a single cot bed, and hanging on the right wall was Paul's twin gun rack, which held his .22 rifle and an old single-shot 12-gage shotgun. Back around to the left was a small two-by-two foot, four-foot high closet (under the eaves) at the foot of the bed, and past the closet was the door under the peak into the rest of the attic. Although we couldn't stand up straight in the room and it wasn't big, it was perfect for studying. I couldn't wait to get it for my room when Paul left for graduate school. The trapdoor could be held open with a hook on the wall behind it, or it could be lowered again for privacy and quiet while sleeping and/or studying. It was a lot of work, and I helped Dad a little with it.

I remember our first Christmas there. Money was tight, but all I wanted was an HO-gauge train. Mom and Dad had hinted around that this was a pretty tall order, and not to get my hopes up with this. When it came time to open presents, I received one small box—an HO boxcar kit! I believe at that time, all you could get were kits to build—no fully ready trains as you can buy today. I was so happy!

A few minutes later they gave me another small box—a tank car kit! And then a caboose. Then some track, which also had to be put together. But Dad said it wasn't much of a train set—no engine! They handed me the final small box—an engine kit! Wow—my best Christmas! Dad and I had so much fun building those different, highly detailed train kits together. They really came out beautifully, and we built a great little train setup on a four-by-eight foot sheet of plywood. I had hours and hours of fun with that set.

My first year in Ithaca was in sixth grade at an elementary school downtown just about at the bottom of South Hill. No special memories here, except there was a candy store on a corner only a block away. Whenever we could, we would all run over there and buy some candy. My favorite? Little candy dots on a continuous strip of paper about two inches wide. The store clerk would tear off a penny's worth, which was about a foot, or as much as we wanted—fun!

I've been in numerous car accidents. The first one I remember was in 1950 when I was ten years old. We had just moved into our home at 104 Compton Road shortly before. I vividly remember heading downtown Ithaca in Dad's old black 1940 Chrysler one afternoon. The old Chrysler had a bench-type front seat, and I was standing, as usual, between Dad, who was driving, and Mom, who was sitting at the far end in the passenger's seat. This was prior to the seatbelt era, so I enjoyed standing between my parents, looking out the windshield most of the time. Paul was not with us that day.

About a mile from our home, there was a four-way intersection. The speed limit on Danby Road heading into town at that time was 50 mph, and Dad was complying. As we approached the intersection from the south heading north, a southbound car had seen us, and was waiting for us to pass before making a left turn. He had his left turn signal on, and his wheels were cocked to the left in anticipation of making his turn. Suddenly, another car raced up behind him, and he was not slowing down. Sure enough, that car slammed into the rear of the stopped car at full force, at least 50 mph, and catapulted the stopped car, with its cocked wheels, directly in front of us as we approached. The timing and speed of all players was perfect.

As the stopped car shot in front of us, we went right behind him, and in between him and the car that hit him, as he ricocheted off. Both our front bumpers were damaged simultaneously as we narrowly passed between the two vehicles. As I noticed in this and my future car accidents, everything seemed to happen in very slow motion. It was an incredible experience. We weren't hurt, but the man, wife, and small child in the stopped car had quite a jolt from the rear and had severe whiplash. And the guy who slammed into them? He ended up in the ditch on the right side of the highway. We went over to see if he was okay. As we opened the driver's door, he was nearly unconscious. However, we determined he was not hurt at all—he was so drunk, he was barely awake. That was my first run-in with a drunk driver, but it would not be the last. We were lucky.

The next accident I remember was a few months later. It was winter, and Paul was driving the same Chrysler with Mom in the front passenger seat, and I was in the back. We were returning home on a winding country two-lane road at night, when all of a sudden, the car went into an uncontrollable spin to the left. We did a complete 360-degree spin and slammed into the guardrail on the right side, tail first. The car was dangling precariously on the guardrail, and would not move. As the three of us slowly got out of the car, we not only noticed the road was covered in clear glare ice almost an inch thick, but the car was hanging over a ten-foot drop-off. We weren't injured, but the car needed to be towed to the garage. Again, we were all lucky.

This was the time I went out and landed my first paying job at age eleven—doing yard work for the neighbors for twenty-five cents an hour. After a few days of this in ninety-degree temperatures in the middle of the summer, I decided it was no longer fun. I quit. I moved up in the world of finance, though, as I went on to become a pots and pans washer and kitchen helper at the Ithaca Country Club for fifty cents an hour for a summer job when I was fourteen.

I joined the Boy Scouts at age eleven, and was active in both Boy Scouts and Explorer Scouts until I was sixteen. I learned a lot in scouting, and have many happy memories of those great times—from camping out at forty degrees below zero in mid-winter to being on the wining team in a fire-starting contest with twenty teams competing. My high school friends, Bob Whittier, Larry Bennett and Norm Lacy, were also scouts with me. Ithaca is on the southern end of Cayuga Lake, and we had a great Boy Scout camp on the west shore about twenty miles north that we went to for a week or so during the summers. It was here that I learned canoeing, life saving, many different crafts, and how to row a whaling boat with nine others on a round trip of about four miles across the lake and back in four-foot waves. Great fun!

One of the camp instructors had a pet raccoon named Rackety Coon. What a great way to become familiar with this animal. He was quite friendly, and if you had some food to give him, he would be your friend for life. The instructor rode around the camp on his bike, and Rackety would ride on his shoulder—a real live Daniel Boone 'coon skin hat. What a sight!

It was also during this time that we all decided to get another dog. I recall that we went to someone's house to look at German Shepherd puppies. They were six weeks old, and just beautiful. Paul put his hand over the little fence and called them. They all came running over to him—except one! We all decided he was the one we wanted—the one with a mind of his own! We brought the cuddly, chubby puppy home, and decided to name him Cappy again after our last German Shepherd. This Cappy grew up to be another great companion to all of us, and a great protector as well. He loved us all, but would bark ferociously any time someone besides the four of us would come to the door. He was strictly a one-family dog, and we never had to lock our doors at night.

Grandma and Edna (Dad's mother and sister) came to visit us a couple of times a year during this time. I remember one such time during a visit when we were all home and had finished dinner. Dad and Grandma were in the living room, I was playing near the kitchen, Cappy was lying in a corner of the kitchen, and Mom and Edna were doing the dishes. Mom and Edna started joking around with each other, and Edna took her dishtowel and playfully flicked it at Mom. In a split second, Cappy leaped up, and with a half-bark, half-growl, nipped Edna in the rear—*you don't mess with Mom!*

Christmas 1959 in Ithaca. Standing (L-R) me; Paul's wife, Mae; Dad; Sitting (L-R) Edna; Grandma; & Mom with our second German Shepherd, Cappy. Edna's watching him very closely! My brother, Paul, took the picture.

Although he had only broken the skin slightly, it was obviously just a warning, as this muscular hundred - pound dog could have done much more damage if desired. We all decided he did the right thing, and praised him for his protection. Edna walked backwards for the rest of her visit, making sure she kept Cappy in sight at all times — and Cappy kept her under close surveillance, too.

Seventh and eighth grade were spent in Boynton Junior High School further downtown. Mr. Homer DeGraff was my homeroom teacher as well as math teacher. Several years later, it turned out he was the father of my wife Carol's best friend, Maggie DeGraff. The few times we visited his home, I was fascinated with his extensive antique shotgun collection. I don't know exactly how many he had, but all the walls in every room of his large house were covered with gun racks several deep in old and rare guns. I wonder what ever happened to this collection from the early 1950's.

Again, not many memories during these two school years. At home, Dad was busy building our new kitchen. I helped some

31

with this big project, but a lot of the time I spent next door at a neighbor's helping them build a house. This was more fascinating to me than helping Dad, but I'm sure it hurt Dad a little that I would rather work next door than help him at home. I guess that's typical of a young twelve-year-old boy. In retrospect, it's too bad I helped them at all, as our two families had a few run-ins with each other and ended up not speaking. A little of this may have been due to an incident with my boomerang.

Boomerangs have always fascinated me. They're not just curved sticks that are thrown, hoping they will return to the thrower. On the contrary, they are made as an airfoil, creating lift as they are thrown and spinning. Quite an invention for the Aborigines of the Australian Outback ten thousand years ago. Anyway, I had one, and I was out "flying" it one day in the large open field in front of our house.

Gordon, the boy next door who was about my age, came over to see what I was doing. He was quite a boaster and very fond of himself—and a real know-it-all. I explained the boomerang to him, and told him to make sure he stood behind me and ducked when it came back. "Yeah, yeah—sure, sure..." Unfortunately, he ignored my warning, and when it came back to us after a near-perfect throw, I ducked, but he didn't—*Smack!* It knocked him to the ground, and with blood running from his head, he ran off screaming to his house. I followed and explained to his parents what had happened. They, of course, blamed me for their son's stupidity—and six stitches.

About a quarter mile away towards town was the home of my closest friend at that time, Ralph Thorpe. He lived on a large farm with his Mom, Dad and older sister. I spent a lot of time there, and really enjoyed helping around the farm with different chores. Even loading bales of hay onto tractor-drawn hay wagons was fun.

Ralph and I made homemade cannons out of one-inch diameter pipe about fifteen inches long. We drilled a little hole for the fuse at one end with the pipe cap, and welded two legs toward the other end so the cannon would sit at about a 30-degree angle. The really interesting part of all this was making our own gunpowder. It was quite simple, because it only has three ingredients that, at the time, could be purchased downtown at the drugstore. My brother's chemistry set manual gave us the correct mixture. With some fine adjustments to this basic mixture, Ralph and I could fire an 18-inch long, half-inch diameter steel rod almost 200 yards—two football fields! That was neat, as we could see it moving end over end downrange toward the side of his barn. We would also use small nuts and stones, but they were much harder to see. However, his dad did not appreciate the damage we were doing to his barn, so we had to go elsewhere.

One episode sticks in my mind here. Ralph and I were out firing our cannons one day down in his pasture. It was a winter day, and there was an inch or two of snow on the ground. For some unknown reason, I was standing in front of my cannon when it was my turn to shoot. Behind the cannon was a streambed, so we had to be on the sides--or in my case, in front. After lighting the five-inch fuse, which burned for about four to five seconds, I turned and started to run; however, I slipped on the snow and fell to my hands and knees. I was struggling to get back on my feet just as the cannon with a large steel nut as the projectile went off behind me, and I felt and heard the *"Wizzzz"* as the nut shot past my right ear. Needless to say, that gave me renewed respect for firearms and firearm safety, and that was the end of my cannon shots for that day!

Another memory I have of this time has stayed with me to this day. Ralph's farm had a large apple orchard that bordered on the busy two-lane highway from Ithaca to Danby. One night

Ralph and I thought it would be really neat if we had a contest. We decided to hide in the orchard and throw apples at cars and trucks as they went by about a hundred feet away. We decided to keep track of the hits, and see who was the better shot. You could tell if you hit or missed, because you could hear the loud *thud* when an apple hit its mark. We were having a great time until one of us hit a car, and it immediately slammed on its brakes, backed up, turned on its siren and flashing lights, and pointed its spotlight towards us. We hit a police car!

Both Ralph and I started running down through his orchard away from the highway. We heard the police officer get out of his car. We ran further down into the backwoods and pastures. We ran for at least fifteen minutes. We were scared to death. We finally stopped and hid in thick underbrush in a dark shadow of an old out building. We waited, but we heard nothing. We stayed there anyway for another three hours before we ventured out and went to our separate homes. That was the end of that game.

Sadly, it was only then that we realized how dangerous it was to throw hard apples at cars going fifty mph at night, or anytime. We were throwing them as hard as we could, and, not only could we have caused damage to the cars and trucks, but worse, could have caused an accident that could have killed someone. To this day, it's hard to imagine why both of us at eleven years of age didn't realize this until it was almost too late. It was a very scary night for all involved. I did a lot of maturing that night.

Another great gift Dad made for both Paul and me were rings. Both were meticulously machined out of solid blocks of stainless steel. Paul's had a flat oval top surface in which Dad painstakingly engraved Paul's three initials. It was beautiful. Mine also had a flat top surface shaped as a rectangle, with a narrow side facing forward. Diagonally attached to this flat surface were my three initials, which were individually carved out of a solid strip of 14-karat gold. What unique and memorable gifts from our Dad!

I don't know what happened to Paul's ring, but, regrettably, I lost mine shortly after I received it. I was down at Ralph's playing football on his lawn, and when I got home that night, I noticed it was not on my finger. I went back the next day, and both Ralph and I looked for it for hours, but never found it. It was a great loss, but I'm sure, an even greater disappointment for Dad. I think I was too young to be responsible enough to own and wear such a unique treasure.

It was also during this period that I started coin collecting with another good friend from Boy Scouts, Bob Whittier. It was a lot of fun to look through our pocket change and rolls of coins from stores and banks looking for those coins to fill the holes in our little coin books. I remember that he found a 1916-D Mercury Head dime in a local 5&10-cent store. He showed it to me, but we didn't know its worth, but we figured it must be hard to find and maybe worth something, because of its very low mintage figure of 264,000, shown in our little stick-in coin folders, compared to millions of other mintages for dimes of that era. We chipped in and bought a coin book together that had coin values, and when we looked it up, sure enough, it's a very rare dime worth several hundreds of dollars. We both were very happy!

Another way I collected great coins at the time was in parking meter change. Dad had arranged with our local parking meter office for a woman employee to check pennies on a "want list" I had given her. Every Saturday when we were in town, Dad and I would drop by this office and pick up those pennies she had found for me on my list. In those few years, I put together a full set of Lincoln pennies, except for the four keys (1909-S, '09-S VDB, '14-D, and '31-S) to that set—at a penny apiece!

My stamp collecting was also in full swing at this time. Dad and I went around to the basement of a local bank every Saturday to collect stamps torn off letters and packages by their janitor, which he saved for me. Dad had arranged this ahead of time, and this was a great opportunity to get great stamps from all over the world. We brought the box full home every week and soaked them off the paper, then either kept them in my album if I needed them, or sell or trade them to others for stamps I needed. Dad had made two small wood frames for me about twelve-by-twelve inches square with cloth gauze stretched over both frames. After the stamps were soaked off, we placed the wet stamps in between the two frames to keep flat while drying. It was a great time for us.

I recall during this period Dad had come home very happy one day. He had received a raise in his job. I don't remember any of the other facts, except that the raise we were all happy over was for five cents per hour—an extra two dollars for the forty-hour week. However, it meant an extra two bags of groceries at the supermarket! How times have changed.

One of my fondest memories of this time was our large vegetable garden that we all helped in plowing, raking, planting, cultivating, and finally, harvesting. We had a large two-wheel, walk-behind garden tractor that we used for plowing and cultivating. It was steered and controlled by two large clutch handles in between the two handlebars that could be thrown forward to engage, or pulled all the way to the rear to disengage their respective wheels. I enjoyed using it, and Dad was glad, as it was quite a handful for him.

The best part was the harvest. I can remember sitting in the dirt between the rows and pulling up carrots, wiping them on my blue jeans, and eating one after another. Those, along with tomatoes, peas, green peppers, radishes, potatoes, lettuce and all the other vegetables that can be eaten raw, were a true delight to eat that way. You couldn't get them any fresher! We would all pick the rest of the harvest, and Mom would freeze it all and pack our large two-door chest freezer. We had vegetables to last the entire winter and spring. As the last of the frozen packets were used, fresh veggies were available from the next year's garden. What a joy!

Chapter 3
High School and College

I went to ninth through twelfth grade at Ithaca High School from 1953-1957. In the summer of 1954, there was a trip out to Philmont Boy Scout Ranch just south of Cimarron, New Mexico, in the northeastern part of the state. My good friend and fellow scout, Bob Whittier, and I

Our group of twenty-one scouts at Philmont Scout Ranch in northeastern New Mexico in August 1954. Bob Whittier is forth from right, top row. I'm on left end of middle row.

decided to go. It was a thirty-day trip for twenty-one scouts on a leased Greyhound bus. We started out from Ithaca; went up into Canada; over to Sault Ste. Marie, Michigan; continued on to the Badlands and Mount Rushmore in South Dakota; and then south to Rocky Mountain National Park in Colorado. Taking the Greyhound bus on the narrow, twisting back roads of Rocky Mountain National Park was no easy feat for our driver. We came upon a tunnel through a rock outcropping so tight that it scratched the paint on both sides of the bus simultaneously as it went through! Our driver had made us all get off before he attempted it in case the bus got jammed inside, and it took him several minutes of aligning the bus just right before starting through. We all guaranteed that no larger bus would ever go through that tunnel!

We camped for a couple of days in that beautiful Park and climbed 14,255-foot Longs Peak. It was a twelve-hour round trip hike up to the summit and back down—a once-in-a-lifetime experience. You learn a lot about yourself and others on a trip like that—what you can and cannot do. We left the Park and went south into Philmont.

Our main event at Philmont was a seven-day camping and horseback trip into the backcountry of beautiful northern New Mexico. My horse's name was Hombre—quite a spirited critter with a mind of his own, and it was the first time I ever rode at a full gallop—not as easy as it looks in the movies—especially when you weren't trying and the horse just wanted to! We took some food with us, but we also lived off the land by catching fish in the many streams and cooking them over a campfire each night. We were also eating berries from numerous wild berry patches along the way. This trip was another once-in-a-lifetime experience, and it was simply outstanding.

It was sad to say goodbye to beautiful Philmont, but it was time to go home. We headed east into Texas, and stopped at a ranch for an all-you-could eat steak cook-out on the open range. It was absolutely outstanding. After dinner, Bob Whittier and I went for a walk through the desert a few hundred yards to get a closer look at a ravine we had noticed earlier. As we walked along talking, all of a sudden we heard a loud rattling noise. We looked down in front of us, and there, coiled and ready to strike, was a five-foot rattlesnake! Luckily, he was as scared as we were. Bob and I stayed perfectly still, and about two minutes later, the snake slowly uncoiled and crawled away from us. What an experience! Luckily, he gave us a warning, or we would have stepped on him.

We then drove north into Dodge City, Kansas, with its famous Boot Hill Cemetery. We got back to Ithaca a few days later, and the thirty-day trip was over, but we all had memories to last a lifetime. I was a Boy Scout and Explorer Scout for five years, and I enjoyed it immensely. I truly believe every young boy—and girl—should be in scouting. You learn things and have experiences just not found anywhere else. Things I learned in scouting I still use almost daily.

It was during this time that I would ride with Dad some Friday nights when he went to work at 5:00 p.m. He worked the night shift—5 p.m. to 2 a.m. I would spend a little time with Dad as he worked, and then would run all the way downtown about a mile or so to see a movie. It was downhill all the way, so I could really pick up a good head of steam. One movie in particular that stands out in my mind was "Blackboard Jungle" from 1955 starring Glenn Ford, Vic Morrow, and Sidney Poitier. I had heard from my classmates that it was a good movie, so I decided to go one Friday night. The theater was packed with teenagers, but I found a great seat up in the balcony of the large State Theater in downtown Ithaca. I enjoyed the movie, but the most unforgettable experience started when Bill Haley and the Comets began singing "Rock Around the Clock." The entire audience of several hundred teens started singing, stomping their feet, and clapping to this incredible tune—"1, 2, 3 o'clock, 4 o'clock rock...!" That was spectacular in itself, but equally impressive was the way the whole balcony started to sway as we all clapped and moved in unison. I guess a few of us wondered if the balcony would collapse, but we were having too much fun to worry! It did not. It was the beginning of my memories of Rock and Roll, and this song, recorded 12 April 1954, is considered the dawn of this fantastic era. What a great time—and a great memory.

As a side note, I went back to my 50th high school reunion in June 2007, and one of the tours set up by the reunion committee was a visit to this historic old State Theater. It had been closed in the early 1970s and was in a medium state of disrepair. It had been scheduled to be torn down for some other new construction, but a group was formed at the eleventh hour to try and preserve the beautiful old brick building as a historical site. This was finally approved, and the extensive renovation was soon to begin. It was absolutely fantastic to once again walk into this old theater fifty years later and remember all the times I had watched movies— especially "Blackboard Jungle" and the hundreds of kids clapping our hands and stomping our feet to "Rock Around the Clock." I can still feel the balcony shaking and swaying in time to our movements. I told this story to our tour guide, and told him I had a concern at the time about the integrity of the balcony to withstand the sway. He said not to worry—the balcony was about the strongest part of the theater. Now I feel better!

After the movie ended, I would walk around the corner to the diner where Dad went for his one-hour "lunch" at nine o'clock. I would have a hamburger (twenty-five cents) or a bowl of homemade clam chowder with Dad, and then he would take me the three miles home before driving back to work. It was a lot of fun, and a great way for me to spend a Friday night.

"Morgan" was one of the men that worked with Dad at Therm. He, too, lived out in the country, and in the spring of 1956, found a nest of crows. He asked us if we would like to have a baby crow to raise as a pet. Sure! Sure enough, about a week later when the young birds were old enough, Morgan brought in a baby crow for

Moe The Crow and me in July 1956.

us that was about the size of a cardinal. What a cute little guy he was! We named him Moe the Crow. He became quite friendly, and would love to ride around on our shoulders even when he reached full maturity. We had heard that crows are one of the most intelligent birds, and we could tell it was true. He used to love to tease Cappy.

The way our house was made, we could walk around in a circle through the kitchen, around into a bedroom, through another bedroom, then into the freezer room back into the kitchen. Moe would *caw-caw-caw* at Cappy, and then half hop, half fly around this circular path, as Cappy would chase him on the slippery linoleum floor. Poor Cappy! His feet and legs were going twice as fast as the rest of his body as he tried to catch up with that pesky bird! Moe would just flap and flutter around and around the circle only a foot or two in front of Cappy's nose. Whenever Cappy barked at Moe, which was quite often, Moe would imitate him and "bark" back at him —which would further irritate the out-classed dog. What a sight! Cappy hated that bird.

Cappy and his "dear friend," Moe The Crow in our backyard under our old apple tree!

About a year later, Mom and Dad went on vacation and left Moe outside in our large apple tree in the backyard with plenty of food and water nearby. When they returned home two weeks later, Moe was gone—nowhere to be found. We all hoped he had just flown away and not met with an accident. Ten months later, Mom heard a crow in our apple tree. She went outside, and the crow was still *caw-caw-caw*'ing. Mom walked over to within five feet of him. It was Moe! He stayed around for a few minutes, and then flew off. He was safe, happy—and free. He must have sensed that we were worried about him, and came back to reassure us. We never saw him again. What a great experience he was for us.

I was interested in mathematics and science, so my schedule was heavy with those classes. Chemistry, physics and the math courses were absolutely great. I had taken drum lessons for a couple of years, but was never really good at it. I tried Hawaiian steel guitar for another two years and trumpet for another year, but had the same luck. That was the extent of my musical instrument endeavors. Looking back on my life, that is one thing I would change. I wish I had picked some instrument, stayed with it, and learned to play it well.

I tried out for football as a tailback and cross-country track, but my serious sport was four years on the varsity rifle team. The rifle team used .22 caliber target rifles, and we shot at standard 50-foot targets. It was here that I met Carol Bly, a year my junior in the Class of 1958, who was on the girls' team with Maggie DeGraff and Betsy Eardman.

The team coaches were Ralph and Lou Bowles, a couple in their thirties. They had an old black hearse that we all packed into to go to rifle matches at other area schools. It was great fun to give people fright, seeing us suddenly open the back hatch and eight of us come pouring out at a McDonald's stop! Our boys and girls rifle team did quite well over those four years, and gave me more experience in the use and handling of firearms. Carol was also a very good shot, and she had Ralph make her a beautiful rifle stock for her own target rifle out of bird's eye maple. It was a very light-colored wood with many small dark brown knots—absolutely beautiful.

My first date with Carol was a Halloween party at Horace "Dody" Mann's house in 1956. Dody was a mutual friend of ours, and we had a great time. We went steady after that. The photo on the next page was taken three days later at the Legislative Dance on 3 November 1956.

I graduated in 1957, and Carol graduated in 1958, and went off to Rochester, N.Y. for nursing school. We would see each other only two or three times a month on weekends.

My first car was a hand-me-down from my brother Paul. He sold me his old 1940 light blue-gray Chrysler four-door sedan for a dollar in early 1956. It was a good car, but the rear end went out only a few weeks after I had it. It was not worth fixing, so I sold it for junk for $35. My next car in late 1956 was a black 1946 Dodge convertible —complete with a chrome spotlight on the outside of the driver's window. It had an automatic transmission called Hydromatic, I believe. Whenever I tried going up some of the steep hills in Ithaca, that poor transmission didn't know what to do. It shifted up and down about ten times before I went fifty feet. I called it "Slush-o-matic." It was much more fun driving Dad's brand new 1957 Plymouth, and my poor Dodge finally met the same fate as the Chrysler.

Photo taken at our High School Legislative Dance on 3 November 1956.

After High School graduation in June 1957 I had a summer job working as a helper for Dad at Therm. It was a great experience for me, as Dad taught me a lot more about the use of tools. It was also great fun to play blackjack at lunch with many of the other workers!

I was very interested in math and USAF fighters, and my high school classes reflected this, as I took all the mathematics courses offered, as well as most of the science courses. I planned on going to a college that was strong in both, and decided on the University of Buffalo, in Buffalo, New York. They had a great math department and Air Force Reserve Officer Training Corps (AFROTC).

An investment I made during that summer of 1957 was a yellow motor scooter from Montgomery Ward, or as my Dad used to call them, "Monkey Wards." This thing was always hard to start, and had a top speed of 45 mph. On one of my trips home, I decided to drive this thing back to Buffalo so I had wheels. That was a major trip, but I finally made it. Prior to that, I used to hitchhike home on long weekends. I would make a sign that said "Ithaca," put on a coat and tie, and stand out on the highway going east. I wouldn't have to wait more than five or ten minutes before some nice older couple would stop and pick me up—sometimes actually dropping me at my house. I'm afraid those days are gone forever.

At the end of the summer, I left Ithaca to go to Buffalo. Mom and Dad took me with all my clothes and school supplies, and I was assigned to a room on the ninth floor of the brand new freshmen men's eleven-story Tower Dormitory. It was quite nice, and it had just been completed a few days earlier in time for this new class of students. We dumped all my stuff in the room, met my roommate, had lunch with Mom and Dad, and then said goodbye as they headed back home to Ithaca. I was on my own.

That night, when all the guys went to take showers, we noticed something wrong—the water wasn't draining—the large, open bay twelve-head shower area was four inches deep in water. After a few phone calls to the dorm manager and inspection, we found out what the problem was. In their haste to complete the dorm for us to move in, the workers had tiled over the shower drains—on all eleven floors! The tile workers were back early the next morning to uncover the drains and retile around them. By the next night, we were all set.

Another great memory I have of the Tower Dorm was the fact that all eleven floors were laid out exactly the same; rooms over similar rooms, each floor's lounge area over each other, and, of course, the large bathrooms capable of handling about ten guys at a time. It was noted by a few of us conversant in laws of physics (and owners of great little items known as cherry bombs), that we could have a lot of fun with our fellow freshmen. Cherry bombs were very powerful firecrackers you could buy in the states that sold fireworks. Unfortunately, New York was not one of them, so stealth, cunning, and secrecy were of the utmost priority. I, who absolutely loved firecrackers, and who would buy them whenever Mom, Dad, and I drove through a state that sold them, happened to have a few with me—you never know when a college freshman may need some.

A cherry bomb was a dark red ball, about one inch in diameter, with a green two-inch fuse—hence its name. Not only were they very powerful and could severely injure you if it went off in your hand, but their biggest asset was that they were completely waterproof. They could be lit and dropped in water! Well, with some high-level careful planning and a system of code banging on pipes, it was time for our adventure.

One of us (gee, I don't remember who that was...) would have a cherry bomb and a cigarette on the top floor bathroom. He would wait for the signal as to where our target was. When an individual went into the bathroom on the floor directly below and sat down on one of the commodes, another of our team would knock on the pipes X number of times, to signal the target on throne number X from the entrance door had just planted himself. That was the signal to the man over head to go to that toilet, light the bomb, drop it in the commode, and flush! By the time the two-inch fuse burned down and this thing detonated (that's precisely the magnitude), it had traveled down through the pipes to about the floor below—where our unsuspecting mark was sitting fat, dumb, and happy. Baaa-*LOOSH!* With our complete mastery of the laws of physics, we knew that water couldn't be compressed; therefore, if a blast went off inside a confined water pipe full of water, the result would be a tremendous tidal surge to the nearest outlet—which happened to be the toilet where our friend the mark was sitting! As planned, the surge would cover our friend from head to toe with the water and other items under him. What fun to see his face!

Unfortunately, the powers that be didn't share an appreciation for our team's handiwork, so we had to shut down our project — had something to do with splitting brand new water pipes due to over-pressure. After that, all we did was to sneak into girl's bathrooms and Saran-Wrap their commodes under the seats. It must have worked quite well, as it was the talk of the campus.

Dropping water balloons from the eleventh story windows was another sport most of us enjoyed. We would fill a strong balloon with water and wait for other students to walk by far below. If timed just right, the balloon would hit a few feet from the unsuspecting individual and instantly cover his feet and legs from the knees down with water. However, after a few near misses where people were almost hit on the heads with these eight-pound balloons traveling about 65 mph, this escapade also came to an end.

During that first year of college, Elizabeth Taylor and her husband at that time, Mike Todd, had come to our homecoming football game. They found out we were leasing our school mascot bull from a farmer. As a gift to our school, they bought it for us—a very nice gesture on their part, and we all thought the world of them. All the students living in the Tower Dorm had a chance to meet them in the cafeteria. I was within three feet of them, and she was very pretty in 1957. He was very protective, but what impressed me the most was that she seemed to be pulled and guided at every move by her husband, who constantly had her arm in his. It was my first encounter with celebrities.

After my freshman year of college in 1958, I got a summer job in Stewart Park on the north end of town right on Cayuga Lake. The job was both fun and a lot of work. The owner let me drive the small train and operate the merry-go-round, as well as the few other rides, but he also had me

Carousel operator, complete with coin-changer, at Stewart Park, Ithaca, NY, in August 1958

Simonize the train when we were not busy. Simonize was a very hard, good wax, but quite a challenge to put on. When you applied it and waited more than a minute or two, it would turn into, what I thought was concrete. It really built up my arm muscles that summer. However, all the work was worth the contact with the people that came to have fun on the rides.

I remember vividly a mother with her beautiful little four-year old daughter. The little blonde, pony-tailed girl loved to ride the merry-go-round. They came over to say thank you to me after a few rides, and the little girl just kept looking up at me with her big, beautiful blue eyes. She then tugged on her mother's slacks, and her mom leaned over to see what she wanted. She stood up, smiled at me, and said her daughter wanted to give me a kiss. How could I refuse? I picked her up, and she gave me a big hug and kiss. I guess I was her hero—I made the merry-go-round run!

I made good money—a dollar an hour. I used all my money to take pilot training lessons at a local small airstrip. I took lessons and learned to fly in a yellow Piper J-3 Cub. The minimum time needed before soloing was eight hours of instruction—I soloed in exactly eight hours. I was very proud, and loved it. What an indescribable thrill and feeling of freedom it was to have the instructor tell me to pull over and stop during one of my practice landings, and to have him get out of the plane! He asked me if I was ready to do it alone. My answer? "You bet!"

"Well, then," he said, "Go do it — and don't bust your ass!"

Piper J-3 Cub. With its 65 HP engine, it basically took off at 60 mph, flew at 60, and landed at 60. It had a top speed of 85 mph.

That was very good advice, and I remembered it for the rest of my flying career. Soloing a plane was about a hundred times the thrill of driving a car for the first time by myself—pure ecstasy. I had actually flown an airplane solo—successfully! It was now time to tell Mom and Dad. I had not mentioned anything to them all summer about wanting to learn to fly, or that I was taking lessons—or even if I could! I figured if I couldn't stand the answer, I shouldn't ask the question. The next weekend I reserved the Cub, and told my instructor that I was going to bring my Mom and Dad down to the field to show them how I could fly. All was set.

On Saturday afternoon, Mom, Dad and I drove the five miles to the airport as I told them I had a surprise to show them. I parked the car so they had a great view of the airfield and the Cub sitting by the little operations house. I got out of the car, walked inside the house, signed the flight clearance log, walked back outside, waved to Mom and Dad as I climbed into the Cub, had the instructor spin the prop for me to start the bird, and off I

Vast array of the Cub's 6 complex instruments!

went! What a surprise for my parents! I took off, flew around the traffic pattern a few times, landed, taxied in in front of them, shut down, and climbed out —their eyes were as big as their grins! It was a very happy moment for all of us, as they knew I had decided long ago on flying as a career.

My next car accident occurred when I was about twenty. I was home from college on summer break, and Mom, Dad and I were heading north on the east side of Cayuga Lake on a two-lane country highway on our way to a smorgasbord for dinner. I was driving Dad's 1961 black Cadillac, and as we approached a slight bend to the left, I noticed another car approaching us from the opposite direction. We were both traveling at about 55 mph, so the closure rate of 110 mph was significant. The other car approaching us coming around his right bend slowly drifted across the solid centerline onto our side of the highway. Sure enough, as we sped past each other, he was at least five to six feet on our side of the centerline, taking up most of our lane. I swerved onto the right shoulder at the last moment, but he managed to sideswipe us anyway. We pulled over and stopped. The three of us were okay. The other car had come to a stop in his ditch heading south. Dad and I went over to see if he was okay. As we approached, he opened his door and stumbled out—almost too drunk to walk. He was quite belligerent and tried to pick a fight with Dad. We didn't let him get to us, and when the police came, they hauled him away. Once again, Mom, Dad and I were unscathed.

Of course, college life wouldn't be complete without belonging to a fraternity. There were many at this school, and the one I liked the most was Sigma Phi Epsilon—"Sig Ep." It had the greatest number of guys that I wanted to be associated with, and they had a good national reputation. After the lengthy rushing, pledging and acceptance procedures, I was a fraternity guy. Unfortunately it took a lot of time, and in my sophomore year of 1958 –1959, I lived in the fraternity house off campus with one other brother—Joe Mastromonico. He was a senior at the time, and a great guy. I don't recall his subject major, but he was in the AFROTC Program and was about to graduate and get commissioned as a second lieutenant—one of my goals.

The house was old, with two stories, and Joe and I had our bedrooms upstairs with a bathroom, living room, and kitchen. One Saturday after a particularly grueling week, we were having breakfast together in the kitchen, when one of us decided to flick a small piece of food at the other. That, of course, demanded instant retaliation, so a little larger piece of food was flicked back. Well, I'm sure this is where the term "escalation" was born. After approximately two hours of the biggest food fight ever held in the western hemisphere, we decided to quit—it was getting just too slippery. The entire house, upstairs and down, was a complete shambles—food, with appropriate condiments, was everywhere—about an inch deep in most places.

We decided to go up to the gym on the campus (about a mile away) to shower and clean up. So we each packed a clean change of clothes, jumped on my trusty motor scooter, and off we went. We sure got some very strange stares—two guys on a yellow scooter covered from head to toe in a variety of food: spaghetti, mustard, catsup, mayonnaise, pancake syrup, butter, etc., driving through the streets of Buffalo. For some unknown reason we were never stopped.

In those first two years of college, I didn't set any academic excellence records. In fact, with all the fraternity activities, I almost flunked out. Most of that was certainly my fault; however, some was the fault within the math department at that time. In my first year of calculus, there were about twenty students. Out of those twenty, two received C's, two of us were awarded D's, and the other sixteen failed. True, I wasn't all I could be at that time, but all twenty of us? Something else was wrong, and the instructor was found to be at fault, too. I guess all that had its blessings in disguise, as I seemed to mature a lot after my sophomore year. The party was over.

The United States Air Force Academy started up in 1954. This was exactly what I wanted to begin my Air Force career. I applied two years—in 1957-58 and 1958-59. The entrance exams were quite complex, both physical and written. Unfortunately, I was Second Alternate both years. After the second try, I was offered their one-year prep school, which would have almost guaranteed entrance to the Academy, but by then I was going to be a junior, and I decided there was no sense wasting three years to start over at the Academy. The ROTC Program should work just as well. As a side note, the guy who received the nomination from my district in 1958 went to the Academy and promptly quit after the first week. That slot remained unfilled for the next four years.

As in high school, the only sport I did in college was four years on the varsity rifle team. Our team traveled to West Point, Citadel, Virginia Military Institute, plus other colleges and universities for matches. We had a lot of fun and did quite well. We were privileged on one of our visits to meet General Mark Clark, the highest-ranking POW during the Korean War, who was the Commandant of the Citadel.

One of my most serious accidents occurred in the summer of 1959. I was home on summer vacation from college, and Carol's parents let me use their Nash Rambler station wagon to drive up to Rochester to pick Carol up from her nursing school. Carol wanted to drive back, so I was dozing in the front passenger seat, and her younger sister, Sylvia, was sleeping in the back seat. We were heading east on the New York State Turnpike toward the turnoff toward Ithaca. We were traveling about 65 mph on the turnpike, and Carol saw the large sign for our exit. She looked down and reached for her purse on the bench front seat between us to get the ticket and cash for the tollbooth. As she looked and reached to the right, she inadvertently let the car drift to the right. The right two wheels left the right lane and dropped onto the shoulder. Carol looked up, startled, and overcorrected back to the left to get back on the highway. We swerved and ended up heading at an angle to the left and into the left lane. Again, she overcorrected back to the right in an attempt to straighten out the vehicle. This additional swerve sent the Nash into a right-hand spin, skidding sideways back across the right lane, down into a shallow grass-covered ditch, and slamming broadside on Carol's side into the large steel pole on the left side of the exit sign.

We finally came to rest at the bottom of the ditch heading back from where we came wrapped around that steel pole. I woke up as we dropped onto the shoulder, and again, everything seemed to happen in slow motion. "Syb" in the backseat was awake, and wanted to know what happened. We checked each other, and we were all okay. Incredibly, the only injury was a small cut on Carol's right leg caused by a piece of the broken windshield that had dropped and cut her. An 18-wheeler truck driver that was heading westbound on the turnpike stopped, grabbed his first aid kit and ran across the median to help.

"How many killed?" he asked as he peered in the smashed driver's window.

"No one," I said, "We're all okay."

"I don't believe it!" he said. "It looked terrible!"

He radioed the police and wrecker, and that was the end of that episode. Of course, the car was totaled. However, the outstanding construction of the solid frame of that Nash Rambler, I'm sure, saved our lives that day. Although we were bent around that steel pole about 20 degrees, I'm positive with another vehicle without the solid frame of the Nash, we would have been bent totally in half with some very serious injuries. Thanks, Nash.

One of my fondest memories in college ROTC was being selected to be on the twenty-man precision drill team. It was very gratifying to work with the other guys in our exact movements. We really looked sharp in our blue uniforms with white gloves, white scarves, and white shoe coverings.

On my long three-day weekends, I would either go home, if Carol was also going home, or I would go on ROTC trips to different pilot training bases in the South on old C-119s ("Dollar Nineteens"). These were great trips to actually see these facilities, and we got orientation rides in T-28, T-37, and T-33 trainer planes. Some of these bases had Aviation Cadets, which were students in training, and if they graduated, they got their wings and second lieutenant commission at the same time. We would go to their mess hall and eat with them, family style, with big bowls and platters of food brought to the tables—help yourself! They had to eat "square meals," sitting at attention, bringing their forks straight up, then over to their mouth—with their eyes straight ahead. Other bases we visited had lieutenants as students. These students were treated as officers—no hazing.

The old T-28 was a propeller-driven bird, but the other two were jets! My one and only ride in the T-28 was quite an experience. Part of the training curriculum was to practice spins—in case you ever inadvertently entered one, you would know how to recover from it. When we were up flying, the instructor pilot (IP) asked me if I wanted to see a spin. Wow — of course — let's do it! That was the neatest thing — in that bird, you could actually do a precise preplanned spin. We decided to do a three-full-turn spin, and recover on a heading of west. Sure enough, we brought the power to idle, raised the nose, slowed down to the stall, brought the stick full aft, kicked full right rudder, entered the spin, counted one, two, three full rotations, then recovered exactly on the heading of west! Amazing! Yes—this is still what I wanted to do with my life.

The T-28 *Trojan* advanced pilot trainer that could do precision spins.

The little T-37 was my first jet ride. It was a side-by-side two-seat trainer, with the student on the right, IP on the left. It, too, was used in practice spins, but they were less exact, and much faster—everything in a jet is much faster. This would be the first plane I would fly in the Air Force, and I loved it.

On one of these orientation flights during my junior year in college, we flew down to Spence Air Base in Moultrie, Georgia. I had some time off to myself, so I walked through downtown Moultrie to see the sights. An elderly black man stopped me on the sidewalk and asked me, "Sir, would you please go in the diner behind us and get me a hamburger?" He held out fifty cents for me to use. I wasn't accustomed to elderly people calling me, "Sir," and it was quite awkward and embarrassing for me.

I said, "Sure, but why don't you get it yourself?" He explained a new concept to me—segregation. The diner had a large sign over the door and in the window: "Whites only—no coloreds allowed." I took his fifty cents, went in and got the hamburger, brought it out to the old man, and gave him fifty cents change. He couldn't believe it. He was so thankful. I explained to him that I was from the North—New York—and I wasn't aware of this culture. We didn't have it in New York. I told him I was sorry, and that some day I hoped segregation would be gone. That was 1960. How things have changed.

Carol and I were married 21 May 1960 in Danby, N.Y., which is about four miles south of our hometown. Our rifle team coaches and good friends, Lou & Ralph Bowles lived there and stood up for us, as neither of us told our parents. Sadly, Lou was killed a few years later by a runaway eighteen-wheel tractor-trailer truck coming down South Hill in Ithaca. She had just come down the steep hill herself and was stopped at a red light when the truck slammed into her. She never knew what hit her.

That summer I went to Wright Patterson Air Force Base in Ohio for what boiled down to be a boot camp for ROTC cadets. We were hazed, did a lot of PT (physical training) and marching, inspections, had a demerit system, and also had a survival school at Nelsonville south of the base in the mountains of southern Ohio. This was my first experience with the rigors of actual survival. You learn a lot about yourself—and others—in a situation such as this. I was happy with what I saw in myself.

When I returned home that summer, we told our parents we were married, and they accepted it—Carol was twenty, and I was almost twenty-one, so they didn't have too much choice. They were sad though, that we didn't let them know so they could be there. When my senior year started in September, we had already decided that Carol would stay out of school for a while, and we would live together in Buffalo. We had a beautiful little furnished apartment about four miles from my campus. Our daughter Kristen was born 3 March 1961, and what a beautiful—and noisy—baby she was!

I graduated from the University of Buffalo in June 1961 with a BA in Mathematics and was commissioned as a Second Lieutenant, USAF. The first part of my goal had been completed. I was selected for pilot training, and they asked me to pick a date that would be best for me, and they, the Air Force, would see if it was available. That was great, because I wanted to make sure I would get in the brand new supersonic T-38 jet trainer that was coming out in Basic Pilot Training (last six months of a twelve-month course). I figured I should be okay with a one-year delay. That was approved.

In the meantime, I got a job as a Scientific Computer Programmer at Bell Aerosystems, in Niagara Falls, N.Y., with a good friend and fellow classmate, Tom Hendricks. Both of us absolutely loved it. We worked closely with their engineers to write programs for the new IBM 704 mainframe computer for satellite intercept and optimum nozzle design for maximum thrust from rocket engines. The work was fascinating, and I was one of the first ones to work in the morning, and one of the last to leave at night. I decided if I flunked out of pilot training, I would come back to this job. $400 a month gross—what a deal!

Carol, Kris, and I lived in a three-bedroom apartment in Buffalo during that year. It was unfurnished, so we scrounged up some furniture from our parents' attics and made coffee tables and end tables out of wooden orange crates from our local grocery store—they worked just great, and the price was right.

Chapter 4
My Air Force Life begins

But now it was time for the fun to really begin! I received orders to report to Reese AFB, Lubbock, TX, with a RNLT (report not later than) date of 12 March 1962 for Pilot Training Class 63-F. Carol, Kris and I said goodbye to all our friends and families, packed our little pale green 1960 VW Beetle, and off we went to Texas and the Air Force. I was now a second lieutenant on active duty—getting $222 a month base pay.

Air Force Pilot Training is a twelve-month course—the first six months, Primary, concentrated on learning to fly as well as class academics in weather, principles of flight, military bearing, instrument flying, Morse Code, and navigation, plus all the different systems of the T-37 side-by-side twin jet trainer: hydraulic, engines, electrical, fuel, oil, egress and pneumatic systems. The T-37 "Tweet" is a very small bird, but easy to fly and a great

Very misty morning of 28 February 1962 as Carol, Kris, and I said goodbye to Mom and Dad as we left Ithaca for Pilot Training at Reese AFB, in Lubbock, TX. Note our trusty light green 1960 VW Beetle.

trainer. It got its nickname from the very high-pitched whine it made, and some said it was a 3,000-pound dog whistle! That was true—it transformed JP-4 jet fuel into noise!

The instructor pilot sat on the left, and we students were on the right—great setup, as the IP could watch us all the time to make sure we weren't getting into trouble flipping the wrong switches at the right time, or the right switches at the wrong time!

In flight we learned basic takeoffs, landings, handling, maneuvering, stalls, aerobatics, instruments and navigation. Carol

The T-37 side-by-side twin jet trainer

helped me study and memorize all my critical action emergency procedures for the T-37 and later on in Basic.

The last six months, known as Basic, concentrated on formation flying, instruments, navigation, low-level flying, plus more takeoffs and landings for this new bird. Unfortunately, my calculations of when the brand new T-38 Trainer would be available to fly in Basic was slightly in error. After waiting a year to enter training to make sure I did get in it, I missed it by about two months. I was in the next to the last class to be in the old T-33 trainer. The "T-Bird" as it was known, was a single engine, two-seat tandem version of the old single seat F-80 Shooting Star used as a fighter-bomber in the Korean War. It was a very reliable bird, and very popular—just about every unit had one or two.

One of the missions I remember from Basic was going on my first low-level training flight. I was lucky enough to get Capt. Neil Graff, an F-86 pilot from the Korean War, a great fighter pilot, as my instructor pilot. The syllabus called for the IP to enter the low-level route at 1,500 feet above the ground, fly the first leg, and demonstrate airspeed control of 360 knots (nautical miles per hour) while navigating and map reading. Our low-level maps had "tic" marks across the route every six miles, or one minute, as 360 knots equaled six nautical miles per minute. Therefore, while keeping track of the exact time, you could look at the map and outside at the ground to make sure

One of my IP's in T-33's, Korean War F-86 veteran Capt. Neil A. Graff

all looked the same! We did all that, and when we turned to the next heading for the second leg, he gave the controls of the T-Bird to me. I flew on for a few minutes pointing out landmarks on the ground and the corresponding map entries. I then asked, "Is this as low as we can go?"

He said, "This is where we're supposed to be, according to the Student Syllabus."

"Doesn't seem to be a low-level route from way up here," I said.

"Let me have it a minute," he replied. He took control of the bird, did a barrel roll and ended up straight and level at 300 feet! He said, "Okay, you've got it—if you want to go lower, go ahead and try it."

Wow! Purring along at 360 knots, or over 400 mph at 300 feet above the ground. That may not seem like much of a big deal, but at that speed, you're traveling at 587 feet (almost 2 football fields) per second, it would take only half a second to hit the ground if you got distracted. Navigating, flying the bird, and watching outside for other aircraft and obstacles definitely made this a full-time job. We had a ball on that mission, and I received a high grade on the ride.

Soon after all of us soloed in our class, the syllabus called for each of us students to practice our scheduled maneuvers. That was about as much fun as watching paint dry, so some of us decided to do more interesting things. We had almost no formation flying experience, but it was great fun to get a few guys to agree to go practice together. We would call ourselves "Batman Flight," pick some radio frequency at random, say 333.3 on our UHF radios, take off as scheduled, then meet at a pre-selected point, say, over Muleshoe; 20,000 feet; left orbit; 300 knots. A leader was designated, and whoever got there next was number two, then number three, and the last guy there was number four.

We knew this was the way to practice formation join-ups, but most of us had not done any. When you get the guy in front of you in sight, you get inside his turn, have a little more airspeed then he, aim out in front of him, and close in on him until rejoined. You watch him on your canopy—if he's moving backward, you're moving out in front. If he's moving forward on your canopy, then you're falling behind. And if he isn't moving on your canopy, you're on a collision course—or he's going directly away from you. Piece of cake!

When he's out in front a mile or so, nothing seems to be happening, so you add a little power to get more speed, then, all of a sudden, you begin to realize that bird in front of you is getting as big as a whale's ass—fast! You look down, and you're going 375 knots—almost 100 miles per hour faster than your target! *Wizzzzz!* You push the stick forward and shoot past under him, and now what—you've lost sight of him!! You bank hard to the left to regain a visual on him, and that takes you back toward him—and the others who are behind you and closing on both of you! After a few more *Wizzzes* and near misses, we got joined up. What a sight—four new solo students bobbing up and down, right and left, forward and backwards in what we called "close

62

formation!" We didn't exactly look like the Thunderbirds. It was a true white-knuckle experience if one knew what danger we were in, but we didn't, so it was fun and exciting.

Flight of four T-Birds

On one occasion, we decided to fly over to the Grand Canyon. When we arrived, we thought it would be neat if we flew through the canyon in formation. We did, and what a thrill to see the stone walls race by as we flew our best formation through the canyon. A few days after we returned to the base and landed, we found out there were large steel maintenance suspension cables running across the canyon in many locations. We, of Batman Flight, became pale as ghosts, as we reflected on what could have happened to us in the canyon. That was the end of our Grand Canyon air shows.

SILVER WINGS

Some people think of those silver wings
As glorious, glamorous li'l ole things
That shine like a beacon while a pilot makes love,
And reflect all the moonlight that comes from above.
But to a flyer they're not that at all,
Those wings are an emblem of an uphill haul.
It's just a small way that a man's reimbursed
For the numerous times he's been viciously cursed;
A hunk of cheap silver that's been shaped into wings,
The representation of lots of fine things,
Of sweating and swearing and laughing and tears,
Of a few open posts with the boys and some beers.
It just adds up to this in a pilot's eye:
The stuff he went through to learn how to fly,
Day after day in a classroom or cloud,
By God, it's enough to make any man proud.

Author unknown

Pilot Training Graduation
27 March 1963

In spite of everything, I graduated on 27 March 1963. Carol, Kris, Carol's Mom and Dad, and my Mom and Dad were there to see Carol pin on my sterling silver pilot wings. Of the fifty-five guys who entered training in my class, thirty-three graduated, for a 40% washout rate — about standard. My goal was still the same — I was convinced I still wanted to fly fighters. Most of my other classmates felt the same, too.

Carol pinning on wings at pilot training graduation,
27 March 1963

Dad presented a graduation gift to me. It was a five-pointed star he had perfectly machined from a 1939 Walking Liberty half-dollar — my birth year. He had left about an eighth of an inch of the whole rim, but cut away the rest except for the silver star. It is a symbol of what that star means to both Dad and me. I still have it today, along with a brass key chain he made for me with my old Compton Road address stamped on it. What keepsakes they are for me.

Unfortunately, only two of the thirty-three assignments our class received were fighters. One was a single-seat, single-engine F-100, and the other was a single-seat, single-engine F-102 interceptor. Class standing was determined by three equal grades: academics, flying, and military bearing. One of the two who picked a fighter assignment scored very high in academics and military bearing; however, his flying ability was average or below, but his overall grade was high enough to make him number two in the class. In fact, one day when he was flying solo on a training round-robin cross-country flight, he had plotted one of his legs 180 degrees in error, and had become lost. Only at the last minute was he able to receive help from ground controllers to get him turned around and safely back to the field.

And when he got into his F-102 assignment? Yep, you guessed it—he became lost, but this time no one was there to help him. While still lost, he ran out of fuel, flamed out, and ejected. Of course the aircraft was destroyed. He was called before a Flying Evaluation Board (FEB), was found at fault, and his pilot's wings were revoked. Very sad, but quite lucky no one was hurt. What a waste of a perfectly good fighter assignment.

The F-100 went to the number one man in the class, Marc Covington. He was a sharp guy and a great pilot. I don't know what happened to him after we went through survival school together. One of these days, I want to try and track him down.

The other thirty-one assignments for the rest of us ranged anywhere from pilot training instructors in T-37s to helicopters—with T-29 twin engine propeller navigator training aircraft, C-130 four-engine turbo prop tactical airlift aircraft, and KC-135 four-engine jet tankers in between. As the number three man in the class chose his assignment, then number four, and on down, it was my turn as number eight to choose. What a decision! What would be the least difficult to accept of all these unwanted choices? *"Well,"* my reasoning went, *"to one day get into jet fighters, I better stick with a jet aircraft."* The only one available was the KC-135. Luckily, there were five to choose from, so I picked the one at Loring AFB, Maine. Loring is in the far northern tip of Maine—absolutely beautiful country. Not exactly the "Entertainment Capital of the World," but both Carol and I loved the outdoors, so we decided this was the best of the other assignments.

I received orders to Loring with TDY en route to the three-week Survival School at Stead AFB, Reno, Nevada, and four-month KC-135 school at Castle AFB, California. As these assignments, with no facilities for student families, would take from flight school graduation on 27 March 1963 to reporting in

NLT 31 August at Loring, Carol and I decided the best course would be for her and Kris to return east to her parent's house in Ithaca for the summer, and I would pick them up there in mid August and drive up to Loring together. So it came to pass.

All during Pilot Training, I still had my Montgomery Ward yellow motor scooter. It was always very hard to start and not reliable. When I graduated, I sold it to my flight commander and instructor, Capt. Theodore W. Guy. That was the last I saw of him until I watched

My Flight Commander, Capt. Ted W. Guy, in January 1963

him on TV ten years later being repatriated as a Vietnam POW in 1973 during Operation Homecoming. Colonel Guy was quite vocal and active against a few of the POWs whom he thought had become too friendly with the enemy during captivity. He was also very active in Washington pressing our politicians not to forget our POWs and MIAs, and to demand full accounting of their whereabouts in other countries.

Ted had a web site, and I finally found his e-mail address. On 27 May 1997, I sent him an e-mail asking if he remembered me and that wonderful yellow motor scooter I off-loaded on him back in March 1963 at Reese.

"Do I! I damn near killed myself on that damn thing every time I could get it running!" he wrote back. After a couple more e-mails, we lost contact. I received word on 23 April 1999 that Ted had passed away that same day from complications associated with leukemia only six months after his first symptoms.

After he was shot down in an F-4 during the Battle of Khe Sanh in Vietnam on 22 March 1968, he ejected and was captured in Laos by the North Vietnamese. On the second day of his capture, while he was being walked up the Ho Chi Minh Trail to the prisons in Hanoi, they were heavily sprayed accidentally with Agent Orange by our own Air Force. Agent Orange was a strong chemical used by us to defoliate the jungle in order to rob the enemy of the jungle canopy under which to hide. Unfortunately, we later found out that it also caused many health problems. In the ensuing days, Ted walked through many areas that had been previously defoliated. We are all convinced his leukemia was a direct result of this concentrated exposure.

On 14 November 1994, Ted wrote, "I was very proud of my belief that as long as there are people in this world that want to be free and are willing to fight and die for their freedom, that the United States of America has an obligation to help them retain or regain their freedom; even at the cost of our soldiers' blood." He was a true patriot and citizen of the World.

A friend of mine and fellow classmate, Marc Covington, and I drove up to Stead together in my trusty VW Beetle. Marc graduated number one in our class, so he took the F-100 assignment. He was a very sharp troop, and a good pilot. He deserved that bird.

On the drive up to Stead, we decided to spend a night in Las Vegas—shoot, why not, it's on the way! We came up from the south, and by the time we crossed over Hoover Dam, it was dark. What a sight to see—that huge dam all lit up at night. It was beautiful. We continued on through the mountains in the dark until we came through a pass, and as we reached the summit, we broke out of the mountains, and there, down in the flat land below us was a small cluster of lights in the surrounding blackness of the night desert—Las Vegas! What a beautiful and spectacular sight. I can still see it vividly in my mind. The rest of the valley was dark desert, and you could just barely make out the mountains surrounding the valley on the other three sides. The little cluster of lights reminded us of an oasis in the middle of a desert — which was exactly what it was.

LT. MARCUS COVINGTON JR
Texas A&M

Marc's graduation photo from our
Class 63-F Yearbook

As a side note, I have come through that pass numerous times since that first time in March 1963. Each time, that cluster of lights got bigger and bigger. My last time through was in March 1998. It was still the same awesome sight as we came through the dark mountains, and there laid out below us was Las Vegas. Only now, that small cluster of lights completely filled the valley and was half way up the mountains on all four sides. What a breathtaking sight! Las Vegas has probably grown a hundred-fold since 1963.

Marc and I got into town, drove out through the deserted black desert, which is a brightly lit city street today, to Nellis AFB, and got our rooms for the night, then headed downtown. We ended up out on the Strip after visiting the downtown area. There wasn't much out there—only about ten or twelve of the big hotel-casinos at that time: Sahara, Thunderbird, Sands, Dunes, Flamingo, Riviera, Aladdin, Caesar's Palace, the Frontier, the Landmark, a couple of others, and way out, the Hacienda. These were huge, brightly lit hotel-casinos (in those days), but between them was open desert. It was still cold and quite windy that night, so we would run from one to the next—had to see them all!

Another great time I had was looking through silver dollars—real silver dollars. They were on all the gambling tables, and you could go to the cashier's window in any casino and get as many as you wanted. I would get $100 worth, sit down and look through them, pick out the few good ones I wanted, turn the rest in, go to the next casino, and get more. At that time in early 1963, I found some beautiful scarce coins. I threw them all in the bottom of my B-4 bag to take with me. There was nothing like gambling and hearing the unique sound of those beautiful large silver coins clinking together all through the big casinos — from the tables and pay-outs from the slot machines. They had a rich, deep ring, like tapping a fine crystal glass with a silver knife. Today's coins, with no silver at all, only *clunk* when struck — what a difference. I'm afraid that beautiful sound will never be heard again, and it's a great memory of mine to have experienced it.

We ended up sitting in the lounge of the Dunes. A couple of guys came over and sat down at a table next to us. Marc and I were busy talking, and so were the other two. We didn't pay much attention to them, as the lounge was quite dimly lit. After a few minutes, one of them asked if we were military, because of our short haircuts. We said yes, that we had just graduated from Air Force Pilot Training down in Texas, and we were on our way to Survival School up at Stead AFB in Reno. He congratulated us, and asked if he could buy us a drink. Well, who were we to refuse a free drink?

He motioned with his hand, a waitress came over, and he ordered a round for us. We thanked him, and as we all stood up to introduce ourselves, the light became better and we saw who we had been talking to: Nat "King" Cole! We apologized for not recognizing him, but he just laughed and said it was hard to see him in the dim light of the lounge. We all had a good laugh. He was there putting on a show, and he was on one of his breaks. What a treat for us. A few minutes later, we shook hands, he wished us good luck, and we said goodbye. He and his manager went back for his next show. What a fine gentleman, and supporter of the military.

The next morning Marc and I headed north to Reno. We checked in at Survival School and began the three-week course the next day. It was a real eye-opener. The first two weeks were classes and exercises. One of the classes was on interrogation techniques and how to resist, as well as the bounds of the Code of Conduct. An exercise to practice all this was a weekend in solitary confinement in a metal box about the size of a doghouse. Every three to four hours they would come around, bang on the box to make sure you weren't sleeping, then get you out for an interrogation session. I learned two things that weekend: 1) don't get shot down; and 2) don't get captured. It wasn't fun.

The last week of the school was a seven-day trek through the Sierra Nevada Mountain Range of eastern California due west of Reno. We were trucked into a starting location and given our instructions. We had to E&E (escape & evade) from that point to an end location fifty miles away within seven days without being caught. Fifty miles in seven days? That's only a little over seven miles a day—piece of cake, you say? Well, yes...except that we had about fifty professional survival instructors looking for us. If you were caught, you flunked the course and were "washed back" to the next three-week class.

This meant splitting up into pairs and traveling at night, and navigating through unfamiliar mountains away from any LOCs (lines of communication) such as roads, trails, railroad tracks, power lines, and so on, to avoid being sighted and/or caught. It was not a walk in the park. By this time it was April, but there was still six feet of snow at our first night start location.

Fires at night could be seen for miles in the black mountains, as well as smoke during the day. Hot meals? Not for that week! It was here I learned for the first time, and hopefully the last, what being hungry felt like and the importance of eating all food without wasting any. It has stayed with me to this day, and it grinds me to no end to see the waste of food we, as a nation, leave on our plates and throw away each and every meal, while eighty percent of the rest of the world goes hungry. You don't do that if you have ever been hungry.

We were each issued two, eight-ounce high-energy Pemmican bars—a mixture of about 50% ground-up meat of some kind and 50% fat. This was the same ration that was found in our survival kits after a bailout or ejection. Just looking at those gray-white bars was enough to gag a maggot! They were marginally bearable if boiled in water for an hour and eaten as soup with lots of salt, Tabasco sauce, and any other seasoning available; however, this was hard to do without fires. A few teams tried cooking, but were quickly sighted and caught. Marc and I lucked out and were trek partners, and we decided not to waste time with fires. We ate those bars cold like candy bars as we walked. Believe me, they sure didn't taste like candy bars, but after the second or third day, they started tasting better and better.

We were even taught how to make small animal snares so we could catch rabbits, squirrels, and other tasty critters of the woods, but this also took a lot of precious time and required a fire to cook, as eating this game raw would be dangerous. Therefore, we didn't do that, either. Many of the guys decided before the trek that, knowing it was only one week long, they would do without these bars and just tough it out. Marc and I went around and picked up discarded Pemmican bars by the handful and put them in our packs—we had all the Pemmican we wanted!

Marc and I made it to the end point in plenty of time, and without being caught. It was quite an experience, and again, we learned a lot about others and ourselves in stressful situations. Again, I was pleased.

When we graduated, one of the gifts that each graduate received was a five-dollar gambling chip from Harrah's Club in downtown Reno. We all took off that night, and headed downtown to celebrate. We were still very hungry, as we only had a small snack since getting off the trek that afternoon. I thought I would crave steak, but actually, I found myself craving spaghetti! Well, I was in luck—Harrah's had both! I sat at the 50-cent blackjack table and played my favorite game. Whenever I won a couple of dollars, I went to have a spaghetti dinner, then returned to the blackjack table to win a couple more dollars. This time I got a steak! This continued for a while until I was quite full. Thanks, Harrah's, for that five-dollar chip!

Marc and I shook hands and said goodbye, and I again pointed my little light green VW Beetle westward toward Castle AFB, in Merced, California. For the next four months, I learned to fly the four-engine KC-135 jet air refueling tanker. This was the military version of the Boeing 707 airliner. Modern versions of this bird are still in use today, and have refueled countless other fighters, bombers and transports in the last forty-five years.

It was strange learning how to interact with the other three crewmembers, and especially the aircraft commander who flew the bird from the left seat. I, as the copilot, sat in the right seat, and did what the "boss" said. Great.

One weekend, when I had some time off, I went to a nearby park that had a lake and a beach for swimming. As I came out of the water, who should I see—my old fraternity friend and fellow food-fighter, Joe Mastromonico, and his wife, Judy. He was close by at Mather AFB going through navigator training.

We visited for a few minutes, and then went our separate ways. Small world.

One of the other great memories I have of this time was a side trip I took on a weekend to Coulterville, California—about fifty miles directly east of Modesto. It was just a very small crossroads town, but on the northeast corner was an old Western hotel with an old bar, like you see in the Westerns, complete with a brass foot rail and a couple of spittoons on the floor.

What fascinated me the most was the top of the old wooden thirty-foot long bar. There, under glass in an airtight display, were two—yes two—complete sets of mint state Morgan Silver Dollars, which were made between 1878 and 1921. Both sets, one with all the obverses (heads) showing and the other with all the reverses up, were mounted on a large mirror. This allowed one to not only view each coin from the top, but to move slightly to one side to see its other surface. Even at that time, the summer of 1963, some of the key dates in these sets were very rare and expensive. These two sets today, if they are still intact, are worth hundreds of thousands of dollars each. As a coin collector, this was a once-in-a-lifetime experience to see these, not one, but two beautiful sets in their historic Western setting. I asked the barkeeper about them, and he told me that all but two of the coins—the very rare 1895 proof-only coins—came right across the bar in trade during the hotel's heyday! Incredible!

Along with this encounter with these beautiful coins, I had another once-in-a-lifetime experience that summer. I have always been very interested in gold, and what better place to see it or be near it then California—birthplace of the famous 1849 Gold Rush up in the hills not far from Merced. During my time there, I found a few other people who shared my love for that elusive shiny yellow metal. One individual from the base asked if I wanted to go with him one weekend to pan and dig for gold. Did I? You bet!

We decided on the long Fourth of July weekend. He had a tent and all the gear. He also had a sluice box to use. We went up to his favorite place on a stream deep in the "Mother lode" backcountry, and set up our tent and sluice box. The wooden box, which was about five feet long, three feet high, and eighteen inches wide, was set up in the stream bed. It consisted of two inclined troughs—the top one dropping from left to right, and spilling into the lower one about a foot underneath, dropping from right to left, both at about 15 to 20 degree angles. A water pump, powered by a small gas engine, was used to pump water from the stream up to the highest part of the top trough. As sand and dirt from the streambed was shoveled into the top trough, the running water washed away the lighter dirt and sand, while the much heavier gold particles would quickly drop and be caught in the carpet material on the bottoms of both troughs.

Every ten minutes or so, we would stop, turn off the water, and check to see if we collected any gold. Sure enough—there in all its natural brilliance, shining in the bright sunlight, were small particles of pure *GOLD!* We carefully picked it all up and put it in a small jar of water. At the end of our three-day weekend, we divided up our "diggin's," broke camp, and drove back to civilization. Profitable? Not at all—at the current price of thirty-five dollars an ounce at that time, we each got about five dollars worth of gold. Exciting fun? Absolutely! How many of us can say we dug gold in the hills of California like the 49'ers!?

Other side trips that summer included the beautiful scenery of Yosemite National Park, and the giant redwoods in Sequoia National Park. Both were absolutely beautiful.

In early August 1963 I completed KC-135 school, packed my little light green VW Beetle again, and headed east toward Ithaca—3,000 miles away. Unfortunately, I only got about a hundred miles up in the mountains of eastern California. Those

VW's at the time only had forty horsepower and a top speed of 72 mph. There was a tendency, especially going up mountains, to keep the gas pedal floored.

As I was going up through a mountain pass, suddenly the car filled with very dense white smoke. I immediately turned the key off, rolled my window down, and brought the car to a stop as soon as I could on the side of the road. I jumped out and went around back to see what was going on. I saw a flickering glow from under the engine hatch. I opened the hatch, and the entire engine was on fire! My first instinct was to blow out the fire—by some strange quirk of fate, I was able to with five or six good puffs. The engine compartment was a mess. All the wires and hoses were either badly damaged or completely destroyed. That was the end of my travels for that day. I hitchhiked to a phone and called the nearest garage. They came and towed it in, and two days later, after replacing most of the wires and hoses, I was on my way again.

After checking out the engine compartment, I found out what had happened. Those early VWs had thin Neoprene gas lines—one of them running from the fuel pump to the carburetor carried high-pressure fuel. The metal throttle arm hooked to the throttle linkage would lower with the pressing of the gas pedal, and rise back up when the gas pedal was released. However, with the gas pedal fully pushed to the floor, the throttle arm came all the way down and rubbed against that high-pressure rubber gas line! After a while, the inevitable happened—the throttle arm rubbed a hole in the line allowing high-pressure fuel right from the fuel pump to spray all over the hot engine. The replacement line was of much stronger material—I could still keep "the pedal to the metal."

I finally reached Ithaca a few days later. Carol, Kris and I spent a few more days there with our families, and then packed the

Bug again for the trip up to the northern tip of Maine—Loring AFB. It was our first operational assignment—the 42nd Air Refueling Squadron (42nd AREFS) of the 42nd Bomb Wing of Strategic Air Command (SAC). When I reported in to the squadron commander, he told me I was now a first lieutenant. I had been promoted over the summer, but I had never gotten the word.

There's a saying we had at Loring: "We have two seasons up here—winter and the 15th of July!" Well, maybe it wasn't quite that bad, but the winters went from September through mid-May. I loved to fish for trout in all the small streams  around the area, as well as salmon and lake trout in the large lakes. The lakes were not free of ice until mid-April. A hot summer day was 78 degrees. It was beautiful country, and the fall colors in early to mid-September were absolutely gorgeous.

Although the winters were harsh with temperatures down to twenty to thirty degrees below zero, and snow "chin deep to a giraffe" in front of some of the family housing quarters, the streets and roads, both on and off-base, were clear within hours of a major snowstorm or blizzard. Aroostook County, which is the entire northern tip of Maine, had more snow removal equipment than the rest of the whole eastern seaboard combined! They had huge snow blowers that blew snow a hundred feet or more, as well as large snowplows. The base itself had the same equipment, so our runways and taxiways were also clear and dry within hours of a heavy snowfall. As you can see from these

Hickam Drive Winter 1963

Seven feet of snow piled in front of the Loring housing area in 1963.

photos, when the snowplows came through the housing area, they would pile snow seven to eight feet deep in front of your house. What I used to do was to shovel our walkway out to the street, but instead of stopping there waiting for the next snowstorm of ten to twenty inches to ensure you got to do it all over again, I got sheets of plywood to put over the walkway to act as a roof. When it snowed again — no problem, and no more work! I had a tunnel to the street with no further work required. It caught on fast with the neighbors.

Flying the KC-135 was a great experience, but I had not forgotten my goal to fly fighters. How I would ever get out of SAC and into Tactical Air Command (TAC) where the fighters were was a problem I hadn't figured out. Unfortunately once SAC got you, you were in for the duration, and all they had were tankers and bombers.

My first crew was with an aircraft commander named Capt. Ken Brush; our navigator, Capt. Marty Delahanty; and our boom operator, TSgt. Ralph Thomas. Ken and his wife, Jo, were nice people. I was still very much interested in coin collecting, and with a little sales pitch, I got Ken interested in collecting. He started collecting everything—U.S., Canadian, early type coins, etc. I was still concentrating on silver dollars, and would drive around to the banks in the small towns in northern Maine and get silver dollars from their vaults. More scarce and rare beautiful coins were found. As Ken was collecting

78

Canadian coins, and because we were right on the border for a great place to collect, I started collecting Canadian coins, too. I was still mostly interested in large silver coins, so I concentrated

KC-135A of the 42nd AREFS, Loring AFB, Maine in November 1963

on halves and silver dollars. They are also beautiful coins, and Canadian halves are quite scarce, as they have very low mintages compared to U.S. coins, and were not commonly circulated.

One Friday afternoon I was in Base Operations down on the Loring flight line and had just finished flight planning a flight to support a "Chrome Dome" B-52 nuclear airborne alert mission. Those B-52 bomber missions would last about twenty-four hours, and were armed with live nuclear weapons. During this Cold War period, we kept these Chrome Dome missions airborne all the time, 24-7, from SAC bases all over the country in case a war broke out and our bases were attacked and destroyed in a first strike. This ensured a devastating retaliatory strike on any enemy; therefore preventing a war. Our crew was just about to walk out the door on the way to our aircraft when the Dispatcher at the desk came running over to us. "Kennedy has been shot!" he yelled.

Our crew's stunned reply was almost in unison, "Oh, my God!" It was November 22, 1963. I honestly believed it was the beginning of World War III, and we wouldn't be coming back from this mission. I quickly called home, and then went to fly. It was a very tense mission. However, we all came back that terrible day, and spent the rest of the weekend glued to our TVs watching that pathetic drama play out before our eyes on national TV.

Immediately from the start, it was a foregone conclusion that Lee Harvey Oswald acted alone, and was the lone assassin who had fired three shots. It was quite obvious to me and the other 900 million people around the world watching TV and the Zapruder film that weekend that Kennedy was killed by a massive head wound, caused by a shot to his right front as he was slumping forward from hits to his back. To have the right forward side of his head explode as it was snapped backwards from the shot is physically impossible from a "lone assassin" shooting from the elevated rear. Also, watching TV footage, you see many people falling to the ground on the "Grassy Knoll" and looking toward the wooden fence where that shot had come from.

Another clue was the old bolt-action rifle itself. Expert marksmen tried to recreate the assassination with that rifle. They found it again physically impossible for them, or anyone, to aim, fire a shot at a moving, receding target eight inches in diameter from that range, and then operate the bolt action, re-aim, and fire two more times in the extremely short time of approximately 4.2 seconds, hitting the target all three times — and the last shot *from the front!* There were countless numbers of witnesses; however, they were all ignored, and many, including noted reporter, columnist and television celebrity, Dorothy Kilgallen, had strange, untimely accidents ending in their death within a few months. Check out: http://www.jfkresearch.com/morningstar/killgallen.htm for more very interesting information. The official report of the assassination was the Warren Report—"Lee Harvey Oswald acted alone and was the lone assassin that had fired three shots." What an incredible cover-up! Even to this day, scholars are trying to figure out exactly what happened that Friday in Dallas. The multi-part series "The Men Who Killed Kennedy" on the History Channel is an outstanding in-depth look at this blotch in our country's history.

Northern Maine is a beautiful place for scenery and just being outdoors, but as you can see from the photos, snow is chin deep to a giraffe during the winters. There are five lakes in that area connected by streams or channels, and have very fine trout and land-locked salmon fishing. To take advantage of this, Ken and I decided to go in together to lease from a paper company that owned all the land an old rustic cabin on one of the more deserted lakes—Mud Lake.

Snow in the housing area winter of 1964.
Detached garages in the rear.

The four-room cabin, which had a kitchen, living room, and two bedrooms downstairs, and a large bedroom up in the loft, was only accessible by hiking in a mile or by boat. It also had no electricity or indoor plumbing. However, it did have a beautiful rock fireplace, a dock in the lake, and a beautiful view of the length of the lake beyond the dock from a large, screened-in porch. Our two families took turns using it, and we all enjoyed it a lot. The cost? Three hundred dollars a year—$150 each! Ken and I also went in together on a little twelve - foot aluminum boat and a 9.9 horsepower outboard motor. Why 9.9 horsepower? Anything ten horsepower or more needed a license.

These were just what we needed, and could be tossed on top of our cars for easy transport. It was about this time anyway that my little green VW Beetle decided to get very tired, so it was traded in on a 1965 VW Hatchback—another great car, and with a rack on top, was perfect for carrying the boat and motor around.

Dad and I on our way out to fish in our boat from our cabin on Mud Lake on 9 August 1964. Notice the remoteness of the surroundings, and both of us with coats on. Only two cabins on the entire lake.

Our navigator, Marty Delahanty, couldn't swim, but Ken and I talked him into coming over to our cabin for some fishing one weekend. Unfortunately, by the time we arrived at the lake and got all our gear loaded in the boat and ready to go the half-mile over to the cabin, the weather had turned quite windy, and it had begun to rain. It did not take much convincing at all to get Marty to put on his life vest for the trip. When we left the seclusion of the inlet in town and headed out into the lake, we encountered very rough water, high wind and rain. Ken was operating the motor, I was in the bow, and poor Marty was on the middle seat, facing forward, with all our gear in front and in back of him.

As we came out of the relative calm of the inlet and ran into the four-foot waves, I watched Marty's eyes grow from wide open to disks about the size of quarters! He was normally hanging on to both gunwales with white knuckles, but as he saw what we were in for, his grip tightened just short of putting deep dents in the aluminum. For some reason I started laughing, and seeing what was happening, Ken joined in. Within a minute or two, we were all drenched, as wave after wave of water would surge over the bow as the heavily loaded boat dipped into troughs between waves.

Marty was petrified. He started yelling, "Go back, GO BACK!" The more he yelled, the louder Ken and I laughed. I was laughing so hard, I let go of the boat and was doubled over in the hardest laughter I had ever experienced. This, of course, fueled Ken, which in turn, added to my enjoyment of the situation—to the point I fell out of the boat laughing so hard, as a large wave hit us. As I surfaced, I was still laughing so hard, I almost inhaled a large gulp of water. Ken maneuvered the boat to pick me up, but I had to get in myself, as Marty was frozen in time and space with a death grip on the sides of the boat. By this time the boat was half full of water, and there was no way to bail fast enough to empty it. We keep going and finally reached our beach in front of the cabin.

Ken and I jumped out to pull the boat up on the beach, but Marty would not move. We had forgotten to tell him before the trip that the boat would not sink—it couldn't, because of trapped air and foam under the three seats. We told Marty about it then, but it didn't help. As Ken and I were standing next to the boat in water below our knees, we finally convinced Marty that he could also step out into knee-deep water and walk ashore six feet away. He slowly did, and made his way to the safety and security of the beach and dry land. Ken and I decided to show him that, in fact, the boat couldn't be sunk, so we unloaded all our equipment and took it out a little deeper, filled it with water, and showed Marty how it stayed afloat enough where we could be on the outside of it and hang on to stay afloat ourselves. Marty was not impressed—all he wanted was to go inside and sit by the fire. His naval exploits were over for that day!

As time went on I was assigned to another crew run by Capt. Dick Skovgaard, advanced from copilot to Standardization Board (Crews that gave check rides to the other crews—known as Stand Board) Crew copilot, to Lead Stand Board Crew Copilot, to finally getting checked out as Aircraft Commander (AC). I was also promoted to captain along the way. Before I got my own crew, I flew with other crews when their AC was not available.

One day I substituted with Ken's crew with Marty, a new copilot, and Ralph. We were happy to be back together again for this one last flight. We knew that Ken was on leave and was up at the cabin doing some fishing, so after completing our mission with some time to spend, we all decided it would be a great idea to go up to Mud Lake and see if we could find Ken and say hello. We headed north to the lake at about 15,000 feet altitude—it was a beautiful, sunny summer day with unlimited visibility. Sure enough, as we approached, we looked down with our binoculars, and there was Ken, all by himself out in the middle of the calm, secluded lake. We took a quick vote, and it was unanimous that we get a little closer to say hello. He was facing north and we were coming in from the south—perfect.

I brought the four jet engines to idle and lowered the nose of the big bird to aim at a point at the south end of the lake about half a mile from Ken. Even with the engines in idle, we picked up speed in the rapid descent from almost three miles high. As we reached our level-off point, we were indicating 400 knots on our airspeed indicator—about 460 mph. I let down to approximately 300 feet over the water, and as we approached the unsuspecting Ken sitting peacefully in our little boat, I pushed the four throttles up to full power.

WhoooOOOSH! Just as we passed directly over him, and with all four engines at full military power, we slowly pulled the nose up to a 30-degree climb and banked to the left to see what had happened. It was a beautiful sight, and the binoculars confirmed it—Ken was in the water—we had blown him out of the boat! He was shaking his fist at us—I'm sure that meant he enjoyed the experience! Marty was beside himself with glee—we had gotten even with Ken for that white-knuckle boat ride a year earlier. Later that week when Ken returned from his leave, he told me we scared the stuffing out of him—and we were so low that we left a wake on the lake. I guess I had misjudged our altitude slightly.

Unfortunately, Ken was quite a domineering guy to his wife and family. As a young impressionable lieutenant, he was my boss and, therefore a role model for me. Unknowingly, I began to pick up some of his demanding attitudes. This, I am sure, took its toll and did irreparable damage to my marriage to Carol. Regrettably, I didn't realize it at the time, but I can look back and see it now, and I deeply regret my actions to this day. There is an old saying, "Live and learn." Sometimes the tuition for the lessons in life is quite costly.

My son, Mark, was born in the hospital at Loring on 9 July 1964. Unfortunately, I was flying at the time, but the Command Post called us and passed on the great news. First a beautiful, healthy baby girl, and now a beautiful, healthy son— what more could a guy want? I was very proud and happy. It was happy times.

Chapter 5
Vietnam – 1964

*I*n November 1964, Dick Skovgaard's crew was deployed to Clark Air Base in the Philippines. These early tanker deployments were known as Foreign Legion, and were sort of the prototype for later regular tanker rotational deployments from all other tanker bases around the country as the Vietnam War heated up. These follow-on tanker deployments were known as Young Tiger. We were the

KC-135 refueling two F-4's over the Pacific on the way to Southeast Asia (SEA)

second group to go over. On the way over, we were in a task force of two other tankers taking twelve fighters "across the pond" to Vietnam. Sounds simple enough, but the planning, coordination, and communications required were quite

Refueling an F-100 with the "Probe & Drogue" system as seen by the Boom Operator of the tanker. Notice the steel drogue basket leaking fuel from a poor hook-up with the Hun's probe on right wing.

complex—especially if one of the fighters had to abort, or worse, a tanker had problems and had to abort. The Task Force Commander had to be constantly aware of exactly where we all were, where the nearest abort bases were, and who was going to go where if an emergency occurred. It was a very important duty, and went only to the highest qualified aircraft commanders.

When we were refueling fighters over the Pacific, I went back to the Boom Operator's position to watch the refueling procedure. The "boomer" lay on his stomach facing aft talking to the receiver pilot as he watched the fighter slowly slide into refueling position. "Forward 10, down 2," the Boomer might say. The receiver would inch forward and down as the two aircraft,

88

traveling at over 400 mph and four miles high, would finally get within twenty feet of each other and ultimately hook together.

As the fighter aircraft approached the "contact position" with its refueling door open, the Boomer would call, "Stabilize," and the fighter would hold that position. The boom operator would then "fly" the boom into the receptacle and latch it in place. "Red 11—contact," we would say.

"Sundance 21—contact," was the reply from the fighter. After positive confirmation of a viable hookup, the boomer would call the co-pilot on the intercom to turn on the refueling pumps on the overhead panel between the aircraft commander in the left seat and the co-pilot in the right seat, and fuel would be pumped to the receiver.

As I watched this procedure, I couldn't help thinking that some day I would some how be the fighter down there, and someone else, perhaps another young tanker copilot would be up here dreaming the same thing.

Luckily, our group of birds arrived on schedule without mishap. We were assigned quarters, and were briefed on our upcoming mission. We were to takeoff from Clark, fly west across South Vietnam and Thailand, then turn north and fly over Vientiane, the capital of Laos, to refuel fighters much further north going in to strike North Vietnam. Laos was a neutral country, and did not wish to be involved in the expanding war in Southeast Asia (SEA). However, no one honored that choice, and the North Vietnamese used Laos to bring supplies down on what became known as the Ho Chi Minh Trail. The North never admitted they were in Laos, but they were. It was also a fact we had already lost aircraft over Laos being shot down—that certainly did not happen by the neutral people of Laos.

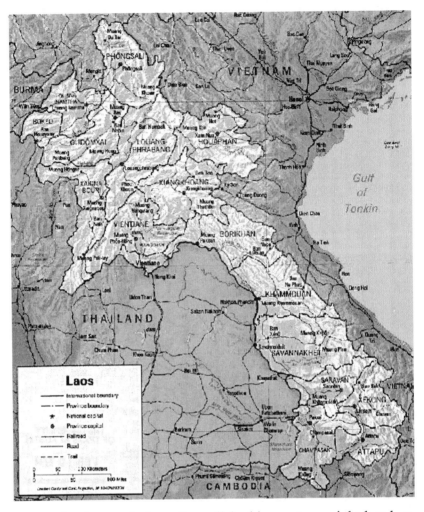

On those missions, I recall looking out my right-hand co-pilot window at the landscape below as we headed north. I remember looking down at the Plaines des Jarres in northern Laos off to our right and noticing how ominous it looked with its dull, light maroon color. I remember thinking that, if we were shot at, we had no armament—nothing to shoot back with. The only armament on a KC-135 was four scared guys with switchblade survival knives.

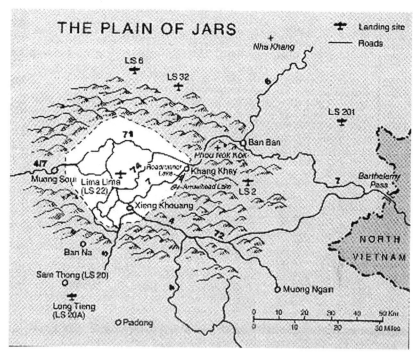

It was also duly noted that, although we wore parachutes, we didn't have ejection seats—in case we had to get out, we had to unstrap, climb out of our seats, go to the exit floor hatch about five feet behind the aircraft commander's left seat, open the hatch, lower a chinning bar over the open hatch, hold on to the bar facing aft, swing down in the open hole, then let go and drop free of the bird into the slipstream before manually pulling your ripcord. Then it was the other three guys' turns. I'm not sure how many times this escape procedure was ever used in KC-135s, but I know it wasn't very many.

After we landed back at Clark, we got some time off, so the best thing to do was head for the Officers' Club. I remember one Friday night in particular I was downstairs in the Stag Bar talking with some fighter pilots who were there blowing off some steam from that day's mission. They were relating how they were assigned to take a four-ship flight of fighters up to hit a small

91

insignificant target, such as a little rope footbridge across a stream. On the way they would pass a truck supply convoy heading south on the Ho Chi Minh Trail. They reported the activity and asked permission to attack it. In every case, permission was denied. They dropped their bombs on the footbridge, and came home. Most fighter pilots aren't world-renowned Rhodes Scholars; however, *they ain't no dummies, neither!* Even they could figure out that, if our Rules of Engagement (ROE) didn't change, there was no way in hell we would ever win this war. This was November 1964. It didn't improve much, and sure enough, eleven years and 58,000+ of our good men and women later, this was the only war in our nation's history that we lost. Are Vietnam veterans bitter? Beyond words.

It's quite basic knowledge that, if you need brain surgery, you get a brain surgeon to do it—not plumbers. In an article by Joe Patrick, he stated:

> The war in Vietnam was a strange war, indeed. It was a conflict that should not have been lost. But the men who ran that war were politicians and bureaucrats, not military professionals. Men like Secretary of Defense Robert Strange McNamara (who brought us the legendary Ford Edsel...) and President Lyndon Baines Johnson, along with Department of Defense bureaucrats, civilian and military, called all the shots. America lost her first war ever because bureaucrats 10,000 miles away from the fighting played a kind of "war monopoly" game, in which the stakes were not play money, but the lives of men sent out to die in the rice paddies and skies of Vietnam.

Called to testify in a civil suit after the war, McNamara said under oath that he had decided as early as December 1965 that "the war could not be won militarily." During the war, President Johnson would talk by telephone to then-Air Force Major John Keeler about what to say during the "Five O'clock Follies," the daily press briefing held every afternoon in Saigon. As Keeler put it, Johnson called so that the press officer could "get the party line." The political agenda in America was obviously more important than the bloodshed on the hills around Khe Sanh. Johnson often bragged, "Those boys can't hit an outhouse without my permission."

He was a world-class plumber trying to do brain surgery. It didn't work.

On one of the weekends we had off, our crew rented a car and drove up to the resort town of Baguio in the mountains of west central Luzon about 100 miles north of Clark Field. It was a pretty town with a hilly, but nice golf course. I remember plugging my electric shaver into the outlet in the bathroom of my hotel room to shave. Unfortunately, I had forgotten they had different electrical current than we did. There was a loud *ZAP*, some white smoke, and that was the end of my shaver.

We relaxed and enjoyed the cool climate for the weekend before driving back to Clark. On the way we stopped at a little mountain village where natives were busy hand-carving "monkey pod" wooden items to be sold to the tourists. Without the middleman involved, we could find some great buys right from the very poor natives that made the items. I picked up a beautiful large salad bowl set, which had the large bowl and eight individual matching bowls, with serving fork and spoon—all hand-carved, for five dollars—less than fifty-cents for each item. Absolutely beautiful, and we still use that set today.

When we returned to Clark, the four of us went back to our hooch where we were staying and opened the door. There, in the middle of the living room, was a local native with an armful of our flight jackets under his left arm—and a thirty-inch machete in his right hand. He crouched into a threatening stance as he came toward us. He wanted out of the door that we were in front of! The four of us talked about overpowering him, but quickly gave it up as a bad idea. The four flight jackets weren't worth the chance of some of us being seriously hurt. (That machete looked about six feet long!) We talked calmly to him, and slowly moved away from the door. Out he went, and he was gone.

We called the Air Police and told them what had happened. They made a report, but nothing was ever done. They said it happened all the time—they even stole a fire truck and drove it right out the front gate a few months before. Six miles of Clark's perimeter chain link fence disappeared one summer, too—they were very good at making other people's belongings vanish.

I spent my twenty-fifth birthday, 19 November 1964, having a steak dinner and wine by myself in the Officers' Club at Clark Air Base. When I walked into the Club to be seated, a very beautiful American girl—the hostess—met me. She showed me to my seat, and I couldn't help thinking how strikingly beautiful she was. The entertainment that Thursday night was a local group that impersonated famous American rock and roll artists. They were absolutely superb. Filipinos were truly outstanding at this. It was a good evening.

Jay E. Riedel

While in the Club, I saw one of my old ROTC friends from the University of Buffalo—I'll call him Ken Bogotti. We talked briefly, and he invited me over to his hooch to visit after dinner. He was stationed there flying C-130 cargo planes. After dinner, I walked over to the address he gave me and knocked on the door. After a couple more knocks, Ken finally opened the door. He wasn't alone—that beautiful hostess from the club was with him, and it was quite obvious they were in the middle of something, and didn't want to be disturbed. I thanked him for the invite, but excused myself. They didn't know I left. I wonder what ever happened to Ken. He and his wife, and Carol and I, used to play cards together occasionally back in Buffalo.

My last great memory of Clark at that time was going up "on the Hill" to the Officers' Club Annex for Mongolian Bar-B-Que on Wednesday nights. Everyone would walk through the line selecting all the different ingredients we wanted, then handed the bowl to a cook who would dump it all on a grill and cook it for you as we watched, just the way you liked it. That was my first introduction to Mongolian Bar-B-Que, and I enjoy it to this day.

Our squadron was a good one. A news clipping at the time reported, "The 42nd AREFS won the 8th AF Golden Boom Award three consecutive times in 1963-1965. Topping that achievement, the 42nd brought home the Saunders Trophy as the best AREFS in SAC for two straight years, 1964 and 1965. A portion of that excellence had been demonstrated in Southeast Asian Combat, where the 42nd had begun sending crew and aircraft in October 1964 in a deployment known as Foreign Legion. Forty-two 42nd crews had served with the Young Tiger tanker task force, the follow-on to Foreign Legion, by January 1969." Unfortunately, I only went on one of those deployments, but its memory is still quite clear.

Chapter 6
Loring – 1965 - 1968

*A*fter a few more weeks, we finally returned to Loring. I was happy to be home. One doesn't realize how extremely fortunate we are to be citizens of this great country until we're outside its borders for a day or two. Seeing how the other ninety percent of the world's population lives is quite an eye-opener. It gives me great disgust to see and hear some of our protesters and celebrities bad-mouth our country.

Only two days ago, as I'm writing this, I heard on CNN that some Hollywood celebrity had won an award. When she went up to receive it, she gave a political speech instead of an acceptance speech. She belittled the president and stated she was "disgusted and ashamed to be an American." I tried to send a message to the station to pass on to her that I would gladly give her a one-way ticket to any other place on earth outside this country—*one way*. And, if she wanted, she could leave behind all her money and other assets that she had acquired in this terrible country so she could start fresh somewhere else. Oh yes—and give up her citizenship that I know she despises…

It was now back to flying and sitting alert. We would sit on nuclear alert about half the time—week on and a week off. There were five tanker crews and five B-52 bomber crews on alert at any one time. During the week off, we would fly once or twice. After seven days living in the alert barracks, we had three-and-a-half days of crew rest off before our week between alert tours. We used this time for our family time. Although we had to live in this building, we could travel around the base to certain areas that had a short response time in case of an alert. We could also have visitors, so it was better than no contact at all.

Sitting on alert for seven days at a time about every other week gave us plenty of time for hobbies. Marty Delahanty's project was to build a flying scale model of a KC-97. This was no small project. Marty had been a navigator on these four-engine propeller-driven aircraft used for in-flight refueling before coming to their replacement—the KC-135. His flying model was to be about seven feet long with a six-foot wingspan. He had mounted four McCoy 35 Red Head model aircraft engines in it, and had designed an elaborate fuel system to prevent fuel starvation to the left wing engines as the model was flying counter-clockwise around a circle on its control cables. I had a few of these control-line model airplanes, and had flown them with some measure of proficiency. Marty had helped me "crew chief," so he became very interested in this type of flying. After we got the model engine started, Marty would hold the bird while I ran to the center of the circle, picked up the up-down control handle, and signaled to him to release the airplane after a quick check of the controls. With any luck, the model would accelerate quickly, and with a little "up" control by me, would jump into the air and fly around in a circle, held tight against the control lines by centrifugal force. These single-engine birds were quite fast and highly maneuverable—being able to do Figure 8s, inverted flight, etc. Fun. It was even possible for two guys to get in a circle at one time with their individual birds with crepe paper streamers attached to their tails, and dog fight each other. I never did this, but it was great to watch as each tried to snip the others paper tail.

Marty spent months on his model, and finally finished it—complete with a great authentic gray paint job. It was now time to fly it. He waited for a perfectly calm day, and we went out to a smooth level school parking lot with the big bird and all the equipment needed to fuel the large model and fly it. Word

KC-97 in-flight refueling tanker

had spread around the base that Marty was going to fly his airplane.

Marty and I filled the four fuel tanks inboard of each engine, and then started the time-consuming process of starting each engine. As one engine started, we went on to the next, while a third crew chief would keep topping off the fuel for the others. Finally, all four engines were started, tuned and running at max speed, and each fuel tank was full—now it was time! I motioned over the loud roar for Marty to run to the center of the circle while I held the monster that was straining to get airborne. To my complete surprise, Marty shook his head and pointed to me. I couldn't believe it! Time was wasting—I nodded, ran to the control handle, checked the up-down controls with my right hand, and waived my left arm horizontally as a signal to release the bird.

The old McCoy 35 Red Head was a pretty good engine that sold for five dollars at the time. Although its .35-inch displacement was large enough for most single engine models, four of these on a model the size and weight of this KC-97 were barely adequate. Marty made sure the bird was pointed slightly outward from the circle, to make sure the control cables stayed tight, and released the giant. This model, as all other control line models, had been built with slight right rudder to keep the model taut against the cables while flying.

I was shaking with adrenaline as I gripped the handle waiting for the bird to surge forward and leap in the air. Instead, it started very slowly to roll around the circle while it picked up speed. As its speed increased, so did the tension in the control cables as the centrifugal force also increased. I let it roll completely around the entire circle waiting for what I guessed would be enough speed for it to takeoff. I gently gave the lumbering giant a little "up" control by pulling back on the top cable, and the huge bird rotated and took off—just like the real thing!

There was a loud roar of applause from the hundred or so spectators as Marty's famous model, which had become the talk of the base, flew around the circle at about six feet off the ground. The tension on the cables was now at its max, and I could no longer hold it with only my right hand. With both hands on the handle and leaning back to help compensate for the incredible pull of this monster, I could only hope that Marty had anchored the bell crank control, which the two control cables are attached to deep inside the model, in such a way as to prevent it from being ripped out through the wing from the tremendous pull. I flew it around a few more times at this altitude to ensure a slight safety margin of avoiding the ground as it porpoised slightly from my over-controlling, but yet low enough to allow a successful landing when the time came, or in an emergency.

After a few more laps, one of the engines quit, so I knew I had better get it on the ground while it was still under control. I inched it down, and as another engine ran out of gas, it touched down in a fairly respectable landing and, with another round of applause from the crowd, it rolled to a stop as the other two engines ran out of fuel and quit. Wow, what an experience! I thanked Marty for letting me fly it, but asked why he did not—he had never flown a model before.

My best memory of coin collecting in Maine came on April 1, 1965. My little four-year old daughter, Kris, and I drove around to some of the small Canadian towns just across the border. I took my entire paycheck—$300—and would go to each bank for coins as we had done many times before. This time I was looking for their elusive half-dollars. We went in to the small bank in Perth-Andover, New Brunswick, and I asked the teller if she had any half-dollars.

"How many would you like?" She said.

"How many do you have?" I answered.

Again she asked, "How many do you want?"

It was now or never. I replied, "$300 worth."

She looked at me kind of funny, then said, "Oh my, I'll have to go in the vault for that many."

As she turned and started to walk away, I called after her, "Please dig deep!"

She returned a few minutes later with an old cloth bank bag. She dumped out thirty-three $10 rolls of halves—and they looked dusty and old. I knew I had hit the jackpot! With the exchange rate at the time, I received $330 dollars worth of these beautiful, hard-to-find silver coins.

I thanked her, and Kris and I went out to our VW bug and started looking through a couple of the rolls. The first roll I opened had beautiful coins—almost each one being in the "keeper" category because of its condition, rarity, or both. In the third roll I opened, about halfway through, I found a coin that really caught my attention. It was a 1947 coin, but I had to look closer.

In 1947, Canada made four different half dollars: the hard-to-find 1947 Straight 7, which had the stem of the 7 straight down; the equally hard-to-find 1947 Curved 7, with the stem of the 7 curving slightly to the right; the scarce 1947 Straight 7 Maple leaf, which had a very small maple leaf just to the right of the 7; and the very rare 1947 Curved 7 Maple Leaf, which had the small leaf just to the right of the curved 7. I got out my Canadian coin book and magnifying glass to make sure. Yes— there it was—the very rare 1947 Curved 7 Maple Leaf in Fine condition! I checked my book—it was a $325 coin at that time! What a find! Today the coin is worth about $2,000. However, that coin, as well as others, would find a fate that upsets me to this day.

In the mid 1960's, we used to pull what was known as "Reflex Alert" up in Goose Bay, Labrador. It was advanced refueling support for our nuclear bombers in the event of a first strike from our Cold War enemies. We flew our KC-135 tanker up there on a Sunday about noon so it could be readied the rest of the day and night to go on ground alert the next morning at 0700. We were then on ground alert, twenty-four hours a day, until the next Monday morning, when we were replaced by another crew.

Although that was a busy time for the ground crew to get the bird ready, we, the four crewmembers, had the rest of those Sundays off. A few times the people at Goose Bay called down to Loring a couple of days before our trip up there, and asked if any of us would like to go fishing. We all said yes, as this would be a great way to spend that free Sunday afternoon. Sure enough, when we landed about noon the following Sunday, they met us at the airplane, took our bags to the BOQ, and loaded us on either a six-passenger DHC-2 Beaver, or a larger DHC-3 Otter outfitted with floats.

Snacks and drinks were also waiting for us, along with all the fishing gear we would need for the afternoon. We took off,

Ten or eleven Passenger DHC-3 *Otter*, above, or its smaller brother the six passenger DHC-2 *Beaver* we used to go fishing.

flew north for about an hour, and landed at a remote VIP camp only accessible by floatplane. I walked about 300 yards down the shoreline of the lake from the camp to a fast-moving stream that emptied into the lake from the left. I walked up the edge of the stream about 100 feet to a place that looked promising. I put a three-inch red-and-white Daredevil lure on my line, and cast it almost all the way across the 100-foot-wide stream. As the fast-moving current swept my lure downstream to the right near its mouth, there was a tremendous pull on the rod. As I slowly reeled in against the full force of the current, the pull was unmistakable—something big was on my line. One of the guides leaned down and reached out with the net to pull in an incredible sight to me—a five-pound rainbow trout—on my first cast! It was the biggest trout I ever caught in my life—what an absolute thrill!

The rest of the afternoon was spent enjoying this outstanding pastime in this pristine location with my crewmembers and friends. When it was time to go, I walked the 300 yards back to camp, and there on the dock waiting for us was a large black bear! He knew we were "in town" fishing, and he was waiting for his share of the take when we cleaned the fish and threw out the remnants. He made quick work of the fish scraps, and finally wandered off into the dense woods—very happy and very full.

These few fishing trips were an experience of a lifetime I'll never forget, and it's as clear to me now as it was then in 1966.

Another great memory I have from 1966 is another Reflex Alert trip. This time we went up to Eielson AFB, twenty-eight miles south of Fairbanks, Alaska. The strategic location of Eielson makes it an important base to this day.

On one of the trips up there during winter, the four of us went into town and ended up in a pizza bar with sawdust on the floor, lots of great pizza, and lots of beer. It was quite cold outside, and we were in dire need of personal antifreeze. In the middle of the large floor was a raised platform that could be viewed easily by everyone there. On this particular night there was a banjo player sitting up there entertaining as we all had a great time. He asked if anyone had a song they'd like played. As someone would call out a request, he proceeded to play it—in two or three different renditions—all by memory! He was absolutely amazing. He was by far the best banjo player I've ever heard in my life—tucked away in a bar on a cold winter's night in the middle of Alaska. What a waste of a great talent.

Another flight I recall from those years while I was on Dick Skovgaard's crew was a long flight up over the North Pole to refuel a reconnaissance aircraft. The vision I remember most vividly is looking out the cockpit windows from our 37,000-foot altitude, and seeing nothing but the Arctic Ocean about ninety-five percent covered with huge chunks of broken ice as far as we could see in all directions—thousands of square miles. We were all very happy to have all four engines running smoothly that day, as there was no reason to be wearing our parachutes!

During the time I was at Loring, Mom and Dad came up to visit during the summers. Mom had very severe hay fever, but we found out that she was virtually free of all allergies in the northern Maine climate. They rented a cabin in the small town of Sinclair between Long and Mud Lakes for a month during her worst season down in Ithaca. It was truly amazing to see her hay fever-free and enjoying the cool climate by the lakes each summer. Dad and I took advantage of the situation and went fishing! We tried Long and Mud Lakes, but with no luck—Long was too large, and you had to know where the good spots were. I did not, and the local residents were not about to tell us. Mud Lake was too small and shallow. However, Cross and Square Lakes were great fishing for trout and salmon. We had many enjoyable days together fishing those two lakes for their fun-to-catch and very tasty yield.

During this time, the war in Vietnam was escalating. More and more pilots were being called to go. USAF Personnel came out with a policy that allowed any pilot to volunteer for duty in Vietnam. This was my chance! I volunteered for "F-anything"—to fly any fighter. That was all I could do. I could only sit and wait now—and hound the "personnel weenies" who made the assignment selections.

In January 1968, I received TDY orders to Squadron Officers' School (SOS) at Maxwell AFB, in Montgomery, Alabama. SOS was a three-month school to teach staff and other need-to-know classes for young officers. Part of the curriculum of the school was physical fitness. Along with other activities, we all had to run twelve minutes every day. However, if we wanted, we could strive for the 50, 75, 100, or additional Mile Clubs that we could shoot for in our off-time. I reached the 100-Mile Club, and I never felt better in all my life—it was a great feeling.

While there in SOS, I met Captain Lee Canh Loi, a South

Vietnamese pilot in the Vietnamese Air Force (VNAF). He was a great individual, and we had many talks together. He gave a very emotional lecture to our class about his country and the war raging in his land. He said the war was *not* a civil war as many around

Down at Aunt Edna's in Sarasota after SOS in April 1968. (L-R) me; Carol, Dad taking a picture of Mom taking the picture of us; Mae, Paul, Mark, Kristen, Paul & Mae's daughter Ellen; and their son, Jack.

the world had claimed. It was out–and-out aggression of one country against another—the North against the South. He was so happy that the United States was helping his country against the invaders. I told Lee that I was trying to get a fighter assignment to Vietnam, and I would like to meet up with him again when I got over there. He gave me his address and phone number in his squadron, and was looking forward to getting together again—he would buy the drinks!

A few months later, our 42nd Air Division Commander, Brig. Gen. Robert J. Dixon, was looking for an aide. Just for the heck of it, I applied. When it was my turn, I was told to report to him in his office for an interview. When I went in, I saluted, and stood at attention while he sat at his desk. He asked me if I wanted this job of being his aide. I said, "Yes, Sir." But then I added that I had a volunteer statement in at Personnel for Vietnam. He asked what for. I told him I wanted to fly fighters, and I had volunteered for any fighter to make it happen.

He then asked, "Well, what do you want to do—be my aide, or fly fighters in Vietnam?" I told him, with all due respect, I'd rather go to Vietnam, because flying fighters was a goal I'd had since I was four years old. In typical Gen. Dixon format, for which he became famous over the next fifteen years as he went on to four stars, he yelled at me, "Well then, GET THE HELL OUT OF HERE, AND QUIT WASTING MY TIME!"

That meant the interview was over. I said, "Yes Sir," saluted, did a crisp about-face, and started for the door. As I was about to leave, I heard him say in an almost fatherly tone, "Good luck in Vietnam, Captain—wish I was going with you." A few weeks later my assignment came down: F-100 school at Luke AFB, Phoenix, Arizona. I wonder to this day if Gen. Dixon had anything to do with that assignment. It was October 1968.

Just prior to me leaving Loring in November on my way to water survival school at Homestead AFB, in southern Florida, I was once again sitting alert. It had snowed about ten inches the day before, and the taxiways, ramps and hardstands where the birds were parked were still icy. Sure enough, the alert klaxon went off, and all the tanker and bomber crews ran to our alert vehicles—six-passenger pickup trucks affectionately known as "six-packs"—and headed at a lively pace to our aircraft about half a mile away. As we skidded to a stop outside the left wing of our forward-facing "cocked" alert bird, we all jumped out and ran toward the ladder underneath the nose to climb up and in.

Unluckily, I slipped and fell on the ice, and landed flat on my back. It felt like a lightning bolt went through my body, and for a few seconds, numbness. I lay still for a minute to see what

106

was going to happen. I tried to move my fingers and toes, and all worked fine. My navigator helped me up, and we slowly climbed into the cockpit; I started number four engine with the large starter cartridge. I put my headset on and, along with the copilot and navigator, got ready to copy the coded message from the Command Post telling us it was just a start-engines exercise; a start and taxi simulated alert launch of the entire alert force; or, God help us, an actual nuclear launch from which I most probably wouldn't be coming back. Thank God, it was just another start-engines exercise, and after all alert birds checked in, we received clearance after a few minutes to shut down, secure the aircraft, and return to our Alert Facility.

I was a little stiff getting out of my left seat, and getting back to the "alert shack." The next morning I could hardly get out of bed. I moved around as best I could, as I didn't want to go to the flight surgeon. Pilots don't like to go to flight surgeons, because if something is seriously wrong, they have the power to ground you—permanently. Pilots don't like to be grounded—at all. As time passed I slowly got better, I thought.

I had an assignment to F-100 school at Luke AFB, Phoenix, Arizona with a "TDY Enroute" to water survival school at Homestead AFB, Florida. Water survival in southern Florida in November, coming from snow chin deep to a giraffe in Northern Maine, was great. We had classes for a few days, and then out on the ocean we went. The school had an old converted WWII landing craft with a flat deck over most of the boat. They also had a motorboat with a large engine—much larger than would be needed to water ski. We were each, in turn, hooked up to a parasail, which looked like a steerable parachute, and we were pulled off the back end of the landing craft. As we picked up speed, we would climb with this chute until we were being towed at about a sixty-degree angle and about 150 feet off the water.

We had our survival kit hooked to us the same way we would have it in the aircraft.

On a signal from the head instructor and an okay from us, we released the tow cable. We deployed our survival kits as we started to float down in our chutes to the ocean below. Great fun! As your feet hit the water (not before!) we were trained to release both parachute Koch fittings at our shoulders, which instantly released the chute from us, and it would, hopefully, blow away from us. This was done to avoid being dragged under water and drowned, which could happen quite easily, even in a light breeze.

However, if there were little or no wind, it was quite possible to have the chute canopy settle on top of you. This was also dangerous, as it could entangle you in the nylon parachute lines, and smother and drown you as it started to sink. But not to worry. We learned in class, and practiced in a swimming pool, what to do if that happened—roll over on your back, reach up and back behind you, and pull the chute up and forward one hand at a time, hand over hand, as you find and follow a seam to prevent going around in circles. This would get you to an edge of the chute and keep an air bubble under the canopy in which to breathe. We then inflated and climbed into our one-man life rafts, and practiced using all our survival gear from our survival kits. They left us out there three to four hours before coming by and picking us up. It was very educational.

With water survival behind me, it was off to F-100 school at Luke. I was to finally become a fighter pilot.

Chapter 7
F-100 School – January – July 1969

*B*y this time, Carol and I decided to trade in our VW Hatchback for something larger and more dependable for the trip west to Luke. We decided on another VW, this time a station wagon, which looks like a present-day minivan. We packed all our loot, said goodbye to our friends at Loring, and headed south to Syracuse to say goodbye to Carol's folks. While there we had a big snowstorm, and I helped out a little shoveling snow off the driveway. This aggravated my back again, but I did not want to make waves over it— it'll go away as it did last time. It finally did, but it took many weeks. We left Carol's parents and drove down to Ithaca to say goodbye to my Mom and Dad. Carol, Kris, Mark, and I left Ithaca and headed west to Phoenix.

We arrived in Phoenix in plenty of time to get settled before my F-100 class started in January 1969. We bought a brand new four-bedroom house that was being built in a new subdivision on the west side of town with easy access to Luke about six miles away. We put a pool in the backyard, and then landscaped both front and back. It was beautiful. Total cost, if I remember correctly, was about $22,500.

My fighter school started in earnest in late January 1969. The first couple of weeks were devoted to more academics as my classmates and I studied the different systems of the Hun. It was now time for my first fighter sortie.

The North American F-100 Super Sabre was nicknamed the Hun—the first in the "Century Series" of fighter aircraft, and it was the first fighter in the USAF active service inventory capable of attaining supersonic performance in level flight. Our class was in the single-seat "D" model of the F-100, which was the most prevalent at that time. However, there was a two-seat "F" model that was used in upgrade training such as this, and most F-100 squadrons had one or two for instrument check rides and such.

There were very minor differences between the "D" and the front seat of the "F."

The F-100D had one Pratt &

The North American F-100D *Super Sabre*

Whitney J57-P-21/21A turbojet engine that had 10,200 pounds of thrust at full military power and 16,000 pounds with afterburner. It had a maximum speed of 770 mph at sea level (clean), 864 mph (Mach 1.3) at 36,000 feet (clean). It had an initial climb rate of 19,000 feet/minute, and it could get to an altitude of 35,000 feet in 2.3 minutes. Weights: 21,000 pounds empty, 28,847 pounds gross, 34,832 pounds maximum takeoff. Armament: Four 20 mm Pontiac M-39 cannon, and six under-wing pylons for up to 7,040 pounds of bombs, fuel tanks or rockets.

My first flight was to be with my instructor pilot (IP), Maj. Al Bartels, in an "F" model. He would be in the back seat, and I would be in front. We taxied out and went through the quick check at the entrance to the runway where ground crews check for any loose items, fuel or hydraulic leaks, cut tires, etc. We received clearance for takeoff, and I taxied on the runway, and held my brakes as I pushed the throttle up to full military power. I quickly scanned all my gauges one last time for any sign of trouble, then released brakes, moved the throttle outboard to light the afterburner (AB), then pushed the "kerosene handle" all the way forward to full AB. The sensation was fantastic!

While holding the brakes at full mil power, the bird was surging and straining to be set free. When I released the brakes, I was pushed back into the seat cushion by the acceleration. But when the AB lit and the throttle was pushed forward to the max AB position, I was thrown back even deeper into my seat. I had never experienced any acceleration like this in my life. I was in a jet fighter hurtling down the runway at over 150 mph ready to takeoff in a matter of a few seconds. I eased back on the control stick with my right hand while holding the throttle in max AB with my left. The bird rotated to the slight nose-high takeoff attitude and smoothly left the ground. I was flying a fighter!

"Gear up," I commanded as I had done for the past five-and-a-half years in a multi-person crew aircraft. Nothing happened. "Gear up," I said again over the intercom to the IP in the back seat.

"Raise the goddamn gear yourself!" came the gentle sound wafting through the intercom from the back seat into my helmet headset. "Who the hell do you think I am, you're &^*%#$@* butler?!"

For the past five-and-a-half years I had flown with three other people as a crew—each of us with our coordinated duties, but now I was training to fly a single-seat fighter with a crew of one: me! That was Al's hint to me that I needed to learn this fact. Everything done or not done in this bird would depend on me, and me alone, from now on. It was a very valuable lesson, and it really made me pay attention to the complex business of flying single-seat, single-engine jet fighters.

After I finally got the gear and flaps up before ripping the gear doors off from excessive speed, we accelerated to climb speed of 300 knots, and headed out into the student practice area and leveled at 15,000 feet. My IP demonstrated different stalls and the proper recovery procedures, and then let me do the same. You don't intentionally stall airplanes—any of them—however, you always practice them in most aircraft to recognize the onset of the stall, the stall itself, and the proper recovery in case you approach and/or enter one unintentionally during critical flight conditions, such as in the landing pattern.

Maj. Bartels also wanted to show me another anomaly with the Super Sabre. He told me to slow down to about 150 knots while maintaining straight-and-level flight. To do this, I needed to keep more and more backward pressure on the stick, because the nose, as in most aircraft, tries to drop as speed is reduced. As our speed decreased, and more and more back stick pressure and back trim was applied, the nose came up higher and higher to maintain level flight. This high nose attitude in relation to the direction of the aircraft is called "Angle of Attack" or AOA.

When I stabilized the bird at 150 knots, only about thirty knots above stall, and 15,000 feet, he told me to light the afterburner. I went through the normal AB lighting procedure as we had done on the runway for takeoff. I pushed the throttle up to full mil, moved it outboard to light the burner, then pushed it forward to max AB. Nothing happened for a few seconds, and then an incredible *BANG!* that actually blew my feet off the rudder pedals! I thought we had hit a brick wall or another airplane. Al told me it was a compressor stall of the engine caused by trying to light the AB at high angles of attack. At these high AOAs, airflow into the engine isn't sufficient for the demands of lighting the AB. "If you need to light the AB, make sure you 'unload' the airplane first by releasing back stick and/or applying forward stick pressure," he told me.

We tried it, and it worked normally. This was another incredibly important lesson I learned about the Hun on this first ride. So what, you may ask? So many pilots were killed in the Hun because of this problem—the most famous of these was the infamous "Sabre Dance" caught on film at Edwards AFB in the early '50s. Every student going through F-100 school was shown this film, showing a pilot coming in for a landing and deciding to go around at the last minute. At normal landing attitude, the angle of attack is high. If you raise the nose higher and try to light the burner, you actually slow down further because the exhaust nozzle opens, but the AB doesn't light, the engine compressor stalls with a belch of fire out of the intake, the aircraft stalls, and, as in this case etched in our minds, crashes into a fireball. The rest of the ride was equally as informative.

After a few more rides with the IP it was time to solo! I would get to fly my own jet fighter with my IP chasing me in his own Hun! What a great experience! It was about tenfold the feeling I had with my first jet T-37 solo and my T-33 solo in pilot training back at Reese in 1962—and it reminded me of that summer day back in Ithaca in 1958 when I soloed for the first time in that little yellow Piper J-3 Cub. But this was no Cub, and this was no trainer. This was the real thing!

After a very detailed and thorough preflight briefing of what we were going to do on the mission, Al and I went into our squadron's life support section to suit-up. We put on our G-suits, checked our helmets to make sure the oxygen mask, and radio transmitter and receiver were all working properly, picked up our parachutes, and headed out back to the waiting crew van to take us to our individual jets. The driver dropped each of us off, and the first thing I did was greet the crew chief, who was at the bird waiting for me. "How's the bird, Chief?" I asked as I climbed the ladder to put my chute and helmet in the cockpit.

"Ready to go, Sir" was his quick, confident reply. That sure made me feel good, but we always checked the Form 781, a book about an inch thick that always stays with each aircraft, for the history and current maintenance write-ups. I reviewed the form and signed it off that I had accepted it for flight—all was in order. I grabbed my checklist, came back down after a quick check of the cockpit instruments and switches to make sure all were in their proper positions, and the crew chief and I walked around the bird for the preflight inspection.

The preflight walk-around is to check for any fuel or hydraulic leaks, tire condition, proper weapons load, loose or missing panels, and any other possible problems that may be in waiting for the unsuspecting pilot. All was normal. I climbed the ladder and the crew chief followed me up. After I climbed in and got seated, he helped me with the parachute harness and shoulder harness. I told him thanks, and he said, "Have a good flight, Sir," as he went down the ladder to man the large fire extinguisher during engine start. Again, using my checklist, I went through the entire cockpit, from back left of the left console around to the back right of the right console, to move the maze of switches to their new positions for engine start. I checked my watch—two minutes to the prebriefed start engines time. The checklist was complete to that point, but my eyes moved around the cockpit again to see if I had missed anything. All was ready.

I could see my IP sitting in his jet a few parking spots away. When it was time, I gave him the start-engine signal—a vertical circular motion of my right hand with index finger raised. We each gave our crew chiefs the same sign, and initiated our start-engine sequence. My bird started normally, I completed my checklist for this sequence, and called my IP to check in. "Dancer 11, check."

"Twoop," was his quick answer.

"Luke Ground, Dancer 11, taxi two Huns."

"Dancer 11, Ground, taxi runway 03 Left."

"Dancer 11, roger."

I gave my crew chief the horizontal two-thumbs-out signal for him to pull the chocks from under the wheels, advanced the throttle slightly to start the bird moving while watching him motioning me forward, checked the brakes by pushing the tops of the rudder pedals to make sure they were working, and taxied out to the quick check area at the entrance to runway 03L. Maj. Bartels fell in behind me as I taxied past his parking spot. I took the downwind side of the taxiway, and Al was on the upwind side, clear of my exhaust.

The ground crews gave our two birds one last check, pulled the pins on our two external fuel tanks to allow quick jettison in an emergency, and gave us the thumbs-up signal that all was okay. When they completed their checks, I called Ground Control, received our clearance, and we were cleared over to Tower frequency. We were ready.

"Luke Tower, Dancer 11 ready for takeoff."

"Dancer 11, Luke Tower, winds three-five-zero at 10, cleared for takeoff."

"Dancer 11, roger—cleared for takeoff."

I taxied onto the runway and lined up in the middle of the right side of the runway, because we were going to make our first turn after airborne to the left. The IP taxied on behind me and lined up in the middle of his half of the 300-foot wide two-mile-long three-foot thick slab of concrete. I gave him the same engine start/run-'em-up signal we used before, and we each went to full mil power and checked our gauges. All was well. I looked back at Al, and he gave me a nod that he was ready, and, because this was my first solo flight and he was the IP responsible for me, I was cleared to go. I released brakes, lit the afterburner, and pushed the throttle forward to full AB. What a feeling! The acceleration was even more dynamic than takeoff in the heavier two-seat "F" model. I brought the nose up smoothly as I reached the pre-calculated takeoff speed, and my bird leaped into the air. I was airborne—solo in a jet fighter!

I raised the gear and flaps, made the required radio call to the control tower, accelerated to our best climb speed of 300 knots, and started my left turn out of traffic toward the north end of the White Tank Mountains west of the field, as I checked the gauges and reset switches that needed resetting. I looked back over my left shoulder to see Al as he was closing on me to join up. With only fifteen seconds spacing behind me on takeoff, he joined up quite easily. Before he settled in on my left wing, he maneuvered underneath me to make sure my bird was okay. He gave me a thumbs-up. I gave him a forward motion of my left index finger, and with a tap of his helmet with his left hand and a raised index finger signifying he was now Number 1, he assumed the lead of the two-ship flight, and I slipped back and checked his bird out. All was not all right.

Al's bird had a very pronounced leak from under his mid-fuselage section. I immediately called him on the radio and told him that it looked like a possible hydraulic leak. He rechecked his gauges, and it was confirmed—he was losing hydraulic fluid quite rapidly. Now what? An IP up with a student on his initial solo flight, and the IP has a serious emergency. That's what long preflight briefings are for—to talk about emergencies and what we would do. In this case, losing all hydraulic fluid would mean losing all your brakes, steering, and some control on landing— time to get it on the ground.

Al immediately declared an emergency with the tower and turned back toward the base, which was now already about fifteen miles behind us. He told me to get clearance to orbit here at the north end of the White Tanks, and he would get another IP to join up with me. On the way back, Al called one of his IP friends who was also airborne at the time with a more advanced student from a more senior class. That IP took his student back and watched him land, and then came out to join up with me. Al had also told him I was on my initial solo flight and required, by the book, chasing through all traffic patterns and landing to make sure I didn't do that "Sabre Dance" thing. After about twenty minutes, the new IP joined up, and all was back to normal. We no longer had time to complete the full mission, so we flew around a little practicing simulated traffic patterns to burn down gas enough to go back to the landing traffic pattern and practice.

The tower relayed to me they were still using runway 03L with a left break. I gave the IP a wing dip to the right, and he slid down, under, and back up to my right wing formation position— wingtip light on the fuselage star. I entered the pattern in the proper way, reduced speed to 300 knots at 1500 feet above the ground, and turned onto initial approach—lined up with the center of the runway flying directly toward it.

"Luke Tower, Dancer 11, Initial, initial solo" I transmitted when we were about five miles out. This was the only time the students needed to give the added "Initial solo" call. It was to alert all who heard it that there was a new guy in that jet. I looked at the IP briefly to make sure he was in position on my right wing away from my pitch, and gave him the circular motion of the index finger signal for pitchout.

On the next page: left, front, and right consoles of the F-100D/F. Notice the bomb sight at eye level; yellow drag chute handle at top left for landing; yellow canopy breaking tool on top of right console to break out if canopy won't open; two yellow ejection seat handles on front of both sides of the seat; gear handle on front of left console; throttle on left console; engine start button very top left of left console with red "panic" button directly below it that jettisons all external stores (easily confused with start button); standby compass is barely visible at very top above the sight. Bottom of rudder pedals can be seen. Gray flap handle is outboard of the throttle; UHF radio is just to the left of the left ejection handle; caution & warning light panel on forward right console; control stick in center. Red "pickle" button to drop bombs on top of stick grip next to the "top hat" trim switch. Gun trigger is on front of grip (not visible). Altimeter, reading about 780 feet, is in center of front console with the attitude indicator to the left—gray is sky; black is ground. Quite different from that Piper Cub ten years before!

Jay E. Riedel

The Office—cockpit of the F-100D *Super Sabre*.

When I reached the point directly over the landing spot at the approach end of the runway, I banked the aircraft 60 degrees hard to the left, brought the throttle back to just above idle, extended the speed brakes to help slow me down, and concentrated on maintaining my altitude of 1500 feet as I pulled the bird around the turn. After 180 degrees of turn, I rolled wings level, checked the runway to make sure I wasn't being blown in or away from it by the wind, checked airspeed below 230 knots, which had bled off rapidly in the "pitch-out," and put the gear handle in the "down" position. In a couple of seconds after three thumps, I checked the landing gear indicators on the front instrument panel for three green lights—all three wheels down and locked. Yes! Now the flap handle down for full flaps, and start the 180-degree base turn to final approach. "Luke Tower, Dancer 11, Base, gear down, low approach, initial solo." was the required call.

"Dancer 11, Luke Tower, roger, winds zero-four-zero at 8, cleared low approach," came from the tower, and they knew I was being chased in fairly close formation by an IP.

During that last base turn to final approach, you not only had to fly the bird precisely to line up with the runway by playing the bank for winds, and be at the right altitude and airspeed, but you had to keep scanning the airspeed, engine RPM, and about twenty other instruments, to make sure you and the bird were both ready to land at the right spot. You also needed to keep track of the other birds in the traffic pattern to make sure you didn't try to get in the same piece of sky at the same time with any of them. The landing pattern is a very busy place—especially when it's full of students.

At about fifty feet over the runway, I smoothly pushed the power up to full mil, raised the gear and flaps, and made my call: "Luke Tower, Dancer 11, on the go, request closed, initial solo."

"Dancer 11, Luke Tower, roger—cleared closed." After a few more low approaches, I made a full stop landing, taxied into the parking spot I came from, shut the bird down, and climbed out. I had just completed my first solo ride in a single-seat, single-engine jet fighter. What a great feeling of accomplishment I had! It was a long-term dream fulfilled. But that was only the beginning of the F-100 school. Many more months of intensive training, both in the classroom and in the jet, were ahead of me to, not only learn how to fly the bird well, but how to use the bird in combat.

Mission complete!

About a month later, I was up flying an Instrument mission with my IP in an "F" model. Al was in the front seat as the Instructor and safety observer, while I was in the back seat. When we were safely airborne, Maj. Bartels turned control of the bird over to me, and I began to fly the preplanned instrument mission. This was done by the student in the back seat sliding a canvas hood from back to front of the canopy and completely blocking any outside viewing from the rear cockpit. The student had to fly the jet only by the reference to his cockpit instruments. This was excellent training, because someday one could be flying in clouds or other weather that would prevent any reference to the ground. Not knowing how to fly solely by instruments would surely mean disorientation and disaster if caught in bad weather. I didn't want that. I paid attention. It paid off later.

However, to get that wonderful heavy canvas hood to slide all the way forward on its wire runners, tall people, like me, had to lower the seat all the way so the hood wouldn't catch and drag on my helmet. If it did, it was very annoying and distracting—not good while concentrating on flying precision instruments. Unfortunately, when the seat was bottomed out, your feet on the rudder pedals were out almost level with your butt. This meant that most of your body weight was resting directly on your tailbone. I flew about half the prescribed mission this way, but the pain in my back was getting to the point that I could no longer concentrate on flying. Finally, I couldn't do it any longer, so I told Al what was going on with my back. He told me to come out from under the hood, and we would abort the mission and go home. Sounded like a great plan to me—I was really hurting.

After we landed, I knew I had to finally go to the flight surgeon to find out the problem and get some pain pills. I told the doctor what had happened in the aircraft. He decided to have some X-Rays taken to see what was going on. When the X-Rays came back about an hour later, he studied them, and then asked me, "When did you break your back?"

I told him what had happened back at Loring many months ago when I fell on the ice, but that it had slowly gotten better. He asked me if I had seen a flight surgeon at the time, but I told him I hadn't, because of the fear of being grounded. He let me know that wasn't a great decision, and my last three vertebrae in my lower back had now fused together. He gave me some pain pills to take when it bothered me a lot, and told me that it would slowly deteriorate over the years, and would be quite prone to arthritis. I wasn't grounded. However, as advertised, my back has slowly gotten worse over the years and constantly bothers me today.

The rest of the school went well. We learned different weapons and their respective deliveries. Five hundred-, 750-, 1000-, and 2000-pound bombs were delivered in either 30- or 45-degree dives, while high-drag weapons, such as napalm and bombs with high-drag fins that opened after release to slow them down, were delivered in level, 15-, or 20-degree attitudes. Strafing with the four 20 mm cannons was the most fun. This was done in a 10 to 15-degree dive, or in some cases depending on the threat, high-angle strafe of 30 degrees so you could recover from the dive at 3,000 to 3,500 feet and stay out of the small arms and automatic weapons fire from the bad guys.

Each of these different deliveries with these different weapons required individual sight settings, which had to be set up prior to the delivery. The Hun had an "iron sight"—not computerized as modern sights are today. The sight reflected in the windscreen and was depressed at different degrees by dialing in different mil settings in an instrument on the left console. This exact sight setting, along with very accurate release airspeed, altitude, and dive angle—while compensating for wind—would result in a very accurate "splash." However, if any of these factors were not "exact," as was the case 99.9% of the time, we were taught how to compensate by adjusting the others so as to still get a very accurate delivery.

Second only to strafe for fun was 50-foot level skip bombing. You approached the target at 50 feet above the ground,

Normal F-100 formation takeoff on the right wing showing the correct position as to line up the small green wingtip light on the star of the fuselage. This photo was taken by the back-seater, which shows him to be slightly aft of the correct "light on the star" position—the front-seater is lined up correctly.

going about 400 knots. When the depressed sight showing in the windscreen passed through the target, you would "pickle" the bomb off, and hopefully, hear that beautiful sound from the Range Officer who monitored the deliveries: "Skip hit in the middle of the box, Lead!" or, as in other bomb deliveries, you may hear, "Shack, Lead—that's a bull!"

We also had a lot of formation flying as well. Except for the first one or two rides, just about all the missions had some amount of formation time with one, two, or three other birds, including formation takeoffs and landings. Rarely do fighters go out single ship. Most always in at least pairs for mutual support.

During these six months at Luke I got my first motorcycle. It was a 350 cc bike from Sears, and about the same quality as that motor scooter from Wards I had in pilot training—

poor. However, it was great fun to ride to and from Luke. In that short six months I had an accident that taught me another lesson: motorcycles are hard to see, and if you're on one, you'd better anticipate the actions of all other vehicles around you.

I was on my way to the base one morning when I approached an intersection that had stop signs for both corners that met my through street. I saw a car stop at the corner to the left of me, the driver looked both ways, and then he pulled right out in front of me as I was entering the intersection. I had to lay my bike down to prevent hitting him full broadside. The man, in his 50's, never saw me...and I had my headlight on. That taught me to become a very defensive driver—all the time. Expect the unexpected. It has paid off well.

Also during this time, little Kris and Mark and I had "fight time" when I got home from work. We would wrestle on the living room floor, and then each of them would take turns climbing up on our couch and riding on my feet as I lay on my back on the floor. I would hold on to their hands while I gave them their ride with my feet on their stomachs. Great fun! We also had lots of fun in our pool in the backyard, and both Kris and Mark learned to swim very well that summer.

After six months of concentrated instruction, I graduated from F-100 school in late July 1969 as a combat-ready Hun driver. All of us in the class received our orders—we were on our way to Vietnam, but to many different squadrons. Some received orders to become Forward Air Controllers (FACs) flying little propeller birds, such as the O-1, O-2, or the newer OV-10, that found and marked targets for the "fast movers"—the fighters. I had survived the luck of the draw, and had received an F-100 assignment instead of a FAC job.

Capt. George R. Andrews was a classmate of mine. He was a good guy, and not as wild as most. He had a bad habit in gunnery, which showed up on his gun camera film. He would attack the target, and then bank and pull to recover from the dive. This was dangerously wrong, as you could drag a wingtip and crash if you didn't have your nose pointed well up above the horizon before turning. You were supposed to attack the target, pull wings level to recover from the dive, and *then*, when the nose of your aircraft was pointed up, bank one way or the other. His instructors pointed this out to him, and he corrected it.

He and his wife and baby stayed with Carol and me a couple of days while their belongings were being packed up and moved. His wife and baby were moving back east while George was in Vietnam for the year. We had a great time together for those few days, and it was great to be able to relax after the intense schooling. As it turned out, we were both assigned to Phan Rang Air Base, South Vietnam, so we were looking forward to flying together over there. George had a slightly earlier reporting date than I did, so they left Phoenix about two weeks before I had to leave.

"I'll see you over there, George—don't end the war before I get there!" I said to him, as he was ready to leave.

"Don't worry," he said. "I'll save a lotta action for you!" We waved goodbye as they drove off.

While I was in F-100 school for this past six months, Carol had decided to go to work. As a Licensed Practical Nurse, she got a job as an assistant to a doctor in Phoenix, and was happy to be working.

Chapter 8
Vietnam – 1969

*W*hen it was time to leave in early August, I said goodbye to Carol, eight-year-old Kris, and five-year-old Mark, and departed Phoenix by commercial air to Travis AFB, CA to catch a military charter flight to Clark Air Base in the Philippines. That was a very emotional departure for me at the Phoenix airport, as I got on the plane, and watched my wife and two children standing there waving goodbye. Many things went through my mind at that moment; one of which was the fact that I had volunteered for fighters in Vietnam a few years earlier, and now this wish was about to become a reality. This is an important point.

When I first put in my volunteer statement back at Loring in the early 1960's, it was something I had to do. It was something I had decided on when I was four years old back on our farm in Pennsylvania. There was no hesitation at all on my part. However, how does a decision like that affect a wife and family? Very few wives can accept this. Very few can accept that their husband and their children's father would rather fly airplanes in combat 12,000 miles away, than be with them.

Unfortunately, very few men can explain why they would want to. To me, it is beyond the family—a higher calling than the family unit. It is at the international level in an unstable world— and the fact that stronger nations that invade weaker ones must be stopped if world peace is to become a reality. Is this true? Was it the right choice? This decision can be debated for years to come, as it has already for centuries as young men go off to war throughout history. The cost can be very high. It was for me, but I have no regrets.

I had orders to the 615th Tactical Fighter Squadron (TFS) at Phan Rang Air Base, South Vietnam, with a TDY (temporary duty) en route to Jungle Survival School at Clark Field, PI. Yet another survival school. After a few days of classes, out into the jungle we went to spend a few days. Living—I mean existing—in the jungle for only a few days reinforced my decision I made back at survival school at Stead: Don't get shot down, and don't get captured. We would be awakened each night by jungle rats moving about; they were huge and sounded like elephants going by. We were also taught how to hide and what to eat in a jungle. They had local Negrito natives come out to look for us to see how well we could hide. They found all of us in less than ten minutes. It was good training.

After a couple more Wednesday nights up on the hill for Mongolian Bar-B-Que, I left Clark Air Base after "Snake School" graduation and got a ride on a C-141 into Cam Ranh Bay. On a map, Phan Rang is about six miles from the coast, just below the eastern-most bend of South Vietnam and only about 50 miles south of Cam Ranh. I jumped on a C-130 and finally got to Phan Rang in mid-August. I reported in to the squadron commander, Lt. Col. Aaronson, and he told me to process in, get set up in our squadron hooch, and we would go fly together in the morning.

My first fighter combat mission was with Lt. Col. Aaronson. The normal checkout was to get a backseat ride in an "F" model to have demonstrated all the procedures and landmarks of the combat area.

We checked in with the FAC, got our target briefing, and set up for the first attack. As we rolled in for that first pass, I

Jay E. Riedel

A post-1975 map of Vietnam. Saigon is now renamed Ho Chi Minh City.

thought to myself, *"Here we go—combat—better bottom out my seat and duck my head!"* I pressed and held the seat elevation control switch down to electrically lower my seat as far as it would go, and scrunched down as low as I could get in the cockpit. I was ready. Bring it on.

Afraid? I don't think it was actually fear, but more the feeling of anxiety one has when entering an unknown, never-before experienced, life-threatening situation.

Sure enough, the FAC said we were drawing small arms and automatic weapons fire during the pull-off. But not being hit that first pass on that first mission gave me a sense of security within the cockpit, and a tremendous feeling of self-confidence in my abilities and the outstanding instruction I had to prepare me for this moment of my chosen profession. It is a great belief and trust in one's self.

Fighter pilots are known to be arrogant and self-centered, but I believe the reason for this is their tremendous confidence in themselves for being able to accomplish any mission by himself. I can honestly say I never experienced fear; only various levels of anxiety during times of increased challenges—of which there were many to come. In retrospect, I noticed that, as the situation of the ground troops we were supporting at the time became more critical, as in friendlies close to being overrun by a larger enemy force, my focus became more intent on helping them rather than on my personal situation. Helping and supporting the ground troops in the Close Air Support (CAS) role gave me the greatest satisfaction over the air-to-air role of one aircraft against another of the classic "dog fight." To turn the tide of a ground battle from near disaster into success is a feeling of tremendous pride and accomplishment. It was here I decided to stay with the air-to-ground CAS mission, which I was lucky enough to do, for the most part, for the rest of my career.

Three missions and one week later after processing in to Phan Rang, I received notification I was to report to the 510th TFS at Bien Hoa Air Base about thirty miles northeast of Saigon and about sixty miles east of the jut of Cambodia to the east known by us as the "Parrot's Beak."

3rd Tactical Fighter Wing Patch from Bien Hoa in 1969

I stopped flying, processed out, hopped on another "trash hauler" C-130 (as fighter pilots referred to any cargo aircraft) down to Bien Hoa, and reported in a couple of days later. It was now the end of August 1969. After processing into this base and getting settled in the Squadron hooch, it was time to get checked out in this new local area. More local procedures had to be memorized, and combat missions started coming again.

There was another fighter squadron in the 3rd TFW at Bien Hoa at this time—the 90th TFS that also had the Super Sabres. Our squadron hooches were side by side, but away from the flight line and aircraft. It was great fun occasionally to attack the other squadron. This was done with great planning and precise coordination—usually around 0300 on a Saturday morning after a rather enjoyable Friday night at the Officers' Club. The attack would start, after all aggressors were in place, with about fifteen of the thirty pilots climbing quietly up on the other squadron's roof. Dress was optional except for flight boots—they were a necessity! On signal, the guys would all start a loud, sustained roof-stomping back and forth the length of the building. This, of course, would cause most of the slightly inebriated inhabitants (after that hearty Friday night at the Club) to come stumbling out to see what was going on. This was the desired reaction, as now the fifteen guys on the roof of the one-floor building, plus the other fifteen on the ground surrounding the "bad guys" started spraying "the enemy" with every pump water fire extinguisher in both hooches—ours and the ones borrowed from the other guys as they slept prior to the breakout of hostilities. This prevented any immediate retaliation. Great fun!

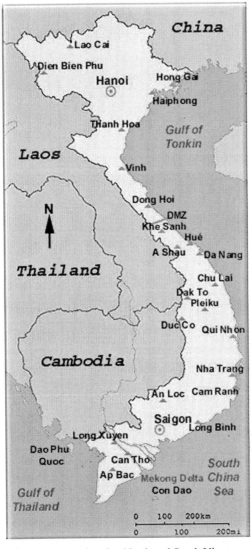

During one of these battles, one of our more energetic pilots lost his balance and fell off the roof, giving himself a cut on the head which required six stitches (no Purple Heart!) and a slight concussion. What to do? Our Squadron Commander had to maintain control and enforce discipline—this chaos could not go unchecked, especially in a combat zone. "Crash," as he would be forever known, was told to report to the squadron commander at 0800 the next morning—in Class "A" uniform. What a

Pre-1975 map showing North and South Vietnam divided by the DMZ (Demilitarized Zone). Notice the relationship to the other four countries.

sight at 0800 as we all went down with him to see what was going to happen. "Crash," in his almost-too-small blue dress uniform, with numerous combat ribbons already awarded for past missions, walking into the commander's office with a slight hangover sway—with a bandage around his head. He looked like one of the Revolutionary War fife and drum players.

The conversation in the commander's office went something like this as we all strained to hear through the closed door what was going to happen:

"WHAT THE HELL WERE YOU DOING LAST NIGHT, CAPTAIN?"

"Sir, I was engaged in an attack on our Squadron's enemy, when I inadvertently lost my footing and fell off their roof," explained Crash.

"WELL, LISTEN UP, CAPTAIN—THE NEXT TIME I CATCH YOU UP ON A ROOF, YOU BETTER HAVE YOUR HELMET ON. NOW GET THE HELL OUT OF HERE!"

The control tower of Bien Hoa in September 1969, and a rescue helicopter at the ready.

With a "Yes, Sir" and a very wobbly about-face, Crash came out to everyone's thunderous applause and laughter. That night, to celebrate, we had another attack on our enemy. Sure enough, there was Crash up on the "enemy's" roof in the heat of battle, in T-shirt, boxer shorts and combat boots, stomping up a storm and pumping away with his fire extinguisher—with his steel infantry helmet on over the bandage around his head! It was the best of times in that environment.

If it weren't for these attacks on each other, we would be brought out of a sound sleep by real attacks and shooting. Occasionally we would have a rocket attack, as the VC (Viet Cong or "Charlie") lobbed rockets onto the base—usually aiming for the pilots' hooches and/or any aircraft out in the open. The birds were usually in individual hardened half-shell shelters, so the pilots were always a better target in their "soft" hooches. We each had a $10,000 price on our heads, so we were controlled where we could and couldn't go. At Bien Hoa at that time, all pilots were confined to the Base. Luckily, during my watch, Charlie didn't do too well. However, with every rocket attack, the Army would answer with their own 105mm Howitzer barrage. Some of these cannons were less than half a block from our quarters, so sleeping was not an option during their response.

The Squadron color for the 510 TFS "Buzzards of Bien Hoa" was purple. We were each fitted for our purple "party suits" the first day we arrived on station. Party suits and flight boots were the uniform for Friday nights at the Club, as well as other social gatherings, such as Hail and Farewell parties for our Squadron mates. Most of us also had small Honda 90 motorcycles that were bought from guys that were DEROSing (Date of Estimated Return from OverSeas) back to the "Land of the Big BX." There was a restriction on buying new ones, so the only ones available were the hand-me-downs from one guy leaving to the next FNG (^&%#*&% New Guy). These were great little bikes for around the Base. They were also a lot of fun to ride to and from the Club. On any given Friday night, we would all suit up in our purple party suits, flight boots and motorcycle helmets,

This official USAF photo was taken at Bien Hoa on/about 13 Oct 1969. These photos were affectionately known to us as "Hero" photos! Photo was taken inside a hardened shelter with an F-100D. My right hand is on a 750-lb M-117 general-purpose bomb with nose fuse and its arming wire showing. To my left is a 100-gallon external fuel drop tank. If the photo were in color, the entire helmet visor cover would be purple—our Squadron color for the 510th TFS.

jump on our trusty Honda 90s, and ride to the Club about a mile away. However, the best part of this was the fact that we all went in a very tight precise "V" formation with handlebars that almost touched. It was a beautiful sight to see—going over. However, the return formation after a few whiskeys was a bit ragged.

On one of the return trips one Friday night, about twenty of us decided to have a Wheelie-Poppin' Contest. All of the guys did pretty well. When it was my turn, I decided I wanted to win. Unfortunately, the way to win was to pop higher than the competition. I did great, only I popped too high, and the bike came straight over on top of me. I started laughing, and during my hilariously great moment of fame, I had forgotten to let go of the throttle, which was the right handlebar grip. I was laughing with the rest of the guys, and as the bike lay on top of me with the throttle still wide open, I was systematically ground, in a clockwise circular motion, into the pavement of the parking lot. We all had a great laugh, and they decided I had won. However, the next morning, I noticed that my right leg of my party suit was ripped to shreds—along with some of my lower leg! Oh well, You gotta expect losses in a big operation!

Bien Hoa in August was very hot and very humid, as it was most of the rest of the year—in the 90s for both, with almost no breeze. We sweated constantly, and our long-sleeved flight suits looked like we took a shower in them.

One day in early September, I was flight planning at a desk in the Squadron Operations building, when suddenly, I felt both of my hands start to go numb with a pins and needles feeling. I didn't think too much of it at first, but within a few minutes, the numbness started up both arms simultaneously. This got my attention, and I started to get hotter than normal. I told one of the guys what was happening, and we decided to jump in the Squadron jeep and head for the hospital.

When we got there, I told the nurse what had happened, and she took my temperature—102. After about five minutes as they were deciding what to do for me, I began to feel quite light-headed with a shortness of breath, and hotter. I told this to the nurse, and we took the temperature again—104.2! Into bed I went. I don't remember much after that, but they said I slept for the next three days at close to twenty-two hours per day as they gave me an IV to keep me hydrated, and to bring down the temp with antibiotics. I had a good case of double pneumonia, and I was in the hospital for ten days. With another week after that before being put back on flying status, my sortie count was getting behind.

Also during this time, there were several trips to take an F-100 up to Tainan in southwestern Taiwan for IRAN (Inspect, Repair And replace, as Necessary) maintenance. You then found your way up to Taipei at the northern end of Taiwan, spent a day, returned to Tainan, and brought another Hun back to Bien Hoa.

I found the train up and back through the middle of the island to be a beautiful trip—quite a nice modern train with hot tea served. These were great R & R trips, and guys were waiting in line to get them. There were many street vendors in Taipei who sold Seiko watches and other great items quite cheep. Seiko watches and little rechargeable pocket flashlights were the most popular goodies at the time. Those little Japanese flashlights were small enough to fit in the cigarette/pencil zipper pocket just below the left shoulder on the flight suit. Once in a while the return fighter wouldn't be ready, so the individual would have to spend an extra day or two TDY in Taipei. Shucks...heck...darn.... Our Ops Officer handed out these trips quite fairly, with everyone getting one or two trips over a period of about forty-five days.

The island of Formosa off the coast of China showing the relationship between Tainan and the capital city Taipei

By this time there were rumors that our squadron may be closing. As soon as I got wind of it, I called my old squadron commander up at Phan Rang, Lt. Col. Aaronson. "Sir, this is Capt. Riedel."

"What can I do for you, Jay?" he said.

"I may need a job in a few weeks, Sir — okay if I come up?"

"You bet—anytime!" was his reply. What a great feeling that was to have this new assignment worked out ahead of time.

Sure enough, the 510th TFS closed up, and a friend of mine, "Buzz" Buzzy and I processed out, packed up, jumped on another trash hauler, bid farewell to Bien Hoa and went back to good old Phan Rang by the sea—a smaller, but much nicer base—cooler and better scenery. This was Halloween, 31 October 1969, and in those past sixty days I had been "in country," I only had twenty-three missions to show for it. It was now time to get busy.

Chapter 9
Vietnam – 1970

Back at the 35th TFW at Phan Rang, Buzz and I processed back in, moved our belongings back into the 615th Squadron hooch, and started flying our combat missions again from this new base—with all new standard operating procedures (SOPs) that had to be relearned. I was one of the guys that hung around the Operations desk, watching for openings that I could jump into to fly more missions. Sitting alert was another way to, most probably, get three missions a day on a "good day."

Sadly, I learned that George Andrews, my friend and classmate from Hun school back at Luke, was killed in action (KIA) 15 October 1969 while I was back at Bien Hoa. I never knew the details, but he was shot down over a target in Kien Tuong Province in the Mekong River Delta of IV Corps. It was my first loss of a friend. Today, George's name can be found on the Vietnam Veterans Memorial Wall on Panel 17W, Row 80—along with 58,226 others engraved on the black granite Memorial Wall in Washington, DC. Rest in peace, George.

Shortly after I got settled in at Phan Rang, I called Capt. Lee Canh Loi, whom I had met in SOS at Maxwell AFB back in January 1968. Lee was now flying A-1 Skyraiders in the Vietnamese Air Force (VNAF). He said that he would stop over at Phan Rang the following week so we could get together again.

Individual revetments (five-foot wide steel partitions filled with dirt to prevent chain reaction fires/explosions) with F-100D's at Phan Rang. This is looking south in December 1969.

Lee flew in, called me at the squadron, and I went down to the parking area to pick him up. It was good to see him again. I brought him back to our squadron building, where we relaxed. When it was time for him to go, we shook hands again, made a tentative date to get together again in a few months, and I watched him take off and leave the area for his home base. It was a great visit for both of us. Sadly, we never got back together. Lee was KIA a few weeks later while attacking another target up in II Corps.

One of my most memorable F-100 missions came on 4 December 1969. "Buzz" Buzzy and I were sitting alert in the brand new George R. Andrews Memorial alert facility. We had the "soft" load that day: 6 x 500-lb high drag "Snake-eye" bombs on Buzz's *Sabre*, and 4 x 750-lb napalm on my bird. Both of us also had a full load of ammo in our four 20 mm Pontiac M-39 cannons. When the klaxon went off, the loud speaker blurted out, "Scramble Alert 3 and 4!" That was us!

Buzz and I raced to our two jets that had been pre-flighted and cocked ahead of time, climbed the ladder, jumped in, and hit the start-engine button. This fired a large cartridge that started the engine rotating, while our crew chiefs followed us up the ladders to help us strap on our 'chutes and fasten our shoulder harness and lap belts. As our engines wound up to 12% RPM, we brought our throttles "around the horn" out of the OFF position, which allowed the igniters and fuel to begin. As we finished strapping in, we heard the deep rumbling as the fuel in our engines ignited, and the engines continued to "spool up" to idle RPM of about 60%. Other crewchiefs were on the ramp in front of us with large fire extinguishers watching our birds to make sure all went well. It did. As our birds reached idle, our helmets and oxygen masks were now on, and the two-thumbs-out signal was given to our crew chiefs to pull the chocks that keep our sleeping birds from moving. It was now time to move!

Alert start of a "cocked" Hun. All switches are set up ready for engine start. The pilot jumps in and hits the engine-start button that fires a starter cartridge about the size of a gallon jug to start the engine rotating. The cart gave off thick black smoke.

We eased our throttles forward slightly—just enough to get us rolling without blowing over equipment and people inside the enclosed alert hanger that kept our birds safe from rocket attacks. As we checked our brakes and cleared the facility, we

Four TER's (triple ejector racks) pre-loaded with 3 x 500-lb MK-82 high drag "Snake-eye" bombs, each ready for uploading.

pushed them up further to get a good taxi speed before pulling into the "Quick-Check" area at the entrance to the runway, only about 100 meters away. As the ground crews checked our birds one more time to make sure all was okay, and the weapons crews armed our weapons by pulling the safety pins with red streamers from each of our bombs, Buzz and I contacted our command post to copy our instructions. It was now that we learned we were headed for a very serious TIC—troops in contact with the enemy.

With our birds ready to go and our weapons armed, we requested and received immediate takeoff clearance. We taxied on the runway, and pushed our throttles forward, outboard to light the afterburner, and then all the way forward for maximum afterburner for our heavy weight takeoffs. Even at max AB, these birds would take 6,000 to 7,000 feet of runway to get enough speed to fly at heavy weight and at the warm temperatures of Vietnam. You had pre-planned exactly how long and at what speed you would rotate the nose to get the Super Sabre airborne.

We also knew exactly at what speed we could still stop on the remaining runway if something very serious happened to prevent flight. We also knew that if any serious emergency happened after that speed, we were committed to

The four-barrel ZPU 14.5-mm KPV heavy machine-guns could reach out and touch you up to an altitude of 4500 feet.

trying to get it in the air and eject, if necessary. Takeoff in a single-seat, single-engine jet fighter was a very busy experience—especially when you had over 3,500 pounds of bombs and ammunition, and 7,000 pounds of jet fuel strapped to your butt. That's why all the very serious emergency procedures, such as "engine failure on takeoff" had to be committed to memory—you didn't have the luxury of digging out your emergency procedures handbook to look it up if it happened.

Our initial heading was 290 degrees for 125 miles from Phan Rang. We were told it was a very critical TIC and to expedite—we did. We were headed for Duc Lap, a very small forward operating base in Darlac Province, II Corps, which was just about due west from Nha Trang and only about two nautical miles from the Cambodian border.

When we were about 75 miles out and within radio range, we contacted the FAC and got our target briefing—what the situation was, the weather, altimeter setting, attack heading, nearest friendlies, and best bailout area if we needed it. Heavy small arms and automatic weapons fire, including ZPU's, were known to be in that area. A couple hundred of our Special Forces were trapped on top of a small hill (836) just south-southwest of the airfield. They were completely surrounded by a vastly superior number of North Vietnamese Army (NVA) enemy troops, which had begun to climb the hill and overrun our forces on top.

The weather in the target area was poor. The ceiling was only 1,000 feet in light rain and getting worse. Because Cambodia was only two miles to the west, which we weren't supposed to fly in at that time, we had a restricted attack heading of south to north with a right break on the pull-off. We were also asked if we could drop our ordnance one at a time. Well, this is three strikes on us already: 1) bad weather. We normally needed about a 5,000-foot ceiling minimum for these munitions to be able to properly and safely deliver; 2) a highly predictable restricted attack heading. After the first two attacks by us, it ain't gonna take no rocket scientist to figure out where our next attack would be coming from—and to have all your guns aimed toward you in barrage fire as you come through that same airspace again; and 3) we normally made one pass to drop our bombs in a high threat area like this so as to minimize exposure. But it was not to be that day.

Buzz and I found a small hole in the clouds about ten miles from the target area and let down through it. We were now skimming under a 900-foot ceiling at close to 500 mph until we got the FAC in sight and the small hill.

We stayed well east of the area to maintain our element of surprise until we were ready to attack. When the FAC had coordinated with the ground commander as to the place he wanted hit, Buzz and I armed our weapons release switches and were ready. The most desperate place was the south side of the hill. A large enemy force was halfway up already. The FAC told us the ground commander wanted us to put our ordnance halfway up that south exposure. With the restricted run-in heading, that meant we would be delivering the ordnance directly toward the friendlies—a no-no. Almost all weapons delivery errors are either long or short; therefore, we always dropped parallel to the friendlies—not over or toward them.

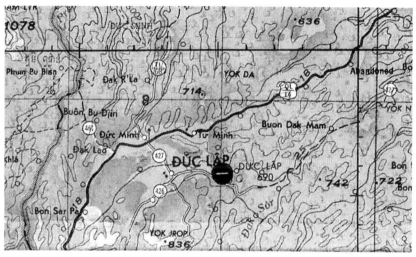

The small outpost of Duc Lap in Darlac Province, II Corps, which was just about due west from Nha Trang and only about 2 nautical miles from the Cambodian border. Note Hill 836 at the lower center of the map and border to the left.

The FAC told us that he knew our restrictions. He said, "I can't ask you to do this, but if you don't, our troops will most probably be overrun within 20 minutes."

Our reply was quite simple, "What do you need us to do?" The situation was critical and the ground commander accepted responsibility for the attack—just do it!

We also had restrictions with these weapons on how close we could drop them to friendlies—500 meters for the 500-pound bombs, 300 meters for the napalm, and 100 meters for strafing. These, too, were waived by the ground commander.

Buzz and I each made individual runs dropping single ordnance each time. After the first pass they told us we were taking heavy small arms and automatic weapons fire. We made sure we "jinked" in the pull-off and around the entire area— never predictably straight and level. All of our attacks used a descending, accelerating curvilinear approach to also minimize our susceptibility of getting "hosed" by the bad guys. The ground commander and FAC were ecstatic.

"Great, lead—two, move yours 20 meters right!"

"Super! Lead, hit another 20 meters right of that last hit."

"Two, move yours 50 meters left!"

We kept pounding that southern slope until all our bombs and napalm were expended. The FAC asked us if we had time to put in a couple of strafe runs. We checked our fuel and the urgency of the situation, and said yes. The weather had now deteriorated to an 800-foot ceiling with two miles visibility in light rain—not the best at over 475mph over the hilly terrain of western Vietnam. We both made three strafe passes up the side of the hill, each time telling the friendlies to keep their heads down as we rolled in. We were now strafing within 25-75 meters of their positions.

At 300 pounds of fuel below our "bingo" quit-and-go-home fuel, Buzz and I safed up our switches, checked out with the FAC, and headed home. The FAC told us on the way out that we had completely stopped the enemy's advance and had sent them back down the hill. What a great feeling we had. There is nothing like it in the world.

We found out later that this siege had lasted from 28 Oct 69 to 27 Dec 69. The same two North Vietnamese Army (NVA) regiments—about 4,000 men—that had besieged Ben Het and Dak To had moved south to besiege Bu Prang and Duc Lap during the cool, dry weather.

Buzz and I were awarded the Distinguished Flying Cross for this mission. My Citation reads as follows:

"Captain Jay E. Riedel distinguished himself by heroism while participating in aerial flight as an F-100 Tactical Fighter Pilot near Duc Lap, Republic of Vietnam on 4 December 1969. On that date, Captain Riedel flew his aircraft from alert status in response to urgently requested close air support for elements of a friendly Regiment completely surrounded by a large hostile force. With complete disregard  for his personal safety, despite intense automatic weapons fire, poor visibility and a ceiling of less than 800 feet, friendly forces within 75 meters of the target, and a highly vulnerable restricted attack heading, Captain Riedel elected to make repeated low angle ordnance passes to ensure pinpoint accuracy and total target coverage, thus completely blunting the hostile offensive. The outstanding heroism and selfless devotion to duty displayed by Captain Riedel reflect great credit upon himself and the United States Air Force."

Just another day at the office!

Another memorable mission came a few weeks later. This time I was again sitting alert, but with the "hard load" of 8 x 500-pound "slick" bombs. This ordnance is delivered by either 30- or 45-degree dive-bombing, or by straight and level at 3,000 to 7,000 feet altitude under the control of a ground radar.

I was sound asleep when the klaxon went off at 0300. The loud speaker called my callsign, so I jumped up, zipped on my flight boots (we slept in our flight and G-suits), and ran to my waiting mount! I jumped in, started the bird, and copied the instructions from the command post—proceed to a specified location and drop the bombs while straight and level on an enemy truck park that had been located. Easy—piece of cake!

After getting armed up in the quick-check area, I received takeoff clearance, pulled on the runway and took off into the very dark night. The weather was solid clouds from 1,500 feet up to

Two TER's pre-loaded with 3 x 500 pound MK-82 "slicks" each. Nose fuses have been installed.

30,000 feet, and this mission, known as a "Sky Spot," (or affectionately called "sky dump" by those of us who did them)

was for me alone—single ship. I reached my level-off altitude of 10,000 feet and reached the area about 30 minutes later. The controlling agency on the ground gave me the briefing, and started giving me headings to fly as they maneuvered me for the proper heading, altitude, and airspeed for the drop. They also passed on some wonderful news—the weather was deteriorating and there were thunderstorms in the area. They finally got me lined up for the target run, and at the precise time, I pressed the small red button on the control stick to release all eight bombs in pairs with 50-foot spacing between pairs. I told the controllers I had dropped, and they gave me a vector back to Home Plate—Phan Rang about 150 miles to the east. I checked out with them, and I was on my own.

My fuel was okay, but the weather was getting worse quite rapidly. I started to see lightning, and I was getting into turbulence. I was about to enter thunderstorms, and I had no way around them. It was pitch black outside, and I was still in solid clouds.

In today's aircraft there is radar that shows weather which you can use to navigate around and avoid strong storms. Unfortunately, the 1950s technology F-100 had no radar at all, and quite primitive instruments. The lightning, rain and turbulence were getting worse—I was in the middle of a large storm.

Suddenly there was a blinding flash, and I could feel the lightning strike hit the aircraft. It was quite obvious I'd been hit, as all my cockpit lights were out. I reached down and got my issued flashlight and switched it on—nothing happened. It was dead, and I'd forgotten to check it prior to flight. Fortunately I had my small Japanese Sanyo rechargeable flashlight about two-thirds the size of a pack of cigarettes that most of us carried. It was one of those really neat items I'd bought from a street vendor in Taipei while I was there on an IRAN trip from Bien Hoa. It sure came in handy that night, because without it, in the thick weather at night with no chance of moonlight, it would have been impossible to see anything inside the cockpit. The next step would have been even more distasteful—eject, lose the bird, and walk home—if I was lucky!

I turned it on and held it in my mouth, as my left hand was on the throttle and right hand on the control stick fighting to keep the bird under control in the severe turbulence. The first thing that went through my mind was that I hoped that little flashlight was fully charged! It worked great, moving my head slightly to see any switch or instrument I needed to from the left control panel, forward instrument panel, to the right panel. The lightning strike had not only knocked out all the cockpit lights, but all the navigation instruments and my radio as well. The only gauges that worked were my engine instruments, airspeed, altimeter, the little standby attitude indicator, and standby compass, and, thank God, the engine was running normally.

So now what? The last weather report I had for Phan Rang was a 1,000-foot ceiling and three miles visibility in light rain. With no way to contact Approach Control or navigate myself to the base over 100 miles away, I was in deep trouble. I decided to gamble. I flew out directly east to a point that I knew was well south of the base and out over open water of the South China Sea. I had to make sure I was over open water so as not to hit mountains in the area. If I hit a mountain, I'd know I screwed up as soon as the windscreen started to crack…. That would've ruined the rest of my night.

When I knew I was far enough east and over water, I turned left to parallel the coast. Phan Rang was only about six miles from the coast. I let down very slowly through the murky darkness as I watched my altimeter closely, so as not to go too low and hit the water. I decided to only go down to 500 feet. If I hadn't broken out of the weather by then, I would go to Plan B—whatever that was.

One thousand feet, 800 feet, 600 feet, 500 feet—still nothing. Time for Plan B—maybe just a little lower—400 feet, 350 feet, and then water and lights from the coast about two miles to my left! I leveled off, headed toward the coast and turned right to fly north towards the inlet that went westward toward Phan Rang. A few miles up the coast; there it was. I turned left and flew the six miles toward the base until I saw the runway strobe lights in the haze off to my right. I turned on a straight-in final approach and put my gear down. Fortunately, all three landing gear came down and, I hope, locked, as I had no positive indication. Luckily, my landing light worked, and I flashed it a few times to get the tower's attention until I got a green light from them, and landed straight in. I was never happier to get back on the ground then I was that night.

Afraid? I don't remember being afraid, as such. I was way too busy to worry about what may happen. I do remember feeling challenged and the very confident feeling I had of being able to overcome this situation, based on the training I had in instrument flying and knowledge of the bird.

That little three-dollar-and-fifty-cent flashlight, bought on the streets of Taipei on one of my maintenance deliveries and pickups from Bien Hoa, literally saved my life that night. After I landed, taxied in, and shut down, I went to unstrap and climb out. It was only then I found that, in my half-alert state of being awakened out of a sound sleep at 0300 with a klaxon loud enough to be heard in Chicago, and in my haste to get airborne, I had forgotten to attach my parachute. If I had ejected from the bird that night, the seat, parachute, and I would have gone our three separate ways. I was more careful from then on.

About a month later I was scheduled for a mission up in II Corps with 6 x 750 pound slick bombs. On takeoff toward the north, I noticed I was getting very warm—I must have forgotten to adjust the air-conditioning rheostat prior to taxing. After I was safely airborne with the gear and flaps up, I checked the switch—it was set normally, but it wasn't working. It was getting much hotter.

There was an emergency in the Hun that happened when a valve fails between the hot engine temperatures and the air-conditioning compressor. This allows very hot 16th-stage air from the jet engine to be blown directly into the cockpit through all the AC ducts without being cooled first. There's no way to fix it in flight, so all you can do is jettison all your external ordnance and fuel drop tanks to reduce weight, slow down by reducing the throttle, and land as soon as possible. If it gets too hot, you should jettison the canopy.

I declared an emergency with the control tower, turned right toward the sea only about six miles from the base, and jettisoned all my external bombs (in safe mode) and fuel tanks when I was over open water. I continued around to the right back toward the base. The temperature in the cockpit was very hot, but I didn't think it was serious enough to blow the canopy off. I would be on the ground in only a few more minutes. I recall turning my head to look at something, and having the large metal quick-release Koch fittings on my parachute harness touch my bare neck and cheeks where my collar had folded down and the hot metal burning my neck. I landed straight-in, slowed down enough to raise my canopy without ripping it off, and opened it.

The blast of fresh 95-degree air felt cold to me. I taxied off the runway and shut down as the emergency vehicles reached me.

Four TER's (triple ejector racks) preloaded with 3 x 750 pound M-117 "slick" bombs each.

Many times after we landed, Red Cross girls, affectionately known as "Donut Dollies," would meet us with ice-cold frozen towels so we could wipe our face and wrap them around our necks.

But this time it was the Flight Surgeon and medical personnel that came up the ladder as soon as the crew chief hooked it on the left side of the bird. It was then that I realized how weak I was. I couldn't move.

They unbuckled my shoulder straps, lap belt, and parachute, but I couldn't get out by myself. They noticed my plastic checklist pages on my right thigh clipboard had melted and fused together. I had red burns on both sides of my face and neck from the parachute Koch fittings. They gave me some cool water to drink, and cold frozen towels for around my neck and over my head. They finally got me up and helped me down the ladder. My legs felt like cooked spaghetti. They took me to the hospital for a checkup, but I was fine. All I needed was a cool shower and a lot of liquids, and the rest of the day off to rest.

It was a very hot ride, but worst of all, it was insidious. I had a false sense of well-being during the flight—a little hot, but no problem…all's well. I had been airborne a total of seven minutes. One of my squadron mates had the same thing happen to him a few weeks later, but he was airborne fifteen minutes and had blown off his canopy. The hot air blowing in on his feet through the air conditioning ducts partially cooked his right foot through his flight boot. He was grounded for over two months. He was lucky.

500-pound MK-82 slick bombs and LAU-3A 19-rocket pods of 2.75" folding fin aerial rockets (FFAR's)

F-100D with 4 x CBU-24 over the bomb-pocked Ho Chi Minh Trail of western Vietnam. "The Trail" was the main supply route from north to south.

A 40-foot munitions trailer loaded with
pre-wired M-117 750-pound bombs.

Two Huns approaching the Vietnamese coast with 4 x 750's each. Two
external fuel tanks on mid pylons were standard.

Bird with 2 x 750-pound BLU-27 napalm on the inboard pylons, two fuel tanks on
the mid pylons, and 2 x 500-pound High Drag bombs outboard.

In early February 1970, I was half way through my tour, and it was time for R&R: rest and recuperation. Carol had made reservations for us at a beautiful beach resort hotel on the island of Kauai, Hawaii. We both flew into Honolulu, and stayed there for a couple of days before going over to the other island. It was great, and so was Kauai. Even the doctor she worked for back in Phoenix called to see how everything was going. How nice. On the way back, we stayed the last night in a hotel back in Honolulu before it was time for me to head back to Phan Rang. It was an outstanding R&R.

Another memorable mission I had after I returned was to the city of Stoeng Treng, Cambodia, a city on the Mekong River about forty-five miles south of the southern tip of Laos and almost 300 miles to the northwest of Phan Rang. My wingman

Another alert start of the Hun showing the dark smoke from the starter cartridge as it fires. It starts the engine rotating before fuel and ignition are added to the start sequence. Also the yellow entrance ladder on left side.

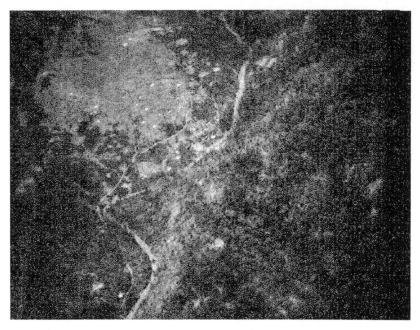

Part of the bomb-pocked Ho Chi Minh Trail—the main north-south supply route from North Vietnam down through Laos into Cambodia and South Vietnam.

and I were scrambled off alert carrying "Snake & Nape." "Snake Eye" and napalm was a favorite weapons load for close air support, because you could get in close to the friendly troops and be quite accurate in their delivery.

"Snake" was 500-pound high-drag bombs with a kit added on the rear of the slick bomb that popped open four metal fins approximately three feet long to a 60 to 70 degree angle. These four fins would slow the bomb considerably causing it to fall slower and quite accurately. They also allowed you to get out of the blast zone before they would detonate. These were carefully fused in such a way that, if the fins didn't open, the wire keeping the arming propeller from spinning in the nose fuse would not be pulled out, and the bomb would not arm. This was always a great idea, because if they did arm when the fins didn't open, the "slick" bombs would be traveling almost as fast as you were, and you and your trusty Super Sabre would be directly over them in the middle of the blast, thus filling your trusty mount with many ugly holes. This was known as a "Low Blow," and the powers that be looked dimly on these...even if you were lucky enough to make it home.

Napalm, or jellied gasoline, was a very good close support weapon when dropped parallel to the friendlies—never toward them, nor from behind. Its nomenclature was BLU-27 (Bomb, Live Unit) for the freefall, unfinned version, which was most commonly used. When delivered in level flight or in a shallow dive, the cans tumbled randomly and were ignited by a very hot white phosphorus fuse on impact. The fireball covered an area close to a football field in size. There was also a finned version, which was delivered like a slick bomb in a 30- to 45-degree dive. These were better suited for pinpoint targets, such as a cave entrance. Napalm was a controversial weapon considered to be inhumane in some circles, and has since been eliminated from our country's weapons stockpile, and from most others around the world. If you must kill your enemy, you must do it nicely.

When we checked in with the FAC, he told us there was heavy construction equipment at the main airport that had been captured by the North Vietnamese, and was on its way up to be used on the Ho Chi Minh Trail—the main north-south supply line from North Vietnam down through Laos into Cambodia and South Vietnam. A large yellow bulldozer, road grader, and numerous other pieces of road equipment were just north of the airport passenger terminal, affectionately known as "Howard Johnson's," as it had a bright orange tile roof. The Ho-Jo terminal was strictly off-limits to any bombing or strafing, as the good guys were going to recapture it any day, and they didn't want it damaged. However, all the heavy equipment was to be destroyed—what a great target!

Both the dozer and the grader were parked side-by-side, facing north on the east side of the north-south runway. There was no enemy thought to be in the area, so I told my wingman we would make multiple passes and attack east to west with a right break. He had the snake eyes and I had the napalm, so I decided this was a great time for me to try my first time at 50-foot level skip bombing in combat—like we practiced so much of at Luke going through F-100 gunnery school. What great fun it would be to slide a can of nape right into a big, yellow bulldozer!

"Skip hit, Lead," was the FAC's call to me after my first pass. This was great! I turned back on the pull-off to look over my right shoulder, and the dozer was engulfed in flames. My wingman and I made multiple passes and completely destroyed the equipment. It was sure a lot of fun, but not too smart.

When all our ordnance was expended, we checked out with the FAC and headed back towards Phan Rang. When my wingman joined up with me on the climb-out and looked me over for the standard battle damage check we always did coming off a target, he called me on the radio, "Lead, I think you're leaking fuel out of your forward fuel tank."

I called for a fuel check, and sure enough, I was 300 pounds less than my wingman. After a few more fuel checks, my fuel was going down rapidly—it was quite evident I wouldn't be able to get all the way back home. We checked each other carefully for any other battle damage, but couldn't see anything else on either bird, although you can only get so close at 400 miles per hour without banging wingtips. After a quick check of the map, I decided to abort into the nearest friendly base with a runway long enough to handle my trusty Hun. This was Pleiku, about 150 miles to the east-northeast. I would attempt Pleiku, and have my wingman continue on home so the bird wasn't tied up for other missions later on that day.

The city of Stoeng Treng in north central Cambodia is on the east side of the Mekong River about forty five miles south of the southern most tip of Laos.

I told my wingman what I was going to do. I contacted Pleiku, declared an emergency with battle damage and rapid loss of fuel, and got their weather. They gave me 1,100 feet overcast, three miles visibility with light rain. I requested radar vectors to a straight-in, full-stop landing. When I knew I had enough fuel to reach Pleiku, I told my wingman I was going to lower my gear to make sure it worked. If it did, he was to leave me and go back to Phan Rang. I put the gear handle down, and those three wonderful green lights came on—all three wheels down and locked! I cleared my wingman to depart, and I was on my own.

The Pleiku controllers gave me headings and altitudes to fly as they vectored me closer to their runway. My fuel was

F-100D landing with drag chute deployed. Note 8,000-foot runway-remaining marker on the right.

dropping steadily. As I descended, I left the beautiful clear blue sky and entered the thick clouds of the undercast below me. I told the controllers to make this a great approach, as I would only have enough fuel for this one try. They told me the same thing! They brought me down to 1,000 feet and told me the runway was off my left wing at one mile. Sure enough, as I broke out of the "soup," I looked to the left, and there was that beautiful runway. I told them I had the runway in sight, and I'd take over visually for the landing. They cleared me to land, and I turned back around to the left, lined up with the sequenced strobe lights that pointed you to the center of the runway in the murky distance, and got ready for the landing.

The runway had standing water on it from the rain. I was also a little fast and a little high in case the engine quit on me. Those three factors made it clear to me that I may have a hard time stopping the bird on the 10,000-foot runway. I touched down as close to the approach end as I could after losing a little excess altitude and airspeed, and popped my landing drag chute,

162

which helps slow the bird. I held the nose of the Hun up as long as I could for aerodynamic braking before letting it settle to the runway. As soon as the nose wheel touched, I got on the brakes—nothing happened! I was hydroplaning—skimming on top of the water—down the runway. I watched the runway-remaining signs go by: 4,000 feet to go; 3,000 feet. I got on the brakes again and felt them start to grab. Two thousand feet; 1,000 feet remaining—and I was still going over 100 knots. I knew I had better put my tail hook down in case I couldn't stop before running off the end of the runway.

The very large steel hook lowered in the rear of the bird drags on the runway, and would snag the large steel barrier cable stretched across the end of the runway, about six inches high, to prevent aircraft from running off the end and into the mud. But before I did that, I had to weigh the fact that I was pouring JP-4 jet fuel out of my forward fuel tank right under me, and lowering the hook would be like dragging a match on sandpaper in the middle of it. I decided to wait a bit longer—800 feet, 300 feet, and my speed was down to 60 knots. I thought I could get it stopped—better drop the hook in case.

GaLOONK! Down came the heavy steel hook as it hit the runway. At this speed, and in the rain for this amount of time, the hook would not have enough time to get hot enough to ignite the fuel running out of the bird...I hoped. I was unstrapping anyway, so I could get out as soon as the bird came to a stop. Luckily, I brought the bird to a stop about ten feet short of the cable just as the fire trucks and other emergency vehicle "meat wagons" pulled up. They started spraying foam on the hook, underneath the bird on the fuel, and they placed brake-cooling fans on the two main landing gear to help cool the very hot brakes. All was okay. I got out and went around to look at what was going on. There was a large bullet hole in my forward fuselage, right under the cockpit, that was leaking fuel. I also found another bullet hole, which had shattered my air refueling light, on the leading edge of the right wing. It was another time I was happy to be on the ground. I also

This photo was taken from the ramp at Pleiku. Pleiku is located about 60 nautical miles due west of Phu Cat. This was a major base with a 10,000-foot instrument runway.

hoped they had stopped teaching 50-foot-level skip bombing in gunnery school. You just don't do that in combat.

I was in luck. There was a trash hauler about to leave for Phan Rang, so I grabbed my gear, jumped on it, and away I went back to my Home Plate. They repaired the Hun, and one of our test pilots went up to get it a few days later. I was back in time to get another mission that day!

Another experience that sticks in my mind was a night mission only a few miles to the west of Phan Rang. There had been some enemy troop movement sighted, and I was scrambled off alert single ship to respond to it. My bird was loaded with four cans of napalm, and the FAC would drop a red marker on the target to give me an aim point. No flares to illuminate the area would be used. The FAC gave me the target briefing as I approached the area after burning down my fuel to the proper attack weight. The weather was good, the terrain was flat, and I was to use a restricted attack heading of south to north with a left break for single passes. Although the weather was clear, there was no moon that night, and it was dark. All was ready, so the FAC flew over the target area and dropped the red spotting ground marker, known as a "log." He asked me if I had the log in sight when it hit the ground and ignited. I acknowledged I had it in sight. He told me that was a good mark: "Hit the log."

I maneuvered the bird to the attack heading and rolled in for the standard 10-degree dive delivery pass for the napalm. I called "In," and he answered with, "Cleared hot." When I reached my release point of 500 feet above the ground, I pickled off a single can and started my wings-level pull-off before turning to the left. I looked back over my left shoulder to see the impact, and the little red marker log disappeared in a huge fireball as the napalm hit and slid into an area about the size of a football field. It was a "shack!" As the initial bright light of the large fireball subsided, I could see past it, and there, only a couple of hundred meters away off my left wing, was a hill and trees above my airplane! I called the FAC and calmly told him, "HOLY SHIT! There's a damn MOUNTAIN off my left wing! I thought you said the terrain was FLAT!"

He answered, "It is. That little hill is only 500 feet high!"

"ONLY 500 feet high!" I yelled back, "That's my RELEASE altitude, and I just bottomed out at 300 FEET!"

Looking southwest at Huns being refueled at Phan Rang.
Note all the "flat" Terrain around the Base.

"Oh," he said, "Sorry 'bout that."

I made one more pass with a release altitude of 1,000 feet, pickled off the other three cans into the target area, and went home.

As time passed and my experience grew, I was checked out as an instructor in the Hun. Fortunately I didn't have too many IP rides in the back seat of the "F" model—*flying* fighters is the best; *riding* in the back seat is as much fun as watching grass grow.

It was about this same time that many of the pilots in the three squadrons of our Wing had a rash of problems with target fixation. They would get so engrossed with the target that they would not be aware of the surrounding terrain until it was time to pull off. They would release their ordnance, and start their recovery—only to look up at a mountain in front of them!

Fortunately, all had been lucky so far, and had been able to plow through the trees and get the crippled bird home with tree limbs sticking out of the leading edge of the wings! This, of course, meant the pilot and F-100 were within fractions of a second, and only one or two feet, from crashing into the high terrain—all at almost 500 mph. Our Wing Commander was not happy with this trend, the damage being done to his jets, nor the

Very low pullout! Once in a while, pilots would bring tree limbs back to the base jammed in the leading edges of the wing.

embarrassing reports he had to make "up the line" to his superiors.

After one such occasion and very close call by one of the Wing pilots, we were all told to form up in front of the alert shack for a pilots' meeting. All of us were there standing at attention when the Wing Commander drove up, slammed on the brakes, got out, and climbed up on the roof of his blue staff car in front of us.

"I'm SICK of this shit!" he yelled. "The next dumb son-of-a-bitch that hits the trees in one of my jets, I'LL SEE TO IT PERSONALLY THAT HE NEVER FLIES AGAIN!"

With that, he climbed down from his car roof, got in, and drove off leaving us still at attention. We all decided he was upset.

Alas, only a few days later, one of our young lieutenants from our squadron returned with a four-inch-diameter limb jammed in his right wing. After a thorough butt-chewing of our Squadron Commander and the young pilot, the colonel made good on his promise. The lieutenant was immediately grounded, and was made officer in charge of the base mess hall. He remained in that capacity until that Wing Commander rotated back to the States about three months later. Only after an appeal to the new commander by our Squadron Commander, was the lieutenant allowed to fly again. The young pilot was very careful from then on—he decided it was better to fly than be in charge of the mess hall.

One Sunday morning at around 0700 while most of us were sleeping, one of our Squadron mates, Maj. Jerry Richards, walked up the small hill from our 615th Squadron pilots' hooch to the O'Club, which was only about 200 feet away. The Club was closed at that time, and he was standing outside reading the new Club schedule that was posted on a bulletin board in a little alcove near the front door. All of a sudden there was a terrific explosion very nearby, followed by others at about five-second intervals at different locations around the base. *WHOMP! WHOMP! WHOMP!* We were under a mortar attack!

The rest of us jumped out of bed; grabbed our flack jackets, boots, and helmets, and ran outside to our bunkers as our base siren went off to signal the attack. Sure enough, none of our hooch maids (local Vietnamese women) were around—a sure sign there would be an attack! They knew when to be at work and when to stay home. What a war. We were always very careful jumping into the bunkers, as they were sometimes known to have sheets of cardboard with dung-dipped razorblades sticking out of them carefully hidden in the sandy floor of the bunker. If you jumped in there without your combat boots, you could get cut up—and infected—quite badly.

Soviet M1943 120mm mortar set up for business without its carriage.

This attack, as with most of the others, only lasted one or two minutes at the most. The most common weapon used was the M1943 Soviet 120mm mortar that had a unique design: it consisted of four components (tube, base-plate, bipod and carriage) that could be quickly broken down for movement over short distances by its five- or six-man crew. For normal travel the whole weapon folded together and could be towed on its two-wheeled carriage or, if necessary, man-packed in its four component parts.

This 170 kg (about 374 lb.) mortar could fire twelve to fifteen 34-pound high explosive (HE) rounds per minute at a range anywhere from 400 to 5,700 meters—a quarter mile out to over three-and-a-half miles away.

This direct hit on an F-100 by a 120mm mortar round happened in May 1969—three months before I arrived at Phan Rang. Another round hit our 615th TFS building down on the flight line. Those extensive shrapnel holes were still visible in the building when I arrived in August.

The Viet Cong (VC) would sneak in to within range of our bases; set up the mortars; aim at vital areas of the bases, such as fuel and ammo dumps, aircraft in the open, pilots' quarters, etc., fire off ten to twenty quick rounds; take the mortars apart; and disperse back into the surrounding jungle before our counter-mortar weapons of our Base Security personnel could locate their positions. Very effective hit and run tactics.

After our attack, Jerry Richards returned to our hooch. He was shaking and white as a ghost. He took me back up the hill to show me what had happened. While he was standing there reading the bulletin board outside the O'Club on that quiet Sunday morning, the first of twenty-two mortar rounds fired at the base landed only nineteen feet to his immediate right and eight feet in front of the building. It landed on the blacktop parking area and blew a hole in it two-and-a-half-feet in diameter and a foot deep. The shrapnel from the HE blast absolutely peppered the entire area of the Club's front doorway, and blew pieces of jagged metal both in front of, and behind him as he stood reading; imbedding into the side of the alcove four feet to his left. He didn't have a scratch on him! After a fifth of Jack Daniels and, most probably, a clean set of shorts, Jerry was as good as new.

Of course the VC weren't aiming for the deserted O'Club; they were trying for our pilots' hooch that had thirty pilots sleeping in that Sunday morning. They had only missed it by about 200 feet. We were all glad.

After a few more months, my one-year Vietnam assignment was coming to an end, and I was "getting short." Ever since I received my F-100 assignment back at Loring almost two years earlier, I had been told by just about everyone, including the "personnel weenies" who made the assignments, that I had come from SAC, I was a SAC asset, and I would be going right back to SAC as soon as I returned from Vietnam. Somehow, I hoped that I'd be able to stay in fighters, but it didn't look good. I watched the other assignments come down to my squadron buddies as they were leaving, and they weren't all that good. Many were getting instructor jobs at pilot training bases. One major, who had flown fighters his entire career, received an assignment to B-52 bombers—*the* ultimate insult to a fighter pilot. Others received fighter assignments, but those coming from SAC were going right back. I had a current assignment preference sheet in my files, so all I could do was wait and hope for the best. About sixty days from my DEROS, my assignment came down—F-4's to Bitburg Air Base, Germany! I was so happy, and the rest of the guys in the Squadron couldn't believe it. What a great assignment! Had I escaped from SAC? It sure looked like it.

All during the year Carol and I had been writing back and forth about where we would like to go for our next assignment. We had decided that we both would really like to go to Europe, so we could travel around the Continent while we were stationed there for the two or three years of a normal tour. As soon as I got the great news, I wrote to tell her. About two weeks later, I received her reply:

> "I'm happy that you received the assignment to Europe that you wanted, but I think it's only fair to tell you that I won't be going with you. This year has taught me that I wasn't cut out to be an Air Force wife."

I read and re-read it over and over, thinking I must have read it wrong, or it must be someone else's letter. But there it was—right there in black and white—my wife of ten years, and high school sweetheart for four years before that, didn't want to be with me anymore. This "Dear John" letter absolutely crushed me. I couldn't believe it. I showed the letter to my Squadron Commander, and he immediately grounded me. I was in no condition to fly. He also said, "Why don't you go home for a few days or so and work things out."

I thanked him, packed a bag, and headed up to Cam Ranh Bay to hop on a "Freedom Bird" back to the States. About a day later I landed at McCord AFB in Washington State, and called home.

"Where are you?" Carol asked.

I told her I was in Washington and would be down in Phoenix the next morning. She asked why I was back. "We have a few things to talk about, don't we?" I replied.

The next day she picked me up at the Phoenix airport, and we went home. We went out to dinner that night, and we talked for a while, but her mind was made up, and I could tell I would not be able to change her mind. She asked me for a divorce. We talked about a settlement—she needed the house, furniture and car, so she could take care of the children. That sounded logical, and I agreed. She told me she would be going to work the next day as usual.

The next day, I was home alone with my five-year old son, Mark, while Kris was in school and Carol was at work at the doctor's office. We were out in our backyard that I had landscaped after we had purchased the new home in January 1969. Mark and I were walking around looking at all the flowers and shrubs, and we came across the beautiful rose bushes I had planted.

"Don't touch those," Mark warned me.

"Why not?" I asked.

"Because those are David's favorite flowers," he answered.

"Who is David?" I queried.

"DOCTOR David!" he said, as if I should have known. Out of the mouth of babes…

Now I knew why Carol had said that she "wasn't cut out to be an Air Force wife." She had decided many weeks prior to be a doctor's wife instead. Needless to say, I was devastated, for I was very much in love with my high school sweetheart and wife.

I packed my bags and remember thinking to myself, *"Well, I might as well go back to Phan Rang where I'm needed."*

When I got back only four days after I had left, the Squadron Commander wanted to know how everything went. I told him what had happened. He said he was sorry. He kept me grounded for another three days until I had settled down. I started flying again, but it was hard to concentrate on business.

I have great memories of my time together with Carol, from that first date on Halloween 1956 to our divorce in late July 1970. She remarried that fall.

Over the years, I've matured and mellowed to the point that I can now accept this. Our situation was not unique. It has happened in the past, and, sadly, will happen in the future, as couples are separated for extended periods of time. There's an old saying: "Absence makes the heart grow fonder." I don't agree. This is, unfortunately, part of life, and you have to accept it, or it will destroy you inside. Carol and I are the best of friends today, and I'm very pleased.

A couple of weeks later, I had my "Champagne Flight"— my last combat mission of that tour. All my Squadron buddies

Getting hosed down on the last mission—the Champagne Flight.

174

met me at the end of the runway as I landed, rolled out and turned onto the taxiway. Most were on their Honda 90s with green smoke canisters taped to their rear fenders. As I turned off the runway on to the taxiway, they all popped their canisters and started spewing dense dark green smoke—our Squadron color. The rest of the guys were in Squadron pickup trucks. All formed into a "V" to lead the Hun to its parking revetment. I taxied in following the escort, pulled into the parking space, and shut down. When I climbed down the ladder, they all hosed me down with a fire hose, then handed me a bottle of champagne that we all shared. It was a long-standing tradition in all the fighter squadrons. It was now time to move on to my next assignment.

When it was time for me to return home to the "Land of the Big BX" in July 1970, I was asked if I wanted to take an F-100 back and give it to the Ohio Air National Guard in Springfield, Ohio. I thought this would be a great experience, so I jumped at the chance—it's not every day one gets to fly a single-seat, single-engine fighter across the Pacific Ocean. The bird I was supposed to take was one from the 31st TFW up at Tuy Hoa, which was another F-100 base about 150 miles north of Phan Rang. I went up there and was briefed on how this was going to be done. Four birds were going back—four F-100's. The four fighters would fly over to Clark Air Base on the wing of an F-4 and meet with a tanker that would take us back across the Pacific.

We departed Tuy Hoa with the F-4 in the lead and ran into some very thick weather. I was on his right wing, and I remember the weather being so thick I could hardly see the fuselage of the F-4—only its wingtip light. I had never flown close formation on an F-4 before, so I was trying to fly formation on the upward bent wingtip of the F-4. This necessitated constant right rudder to keep me flying straight without turning left. It wasn't too bad for me, but the poor guy on *my* right wing was *really* busy! We both fought a very severe case of spatial disorientation for about an hour. We were quite relieved when we finally broke out of the clouds and were in bright sunlight again for the rest of the hop over to Clark.

We landed at Clark, met up with the KC-135 tanker crew, attended a joint briefing on how we were about to get across the "pond" together, got a good night's sleep, and took off early the next morning. Next stop, Guam. As we would get low on fuel, the four of us would cycle on and off the tanker to fill up. The F-100 had what was called a "probe and drogue" refueling system. This consisted of a probe on the right wing of the Hun, which looked like a six-inch diameter pipe, which would hook up with a twenty-four-inch diameter steel basket on the end of a six-inch diameter hose from the end of the boom on the tanker. The idea was to fly up behind the tanker and stab the basket with the probe, then stay in position to maintain contact. This was easier said than done, as the fifty-pound steel basket would bob around in front of you in the 400 mile-per-hour slipstream as you tried to stab it. It also thrashed around if you backed out and disconnected too abruptly, so you had to be very careful, or it could whip over and smash your canopy. That could ruin your whole afternoon.

When it was my turn, I slid in behind the KC-135, the same bird I had flown for five-and-a-half years at Loring, and got my gas. After I stabbed the basket and hooked up, the Boom Operator reported, "Contact tanker."

I checked my gauges and replied, "Contact receiver."

While I sat there flying formation on the tanker and receiving fuel from this big bird out over the Pacific Ocean, four miles high and hundreds of miles from the nearest land, I couldn't help thinking about my time in tankers and how I finally had my dream of flying fighters come true. It was an eerie, yet highly satisfying feeling. I told the tanker crew over the radio, "I used to fly tankers for five and a half years."

They couldn't believe it. "How did you get out?" they asked.

Two-seat F-100F being air-refueled by the "probe and drogue" refueling system.

As I flew the best formation I could on that big bird only twenty feet above me, I pressed the UHF radio transmit button on the throttle in my left hand and said, "Have a goal, and stick to it...and be really lucky!"

We kept island-hopping across the Pacific until we coasted in to the States across southern California. The tanker had brought us back to the States, so he left us and headed back to his home base. All four of the fighters were going to different locations. One was going to Luke, so we all decided to land there for the night as we got close to Phoenix. I called home after we landed, but no one answered.

The next morning I headed out to my waiting bird to make sure it was ready to go. The Transient Alert crews had it all fueled, serviced and ready for me whenever I wanted to leave. I told them to plan on an 1100 departure. I went into Base Operations and flight-planned my route over to McConnell AFB just outside Wichita, Kansas. McConnell was just about the midpoint of the distance from Luke up to Springfield, Ohio, so I thought that would be a good place to stop for gas. I filed my clearance, cranked up the bird, and headed out to McConnell.

I landed at McConnell about 1300, taxied in, and parked in the transient area. I told them I would like to plan on a 1500 takeoff. No problem—they would have it ready. I went into Base Ops, and planned my flight over to Springfield after checking in with the Command Post. They were also tracking me and the whereabouts of the F-100. Again, I filed my clearance and took off at 1500 on what was supposed to be my last mission in the Hun—that last leg up to Ohio.

I was only airborne about five minutes when the Command Post called me to return to McConnell and land. I told them I was too heavy to land immediately, and that I would burn off some fuel and land in about an hour. That was okay with them—I was to contact them after I had landed. I wondered what was wrong.

I landed at 1600, taxied in, shut down again in the transient area, and went into Base Ops to call the Command Post to see what was going on. They told me they had notified the Springfield Air National Guard Base that I was on the way and would get there about 1700. They said that was not a good time—everyone would be gone. Eleven o'clock the next morning would be better. With that, I went back out to the bird, grabbed my bag, let the alert crews know of the planned departure of 0830 the next day, and headed over to the billeting office to get a room for the night. After throwing my bag in the room, I decided to head over to the Officers' Club for a drink.

Once in a while some of us have a life-altering experience—a major fork in the path of life that, depending on which road you take, will change your life forever. One of mine was about to happen.

I walked into the bar in the Officers' Club and ordered a vodka tonic, my usual summer drink. I noticed a major and a captain in Class "A" dress blues at the other end of the bar, while I'm standing there in my well-worn Vietnam subdued flight suit, which was kind of cruddy from flying all day. We started talking to each other. They asked where I was from, and I told them I had just returned from Vietnam and was delivering an F-100 to the Guard base in Springfield, Ohio.

"Where are you heading next?" they asked.

I told them I had an assignment to F-4s at Bitburg AB, Germany, but I had received a "Dear John" letter a month earlier, so I no longer had a great desire to go to Europe anymore. Besides, Bitburg was primarily an air-to-air unit, and I'd like to stay with the air-to-ground role. They told me about the brand new single-seat, single-engine A-7D going in to Myrtle Beach AFB, South Carolina. It was the Air Force's new bird designed specifically for ground attack and Close Air Support. I told them I preferred that mission of supporting the "grunts" on the ground—it gave me more satisfaction than air-to-air. And, the A-7 school was at Luke—back in Phoenix, where I could visit my children. Myrtle Beach was also closer to my aging parents in Ithaca.

"Well, what would you rather do," they said, "take F-4s to Bitburg, or A-7s at Myrtle Beach?"

I couldn't believe what I was hearing. "Who *are* you guys?" I asked.

The major responded, "I'm Chief of Fighter Assignments at AFMPC [Air Force Military Personnel Center]. We're looking for experienced Vietnam fighter pilots to be the initial cadre for the first A-7 squadron at the Beach. If you're interested, we can make it happen!"

"Okay—I'll take the A-7!" I said.

"You got it. We'll send a telegram to your leave address with your change of orders."

I thought to myself, "Yeah, right…I'll believe it when I see it," but I gave them my leave address back home in Ithaca, anyway. We shook hands and had another drink or two. The next morning we all probably wouldn't remember having the conversation. They just happened to be at McConnell that day giving a briefing on the Personnel System to the people on the Base.

Two months earlier, I was sweating out getting a fighter assignment instead of going back into the dungeons of SAC. Now, because of a quirk of fate of being at McConnell on that exact date, getting called back there on that particular night after I had already left, and meeting two strangers over a drink at the bar instead of going right to bed, I had *two* prime assignments from which to choose…offered to me by the very officers who were in charge of handing them out worldwide. It was the best of times in my worst of times.

The next morning I took off at 0830, flew up to Springfield, and turned over the Hun to the Ohio Guard unit at 1100 as I completed my last flight as an F-100 Super Sabre pilot. I sat there for a few minutes in the cockpit to look at the instrument panels one last time. The Hun and I had come a long way together. I'll never forget it.

I found out later that I had ended up with 499.6 hours of Hun time. I should have paid attention to this more closely. Would I ever get that magic figure of 500 hours?

I went in, grabbed a shower, put on some civilian clothes, and headed to the local airport for a flight down to Ithaca. I was now on leave for thirty days. Sure enough, about ten days later, I received a telegram at home from the Fighter Assignments office at AFMPC:

"ORDERS TO BITBURG AB CANCELLED STOP REPORT TO MYRTLE BEACH AFB SC NLT 31 AUGUST 1970 STOP"

My life had been changed forever.

Chapter 10
Myrtle Beach – 1970 - 1972

*I*n the third week of August 1970, I had to pack up and head south to Myrtle Beach. I didn't have time to get a car yet, so Mom and Dad said they would take me down. That was great! We had a fun trip down and arrived at the base about the 25th. I wanted to show them all the

354th Tactical Fighter Wing

brand new A-7s, so I drove down by the flight line. What a surprise—no airplanes at all! I saw a maintenance man by one of the hangers, so I stopped and asked him where all the birds were. He said all the F-100s had already moved out, and the A-7s didn't come in yet. There was one on base borrowed from the training squadron at Luke—maintenance had it in one of the hangers, and they were taking it apart and putting it back together again for practice and learning.

I checked into the billeting office, got a room, and spent the rest of the day with my parents. They spent the night and we went looking around the area the next day. Myrtle Beach at that time was a small town that just about tripled in size during the summers as tourists came down for "fun in the sun" on the beautiful white sand beach and the gorgeous golf courses. Traffic through town during the summer was bumper to bumper. There were also many very fine seafood restaurants in and around the area, which we all enjoyed.

Mom and Dad were quite impressed with the area. After a couple more days of checking out real estate, they said goodbye and headed back home to Ithaca. I found my new car—a red MGB-GT sports car! I had always wanted a red sports car, so now was my chance. It was a great car, but like all British cars, it burned a lot of oil. It went through a quart every 500 miles!

When my leave was up I signed in. Because there weren't any A-7s yet, I stayed current flying the AT-33, a regular T-33 trainer that was modified with some .50 caliber guns and a very crude bombing system. Not much, but it allowed me and the other pilots that were drifting in to be able to stay current on the gunnery range. I found out that I had a class date of November 1970 through February 1971 for A-7 school out at Luke. In the mean time, they assigned me to the Command Post so I could be gainfully employed for those two months. That was about as much fun as watching paint dry. You mention working in a Command Post to a fighter pilot, and he immediately starts to heave.

Those two months were quite hard for me. I found out my divorce had become final in late July, and I was now on my own again—with not much to do. I started drinking and clubbing a lot, but luckily, it only lasted two months, or I may have gotten into trouble with too much drinking. The very prominent anti-war sentiment that was everywhere at that time didn't help, either.

I finally received my orders to A-7 school for a class start date of 4 November. I jumped in my trusty red MGB-GT and headed west to Phoenix. I remember going through Texas and

Al (R) & me at the Super Sabre Society reunion in Las Vegas on 2 April 2009. What a great reunion and to talk over old times—and old stories—in the Hun!

getting stopped for speeding twice within 20 minutes of each other. Both times I was lucky to get a warning.

A-7 school was much the same as the F-100 school I went through two years earlier there at Luke—but now that we were all experienced fighter pilots in the class instead of pilots new to fighters, we did the training in three months instead of six. Incredibly, my instructor was Lt. Col. Al Bartels—my IP from checking out in the F-100 almost two years prior.

His soothing welcome to me was, "Well, I see you didn't bust your ass in the Hun—you gonna try it again in the SLUF, Huh?!" We really did get along great!

The A-7D, made by LTV Aerospace Corporation, was built solely for the air-to-ground mission; hence its designation as "A" for Attack versus "F" for Fighter. It could carry up to 15,000 pounds of ordnance on eight external stations. Its Allison TF41-A-1-2 non-afterburning turbofan engine produced 14,250 pounds of thrust, which gave the bird a max speed at sea level of 698 mph. Although its name was officially the *Corsair II*, it wasn't long before the bird picked up the nickname of SLUF—Short Little Ugly ^%#*. It was a name that became very well-known—and respected—throughout the fighter/attack community worldwide.

A-7D with four external 300-gallon fuel drop tanks

The SLUF was quite easy to fly. We, being experienced "old heads," all learned the basics in just a few hours; however, the rest of the three months were devoted to learning how to employ the bird and use all of its systems. For me coming out of the F-100, it was like leaving a Model "A" Ford and stepping into a new Cadillac.

All the instruments were vastly improved. It had a radar that could be used for weapons delivery, navigation, and monitoring weather. It had an inertial navigation system (INS) that was accurate to within two miles per hour, which was unheard-of at that time. There was also a moving map display on the front instrument panel that looked like a full-color road map, which moved as you flew over the terrain with a small airplane in the center of the display—you. It was tied into the INS, so it, too, had a two-mile accuracy per hour—which could be updated and "zeroed out" by pressing a button as you flew over a pinpoint terrain feature, such as a bend in a river or road intersection. The bird also had a very sophisticated computerized weapons delivery system that was capable of dropping 12 x 30-degree dive bombs, one at a time, all "shacks." Again, unheard-of.

The bird had a 20mm M61A1 Vulcan six-barrel cannon, which had a rate of fire of 6,000 rounds a minute—that's 100 half-pound HE rounds per *second!* This was no machine gun that went rat-a-tat-tat. When you squeezed the trigger on this version of the old Western Gatling Gun, all you could hear was a low-pitched wrRRRRRRrr growl as the hydraulically powered cannon came up to rotation speed, fired and slowed back down. The bird only carried about 1,000 rounds—10 seconds worth.

The first A-7D accident in the Air Force happened in my class at Luke on 15 November 1970. The student, Capt. Ken Blankenship, was an experienced fighter pilot from Vietnam; however, he flew propeller-driven A-1 Skyraiders—not jets. It was his initial solo, and because there were no A-7D two-seater birds at that time, his IP was chasing him in another SLUF. They were in the traffic pattern practicing patterns and landings. When Ken was in his base turn—turning to line up on final approach—he started to get low and slow. His IP told him to "Push it up." Nothing much happened. The IP told him again—"Power in." He was still low and slow. The IP said again, "FULL POWER IN AND GO AROUND!!" The nose of Ken's plane came up, but at the slow speed, he stalled, flipped inverted, and crashed.

The Accident Investigation Board found out what had happened. They focused on the student, as the plane was found to be functioning properly at impact. Throttle response in the propeller-driven A-1 was instant, where as in a jet, it takes a few seconds for the engine to "spool-up" to the new setting. Therefore, in a jet, you have to plan ahead for the power you'll need a few seconds from now. The other factor was, that when you add power in an A-1, you had to push in right rudder at the same time to compensate for the additional torque of the new speed of the propeller. The student's initial small power changes were not enough, and when he finally shoved the throttle to full mil, he reverted to his old habit of pushing in right rudder to compensate for torque that was not present in a jet—not good. Too much rudder at slow speed caused what was known in the A-7 as a "departure" from controlled flight, where the bird literally flips and tumbles through the air. At only 300 feet above the ground, there was no chance of recovery.

The IP was found to be at fault. The Accident Board decided that he should have known about the student's background in prop planes, and anticipated the actions of his student. His career was over.

As a side note, we had our first A-7 reunion thirty years later in Tucson in 2000. At the Saturday night banquet, all of our fallen A-7 drivers were read off and honored. At the end, this same IP stood up, and with tears streaming down his face, announced his student's name, Capt. Kenneth L. Blankenship, the first A-7D fatality, for all to toast. There wasn't a dry eye in the room, as we all stood and toasted our fallen comrade, for we all knew his story in our close, tight-knit A-7D community. That IP, and our good friend, has to live with this brand for the rest of his life.

It was here at Luke that I met a girl we'll call Paula Rodriguez. We started seeing each other, and when it was time for me to return to Myrtle Beach in early February 1971 after the school was over, we decided to get married. She and her little nine-year old daughter (I'll call her Mary Jane) returned with me. We were married in the base chapel at Myrtle Beach on 19 February.

I had noticed while we were dating that Paula had a terrible temper, but I rationalized that it was because of her prior

hard life in her homeland of Spain, and that once we were married, I could change her and live happily ever after. A very noble thought, but unfortunately, I didn't change her—she changed me.

Our squadron was outstanding. When we first returned from Luke, we were in the 511th TFS, but it was redesignated as the 353rd TFS on

353rd Tactical Fighter Squadron patch.

15 July 1971. All the pilots were "old heads"—experienced fighter pilots and Vietnam Vets. Because we all arrived at "The Beach" at about the same time, no one departed or arrived for almost two years. The result was a very close-knit group of guys that learned to fly with each other, and to learn each other's capabilities and limitations. It was a very rare opportunity.

When we returned from A-7 school, each of us was called into the Wing Commander's office. Col. Evan W. Rosencrans told us there was trouble in the past with F-100 pilots buzzing the beach. We were told, "There are twenty pilots around the Air Force waiting in line for each of your jobs, so if you ever decide to buzz the beach, you'll be replaced immediately and will never fly again."

That was clear enough for us. We never had any problems from any of our Myrtle Beach pilots. However, an F-4 from another base buzzed a sailboat one Sunday afternoon about a mile out at sea. He was so low and fast that he almost blew over the sailboat. There was a family on board—a man and his wife, and two small children. They were scared to death. Ironically, the man just so happened to work for the FAA, and was able to not only identify the bird as an Air Force F-4, but got his number and markings from the tail of the bird, as it made multiple low passes. He radioed the information back to the Coast Guard; they called the Command Post and found out there was only one F-4 airborne on the entire East coast that Sunday at that time. They checked his flight plan, and radioed ahead to his destination. When he landed about an hour later, he had quite a reception committee waiting for him. Both the pilot and the Weapons System Operator (WSO) in the back seat were grounded and kicked out of the Air Force. Times were changing, and those types of activities were just not tolerated anymore.

The next year-and-a-half was very busy for all of us. We were all learning more about the bird and how to use it. I was the Squadron Scheduler and a Flight Commander. Before that, I had the job of Mobility Officer—responsible for building the entirely new mobility package of moving an A-7 squadron of twenty-four birds from Myrtle Beach to anywhere in the world with only a few hours notice. We had local as well as higher headquarters exercises and inspections to see how we were progressing. We learned as we went along.

In early 1972, Mom and Dad sold their house in Ithaca and moved down to Garden City, which is only a few miles south of Myrtle Beach. They had been so impressed with the area when we all drove down together in August 1970, and again when they came for the wedding in 1971, that they had decided to move. The cold and snow of the Ithaca winters were just too much for them and also played a large role in their decision. It was good to have them close to us.

During this period we also had an Air National Guard Sister Squadron, for which some of our key squadron people would go to help with inspections and mobility. Our Sister Squadron was an F-100 squadron, and as Mobility Officer, I was one of the team members to visit them. I thought this would be a great opportunity to try and get that last four-tenths of an hour of F-100 time that I had managed to miss.

After my work was finished, I went over to one of the Hun squadrons and told the Operations Officer my plight. I had flown the Hun for eighteen months, a year of that being in Vietnam, and had miscalculated my total time—ending up with 499.6 hours. Was there any way I could get a backseat ride to get that last 25 minutes? "Sure—no problem," he told me, "We have an FCF (functional check flight) on a two-seater going up this afternoon!"

What a deal! I went back to the BOQ room, got my G-suit and helmet, and returned to the squadron to meet and brief with the FCF pilot. The flight was to check out some routine maintenance that had been done on the bird, and the flight would be one hour long We took off, climbed out, and the check pilot did what he had to to sign off the maintenance work. Part of that was to accelerate straight and level to Mach-1—the speed of sound. It was a great ending to my F-100 time. He let me fly the bird around for a while, and when we landed, I was sure to enter our flight time of 1.0 hour in the Form 781. I had not only "broken the sound barrier" on this last flight, but I had also broken the 500-hour mark in the Hun! To this day I still have the 500.6 hours, and as fate would have it, I never had another chance to fly in the F-100. Pure luck.

As our brand new A-7's came off the assembly line at LTV in Dallas, our pilots would take a commercial flight out there with all their flight gear and fly the bird back to the Beach. What an experience! It was like driving a brand new $9 million sports car off the showroom floor! The bird even *smelled* new and clean. These birds had already been inspected and test-flown by their company test pilot, and had been accepted by the Air Force.

Therefore, most of the bugs had already been worked out. However, once in a while one of our pilots had an emergency that necessitated aborting and returning to the company for work. It never happened to me, so I had very enjoyable flights back to Myrtle Beach in my brand new private jets. I was fortunate to get three of those great, unforgettable trips.

I was also checked out as an Instructor Pilot in the bird. With no two-seaters, all instruction was accomplished by chasing the student in your own plane—great flying—especially chasing a student through his gunnery patterns at night!

Four-ship flight of 353rd TFS A-7D's over Myrtle Beach AFB, SC. Note red stripe on tails—our Squadron color.

In early 1972, our Squadron was tasked to demonstrate the weapons delivery capabilities of the A-7 by putting on a firepower demonstration. We deployed to the site at Barksdale AFB, Louisiana, using the mobility package we had developed over the past year-and-a-half. The tasking was to demonstrate every type of delivery currently being used—low & high angle strafe; 10-, 15-, and 20-degree low angle dive bomb; and 30- and 45-degree high-angle dive bomb. Bleachers were set up for the "high rollers" and all their "horse holders" so they could watch the show, and evaluate for themselves the true capabilities and performance of the USAF's newest CAS aircraft. And, for the actual Demo, we were all going to use live ordnance.

With the luck of the draw, my job was 20-degree strafe—with a full 10-second load of ammo. During practice, I was only to fire normal two-second bursts—about 200 rounds—so as not to overheat the barrels, but for the actual Demo, I was to fire one long ten-second burst of all the ammo the bird could carry. Each tenth round was also going to be a red tracer, so the crowd could see the delivery. The other guys in the Squadron had their individual taskings, too, and they would all practice using dummy (concrete) bombs. We all had individual times on target (TOTs) and had different attack headings, so we all attacked the same target, a large pile of old cars, from different positions. Then came the hard part. We were told that our weapons impact timing all had to be within plus or minus *two* seconds!

This precision was unheard of. We always arrived at the target on our TOT within a couple of minutes or so, and the FAC then put us to work when he wanted us. This was different. We all studied our weapons delivery manuals for time of flight for our different ordnance. Our weapons officers checked our figures to make sure they were correct. They also worked with us in group meetings to brainstorm ideas and techniques to precisely add or subtract time from our weapons impact times.

We started our practices. Our first one was over a minute off, and one guy, Maj. Layne, was so tense, he pushed the wrong button (nose-wheel steering) on his control stick and never dropped his bombs. The second run through wasn't much better, and Maj. Layne did the same thing! To add to the tension, there had been some errors by the arming crews, and some bombs were "hung" and couldn't be dropped. We were all called together in a meeting and told that, from now on, if we screwed up, we would be sent home, and it would be reflected in our Performance Reports.

Our weapons officer, Capt. Barry Barrineau, one of the sharpest pilots I ever met in my entire career, came up with a fix to Layne's problem—a thumbtack taped to the wrong button! It worked, and it was used for all subsequent drops! Our timing got better, and by the time we had our dress rehearsal, we were within 10 seconds. I didn't use the tracer ammo in dress rehearsal, because we only had enough for the actual Demo. No problem, because the speed and trajectory of tracer ammo was the same as regular HEI—high explosive incendiary.

The day of the Demo came, and we were all as tight as banjo strings. We were reminded again for the hundredth time that we were all to have the plus or minus 2 second timing of our first weapon's impact. We knew that. You could see the tension.

We had a mass briefing of exactly how the entire Demo was going to go. We all received the official Demo time-hack from which the official timing would be checked. We went to our planes and started at our individual predetermined times. Spare planes, one for each weapons load, were cocked and waiting in case someone had to abort their primary bird. We taxied out to the arming area, and there was a General officer checking the arming crews to make sure all was right. We all got airborne and out to our individual holding points. It was show time!

I maneuvered my trusty mount around my holding point, and at exactly my predetermined time, I punched the stopwatch on the right side of the forward instrument panel and headed inbound to the target, which was twelve miles away. At the precise ground speed of 360 knots and 6,000 feet altitude, it was exactly two minutes to the target. I set up my weapons delivery computer for the cannon, made sure my right index finger was off the trigger on the control stick, and moved the Master Arm Switch to ARM. The gun was now hot.

The myriad details flashed through my mind as I kept checking over and over my speed, altitude, heading, switches, time, position, late/early, how to correct, etc.

One minute out—I pushed it up a little to allow time needed to roll in on the target. I could then modify that roll-in for time needed or lost to make sure I was pointed at the pile of cars (the old ones—not the new ones in the parking lot behind the stands...) at the precise time to shoot. All was going according to plan.

Ten seconds to go as I rolled in, put the computerized aiming symbol "pipper" on the cars, stabilized the bird, and squeezed the trigger as the sweep second hand of the stop watch passed one second to twelve. WRRRRR went the gun as I held the trigger down for the start of the full ten-second burst.

HOLY SHIT! WHAT THE HELL IS GOING ON?! Although the pipper was on the target, the red tracer rounds spraying out in front of me were going UP! Something was wrong. The weapons delivery computer must be malfunctioning! I immediately pushed the stick forward to put the tracers on the target. With the trigger still mashed for the remaining couple of seconds, I watched as the tracers hit the target and marched backward to about fifty meters short of the target. When the gun stopped firing, I started my pull-off and recovery as I looked back over my right shoulder to see the entire target area smoking from the 1,000 half-pound HEI rounds.

Only then did I figure out what had happened. At the extended open-fire range from the target needed to get in the full ten-second burst without flying into the ground, the bullets had to go up in a trajectory arc before dropping back down to the target. Therefore, the computerized aiming pipper was correctly on the target, and all would have gone unnoticed, as it had in the dress rehearsal, without visual tracer rounds. However, with the tracers, they *were* going up in an arc to finally drop into the target. I had never fired tracer ammo before, and I learned another lesson that day.

When I landed, I thought I'd really get chewed out by the Heavies for not putting all 1,000 rounds into the center of the pile of cars; however, they all thought it was great to get the complete target coverage of the whole area by "walking" the rounds up and down through the target! I lucked out again! As for the timing? My timing was right on, and the official time for the *entire* Fire Power Demonstration was a total cumulative error of plus two seconds. And Maj. Thair D. Layne finally dropped his bombs. I can honestly say that was the most stress I've ever had, and I'm sure the rest of the Squadron will agree with me.

We were able, on occasion, to take a bird cross-country over a weekend to get some navigation and strange field training. These were always fun, as you could pretty much go where you wanted—as long as we stayed in the continental U.S., the base had a barrier at the end of the runway in case of an emergency, and the base could support the A-7 with light routine maintenance. This was about eighty percent of all the military bases around the Country. We normally left about 1300 on a Friday afternoon and returned not later than 1700 on Sunday. This would allow the bird to fly once that Friday morning and be back in time to be ready to go for Monday morning flying.

On one such cross-country, I was on my way from Myrtle Beach to Nellis AFB in Las Vegas. I had arranged for a tanker from a Guard unit, and we were to join up and both get some in-flight refueling practice. I had been cruising at 31,000 feet westbound until it was time to descend to 20,000 feet for refueling. As soon as I retarded the throttle to start my descent, the engine started to compressor stall—loud pops and bangs that are not good for the engine to experience. I quickly tried to clear the stalls, but no luck. I declared an emergency and shut down the engine. I was now in the world's heaviest glider—a Simonized brick. As I slowed to my optimum glide speed of 230 knots, the FAA ground controllers suggested McConnell AFB, which was off my right wing for approximately thirty-five miles—perfect. I knew McConnell well, as it was here I met those two AFMPC Personnel guys that I got the A-7 assignment from two years earlier.

Kansas City Center handed me over to McConnell Approach Control. I gave them a brief description of my emergency, and asked for radar vectors to a straight in flame out landing. Now at 30,000 feet with the base thirty-five miles away, I was confident I could get there, as the SLUF had a 6-to-1-glide ratio; that is, for every one mile high, it would glide about six miles. I was almost six miles high, so I should get about thirty-six miles of glide distance. Also, if clearing the compressor stall fails with the engine running, there was also a very good chance of the engine starting normally with an air-start after it had been shut down—if there was no damage to the engine, such as ingesting a bird. This I was counting on.

As I approached the base and got it in sight, I asked them for clearance to land. Done. Emergencies have priority, so the traffic pattern was mine. My altitude was doing well. I would arrive directly overhead the base at 10,000 feet—known as "high key" for a flameout pattern, to allow a pad in case something else goes wrong. It was now time to try an air-start of the engine.

I went through the engine air-start procedures, and sure enough, the engine rumbled into life! I never realized how beautiful that sound was until then! The engine came up to idle normally, but I left the throttle in idle and decided I would continue with my planned flameout pattern. I would use the engine only if I screw up the pattern and needed it, as I didn't know what would happen if I moved that throttle again. If I converted to a normal power-on approach and the engine once again decided to stall, I would have no option except eject. I didn't want that.

With the engine in idle instead of off, I received slightly more glide distance. This was all gravy, but airspeed and altitude were two valuable commodities a pilot never turns down. One could give you the other, and if you had both, you were in tall cotton!

I arrived overhead at the high key position, put the gear down with partial flaps, and started my left 360-degree descending flameout pattern after changing over to the control tower frequency. After 180 degrees of turn at low key, my altitude and airspeed were slightly high—I liked that. I continued around playing the left turn to line up with the runway as I started to slowly bleed-off the access speed and altitude. Without needing the engine, I touched down on airspeed in the first 1,000 feet of runway—a normal landing. The rest of the rollout was uneventful. The maintainers checked the bird out that night, and couldn't find anything wrong.

After coordinating with my command post back at Myrtle Beach, I was cleared to depart the next morning to continue the cross-country. The rest of the trip went normally. Luckily those compressor stalls were an isolated case on that engine at those exact parameters. It was my first, but not the only time, I had to shut an engine down in-flight.

After two years of getting the birds and getting up to speed, our three squadrons of the 354th Tactical Fighter Wing finally had our last Higher Headquarters Inspection—an Operational Readiness Inspection—ORI—to be certified as one hundred percent OR—Operationally Ready. We were now ready to take the SLUF to war.

Chapter 11
Back to Vietnam – 1972 - 1973

*O*n 4 October 1972, we received our execute orders for *Constant Guard VI*—the largest A-7D deployment in history. The entire 354th TFW, consisting of the 353rd, 355th, and 356th TFSs was to deploy its seventy-two birds (twenty-four of each squadron) to Korat Royal Thai Air Base, Thailand —about 150 miles northeast of Bangkok. We were ready and chomping at the bit to show off the awesome capabilities of the SLUF.

12 October 1972. Shaking hands with our Black Panther outside our 353rd TFS building on the way from Myrtle Beach, SC to Korat AB, Thailand. Note G-suit, survival vest, and parachute harness. Our Squadron color was red, so we all wore red scarves until we took them off in the bird.

This huge deployment began on 9 October, after our mobility packages were all packed and ready, and all seventy-two aircraft were in place at Korat by 16 October—the same day the Wing flew its first combat CAS missions in SEA. However, this deployment consisted of much more than just the seventy-two birds with their seventy-two pilots. According to our official Wing History, a total of forty-two C-141s and four C-130 cargo planes, as well as five Military Airlift Command civilian charter flights, transported the 665 tons of equipment and 1,574 personnel required for these seventy-two birds to operate at Korat. Maybe we could change the course of the war...

However, when I started flying over there again this third time, it was quite evident the War was not going well. The first time over in 1964, when I was flying tankers across Vietnam and north up through Laos, there were no threats outside North Vietnam larger than small arms and automatic weapons. If you stayed above 2,500 feet, you were out of range and safe. My second time over in 1969-1970, larger guns were over in Laos, and larger caliber weapons, such as ZPU, were in South Vietnam in certain places. But now on this third trip back only twenty-seven months later, our Intelligence briefings pointed out SA-2 and SA-3 SAMs, not only in the North, but in the PDJ of Laos along with 23, 37, 57 and 85mm AAA guns that could reach out and touch you at 30,000 feet and above. Even in the relatively low-threat "safe" environment of the South, certain places around the DMZ and the Parrot's Beak west of Saigon had, along with the standard small arms, automatic weapons, and ZPU, SA-7 shoulder-fired SAMs as well as 23 and 37mm guns. It didn't take a rocket scientist to figure out the War wasn't going well.

Anti-aircraft weapons encountered on my way to work

The four-barrel ZPU 14.5mm KPV heavy machine-guns

The ZU-23 comprises twin 23mm cannons on a towed two-wheel carriage

The deadly ZSU-23-4 is a fully integrated, SP AA system with four liquid-cooled 23-mm automatic cannons mounted on the front of a large, flat, armored turret.

ZSU-57-2 Self-Propelled 57mm Anti-aircraft Gun System. Rate of fire up to 120 rounds per barrel per minute. Maximum altitude of 26,000 feet.

SA-2 *GUIDELINE* Medium-to-high Altitude Surface-to-air Missile System. At medium to low levels against fighter sized targets the kill radius is about 65 m and the blast radius for severe damage is 100-120 m. The weapon has a CEP figure of 75 m with the large blast radius compensating for any system inaccuracies. The Mach 4 missile had a maximum altitude of over 100,000 feet.

SA-7 *GRAIL* shoulder-fired, heat seeking missile for low flying targets.

SA-3 *GOA* Medium Altitude Surface-to-air Missile System. A SIDE NET 180 km range 32,000m altitude E-band height-finder radar is also used. Maximum acquisition range is 110 km and tracking range of the I-band system is between 40-85 km. It can track six aircraft simultaneously and guide one or two missiles at once. The Mach 3+ missile had a maximum altitude of 80,000 feet at a range of 15 miles.

Our first missions were in the relatively "easy" areas of III and IV Corps—the southern half of South Vietnam—until we learned the ropes. Our capabilities and reputation of destroying any and all assigned targets grew almost overnight. Not only could we destroy a target with (usually) a single bomb, but also we had much more "play time"—time in the target area, before we reached bingo fuel and had to head home. When the FACs had a tough target that really needed hitting, they requested our A-7s and had the other types, such as the F-4s, hold high and dry while they put us in.

Pre-1975 map of North and South Vietnam separated by the Demilitarized Zone (DMZ)

On 3 November 1972, our Boss, 7th Air Force, tasked our Wing to replace the aging A-1s in the Sandy role of Search and Rescue (SAR). Very heavily concentrated training, coordination, and planning took place to learn everything we could from the old, slow A-1 propeller SAR guys, callsign "Sandy," and to convert their knowledge and expertise into much faster A-7D jet procedures. These were very busy times. Along with the SAR mission, we also picked up the helicopter escort mission at the same time. These were known as HOBO missions.

On 18 November, only fifteen days after our initial tasking, we flew the first A-7 SAR mission—nine Sandys that went after Bobbin 05 Alpha and Bravo— the front- and back-

Retired prop-driven A-1 *"Skyraider."* These birds were being turned over to the VNAF.

seaters of a Wild Weasel F-105 from our host 388th TFW there at Korat. The two successful rescues took place in the vicinity of Thanh Hoa, North Vietnam—a very dangerous and hard to get to location about a hundred miles south south-east of Hanoi. Several A-7s received battle damage. I was not on that mission, but it was a good one—the leader of that SAR package, Maj. Arnie Clarke as Sandy 01, logged 8.8 hours on that mission. Not only did he fly it in poor 2,000-foot overcast weather in mountainous terrain, but he was hit by small arms fire in his right external fuel tank, which exploded and peppered the entire right side of the aircraft with tank fragments.

After the two survivors were picked up and on their way out escorted by others, Arnie headed out "feet wet" over the Gulf of Tonkin in case he had to eject, but he managed to recover into Da Nang—the first major air base south of the DMZ. Arnie was awarded the Air Force Cross—second only to the Medal of Honor for heroism—for this historic mission. That aircraft,

#70970, has been restored and now resides in a display at the Air Force Museum at Wright-Patterson AFB in Ohio as a tribute to our A-7D in combat and this mission.

Arnie Clarke, "Sandy 01," after landing from the first A-7D SAR mission 18 November 1972. (Official USAF photo)

Although many of us had picked up battle damage while flying missions all over SEA, we didn't lose anyone until two weeks later. Captain Anthony Shine was flying on a HOBO reconnaissance and escort mission on 2 December 1972, near the border of Laos and North Vietnam. He radioed his wingman and said he was descending below cloud cover for a closer look at their target area—a ten-mile stretch of road called Highway 7.

Ten minutes had passed when the wingman tried to radio Tony. There was no answer. Airborne Command and Control directed an extensive two-day airborne search. Rescue teams reported a fire on the ground, but no aircraft wreckage.

General William W. Momyer, Commander of Tactical Air Command, presents the Air Force Cross to Maj. Colin A. "Arnie" Clarke in ceremonies at Langley AFB, VA. Maj. Clarke received the Nation's second highest decoration for his part in the Bobbin 05 rescue in North Vietnam in November 1972. (Official USAF photo)

It is still unclear what happened to Tony. The area he was in was quite mountainous, and the weather may have been worse than expected as he tried to dip underneath the cloud cover. Or, he may have actually been shot down. We probably will never know. Tony, in aircraft #71-0312, was declared Missing in Action (MIA) on that 2 December 1972.

With no further word or clues, Tony Shine was declared dead on January 8, 1980. The Shine family has remained active in POW-MIA issues. In 1980, Bonnie Shine established an award in honor of her husband and all missing in action from the Southeast Asia conflict. The Anthony C. Shine Award is given each year to a fighter pilot for proficiency and professionalism in flying a fighter aircraft.

This is a quote from a contemporary press report: "I remember the first time I saw the White House was with the 'President Carter, where's my Daddy?' picket sign in my hand," said Colleen Shine. Colleen,

Capt. Tony Shine in front of an F-105 "Thud" during his previous tour in Vietnam.

who was eight years old when her father disappeared over North Vietnam, found the answer to that question twenty-four years later. The answer came not from the White House, but through her own personal struggle. Lt. Col. Anthony Shine's A-7 was downed without a trace on December 2, 1972, and for fourteen years his family heard nothing.

Finally, in 1987, there were leads. Reports of a crash site, witnesses, and a helmet started filtering back to the United States. The government discounted the new information, ignoring the helmet, because the Pentagon said it had no identifiable markings. Colleen grasped the leads as the only link to her missing father.

In 1993, she went to Vietnam to conduct her own personal investigation. She rented a Russian jeep, hired a Vietnamese guide, and set off toward the crash site. After being told by the government that the site had been looted, Colleen did not expect to find many clues about her father.

"I learned from our government that the crash site had been heavily scavenged by villagers, and that there was nothing else to find there. As I started looking at the ground, I started finding pieces of my father's aircraft," she recalled. She later found the man who had her father's helmet, which had her father's name hand-written on the inside. Colleen's findings gave the investigation new information, said James Wold, deputy assistant secretary for POW/MIA affairs. A fuller probe of the site and a nearby grave yielded plane parts with serial numbers, a dog tag and remains with matching DNA.

Tony's remains were repatriated 6 June 1995. On 2 August 1996, the Armed Forces Identification Review Board approved the identification of the remains as those of Anthony C. Shine.

Almost twenty-four years after he disappeared, the serenity of Arlington National Cemetery was broken by the sharp report of rifle volleys followed by the haunting notes of "Taps." Because of his daughter's efforts, Lt. Col. Shine was buried with full military honors at Arlington National Cemetery. Tony had finally come home to rest. In the peaceful skies above, four F-15s executed the missing man formation while the Air Force Honor Guard folded the American flag over Shine's casket. The U.S. and Prisoner of War – Missing in Action flags rustled in the crisp fall breeze as Lt. Gen. Lloyd W. Newton, Air Force vice chief of staff, presented the flag to Tony's wife, Bonnie Shine, and his mother, Helen Shine. Family members and friends looked on as this warrior was finally laid to rest.

In 1986, I was asked to write about an experience of mine relating to POW/MIAs. This incident took place during this same December 1972 period, so I have included it here:

"POW/MIA". We have all heard these words many times, and they mean different things to each of us. Many of us were glued to our TV sets in February 1973 to watch our POWs get off the C-141s from Hanoi and return to freedom—some after more than seven years in captivity. And a lot of us still feel a twinge deep inside us when we hear those words today in the news—continuing efforts by many to further account for those still missing throughout Southeast Asia.

But some of us, when we hear the words "POW/MIA," have flashbacks in our personal experiences. One such flashback of mine is to 10 December 1972; a day that will always be with me.

I was a captain at the time but had just found out that I was on the new Major's promotion list. My entire wing of 72 A-7Ds (single-seat, single-engine attack jet) had deployed from Myrtle Beach, South Carolina, to Korat Air Base, Thailand about six weeks earlier; the first Air Force A-7D's to deploy to SEA. Although the aircraft was new to SEA, our 354th Tactical Fighter Wing already had many Vietnam veteran fighter pilots that were used for the cadre of the new wing. It was my third time to Vietnam—in my third different aircraft.

Flight of three in the arming area just prior to pulling on Runway 24 to the right for takeoff at Korat. Lead of the flight, Capt. Crow Wilson, took the photo.

We were all quite busy flying close air support (CAS) missions in support of the ground forces, and we were heavily committed to the new search and rescue (SAR) role that the A-7Ds had picked up from the retiring prop-driven A-1 Skyraiders.

On that morning, we had put together a SAR package of thirteen A-7Ds and two "Jolly Green" rescue helicopters to go in, pick up, and recover Kansas 01 Alpha (front-seater) and Bravo (rear-seater), who were an RF-4C reconnaissance crew shot down by a surface-to-air missile (SAM) the day before—only about twenty "klicks" (kilometers) northwest of Vinh, North Vietnam. His wingman had observed his ejection, good 'chute, and had talked to Bravo on his survival radio after he had landed safely, but no contact was ever made with Alpha. Bravo only had slight injuries and had not observed any "bad guys" in his area—a good risk for a SAR package!

Using the "survivor's" (the general term used until positive ID is made) approximate location given to us by his wing man, the five A-7D SAR "birds", call sign "Sandy", took off from Korat at first light. Their job: find the best ingress and egress routes; pinpoint the survivor's location; and locate any defenses that may be a threat to the slow-moving, highly vulnerable helicopters— without calling attention to, or giving away the survivor's location. This, in itself, is quite a job for a few hours! You had to be careful not to look like a flock of buzzards orbiting over your intended target—which could be seen for miles.

A few minutes later, I took off as an element leader in a four-ship flight of "suppression of enemy air defenses" (SEAD) aircraft loaded with 20mm ammo and CBU-52. The CBU-52 is a cluster bomb unit—a canister full of about 650 small bomblets about the size of oranges that are used for area coverage. This canister, in the 750-pound class of air-to-ground munitions, is delivered in a 30- or 45-degree dive like a regular bomb, and as it falls, a fuse in its nose senses a predetermined altitude. When this altitude is reached, the clamshell canister blows open, exposing the 650 individual CBUs to the airstream. These small bomblets disperse and spin-arm as they fall, and detonate like hand grenades as they hit the ground over an area about two to three times the size of a football field.

Another flight of four A-7s, also for SEAD, took off shortly after us. KC-135 tankers, used for air refueling of the A-7s, were already "on station"—orbiting in a safe area, and available to us throughout the mission for fuel. Fuel management for the entire package was a major job—Sandy 3s (number three aircraft of the five-ship Sandy flight.) He kept track of everyone's fuel state and made the decision, based on the leader's (callsign "Sandy Low") overall plan, when to send birds to the tankers, over 200 klicks away, to refuel and be back, with as much fuel as possible, so the whole package would be ready to go at the time set by Sandy Low. This, again, was no easy feat, as all the birds operated at full throttle most of the time, and fuel was used rapidly.

After stopping by the tankers to top-off, my flight ingressed at low altitude to the general area of the Survivor and joined up with the five Sandys—also at low altitude. We did most of our work at low altitude to stay under enemy radar observation—both surveillance and SAM radars. The major drawbacks to low-altitude flying were being highly susceptible to enemy ground fire and the extreme danger of flying into the ground while distracted with other writing duties in the cockpit.

The five Sandys had already determined the best ingress and egress routes for the "Jolly," and the two "Jollys," one primary and one spare, were on their way to their predetermined holding points in a safe area. A few minutes later, Sandy Low had pinpointed the Survivor's location while the rest of us stayed somewhat away from the immediate area—to troll for guns (find enemy air defenses that would fire on us), and to not draw attention to the Survivor's location by numerous aircraft overhead. The other SEAD flight arrived in the area; the survivor's exact location was found and made known to all "players"; Sandy 3 had sent us, at our required intervals, to the tankers for a full load of fuel; and Sandy Low had determined we were ready. All was going like clockwork.

After egressing back out of the area, still at low altitude (below 1,000 feet), we joined up with the two Jollys, briefed them on the survivor, routes in and out, weather, headings, terrain, expected enemy defenses, etc., and we all started in escorting the camouflaged Jolly Green rescue helicopter (the spare would stay at the safe holding point unless needed) at tree-top level to minimize exposure to any defenses.

He was fairly easy to see against the dark green jungle canopy. Earlier in our transition to this SAR role, we had determined they were too hard to see—we would lose them and spend too much time looking for them and not paying attention to navigation and enemy threats. Something had to be done. The older prop-driven A-1 Sandys were much slower and could stay closer to the helicopters as they escorted them—keeping them in sight was not a problem. However, when the faster A-7s tried to use the same tactics to escort the Jollys, it was immediately determined that we would have to fly circles around them as they moved forward. This was called daisy-chaining.

Even with the daisy-chaining, the A-7s flying at 400-450 knots trying to stay close to the Jollys flying at 100 knots is difficult. You must fly very tight circles around the helicopters, or you'd lose sight of them, but as you fly tighter and tighter circles, your airspeed and energy drops off to the point that you don't have enough of either to attack any threat that starts to shoot at you or the Jolly. In other words, you're worthless! To solve the problem, someone had a bright idea: paint the top of one of the chopper's rotor blades white. It worked. Now, it was easy to keep the Jollys in sight with their one white blade making beautiful *whop, whop, whop* white circles against the dark green jungle. Consequently, we could fly larger circles—still keeping the helicopters in sight, and keeping our airspeed and energy up—ready at any time to roll in and attack an enemy.

What a sight that was—Jolly ingressing at 100 knots at tree-top level; the five Sandys daisy-chaining around him at about 500 feet altitude and 450 knots, keeping him in sight, on course, and away from all roads, towns, villages, open areas, and ready to respond to any small threat that may have come up on Jolly; and the two flights of four SEAD A-7s escorting the entire package—ready at any time to roll in on any major threat that came up. Radio chatter was limited to only very brief, essential transmissions of headings to the Jolly on prearranged frequencies. Radio silence was important so as not to be intercepted. All was going well. No problems.

When we approached the survivor's location, radio contact with him was reestablished on another preselected frequency, and using special procedures, positive ID of the individual who was shot down the day before in the F-4 was made. When the survivor heard the Jolly approaching, control was turned over to him for final vectoring of the helicopter to a position directly over him and hovering. He was on a small hill in fairly dense jungle. We couldn't see him, but we knew his exact location. It felt like adrenaline was pumping into our veins by the cup full. All was going without a hitch.

"Come left two degrees, 700 meters," the survivor instructed the Jolly.

"Roger," the Jolly aircraft commander acknowledged as he made the small, precise left turn and started to slow down.

"500 meters."

"Left one degree, 300 meters."

"200 meters."

"100 meters, come right 10 meters," said the survivor. Then…"50…30…20…10…5…*STOP!*" yelled the anxious survivor.

Jolly came to a stop and hovered over the survivor, and after further positive ID procedures to make sure it really was the real survivor and not the enemy, the pararescueman (PJ) lowered the jungle penetrator—a heavy metal apparatus on the end of a cable that is lowered to punch through the trees, with three sides that folded down to be used as seats for the survivor(s) as he's hoisted back up to the chopper.

The five Sandys and the eight SEAD birds were buzzing around him like flies—ready to respond to any challenge. What a thrill! What a beautiful sight! Although our hearts were pounding, all else was quiet...too quiet.

Then it happened. As soon as the jungle penetrator disappeared down into the trees, the most vulnerable time for the

SA-2 *Guideline* Surface-to-air missile (SAM)

entire SAR package, the whole sky lit up with white, gray, and orange flashes of numerous AAA guns, and red tracers from small arms and automatic weapons. It was coming from everywhere! My RHAW (radar homing and warning) scope (which displays numbers, types, and locations of threats) was lit up like a video arcade game, and the different audio warning tones from each coming through my headset blended together into indistinguishable noise. Then came the unmistakable rattlesnake sound of the Fan Song guidance radar of an SA-2 surface-to-air missile.

Instantaneously, the warning call "SAMs!" was transmitted; RHAW scope checked, and the white smoke plume of the large thirty-three-foot long telephone pole-shaped SA-2 was located visually as it left its launcher. We were too low and too close for it to guide properly, so it was "easy" to out

217

maneuver as the enemy gunners tried desperately to spear us with the unguided SAM. All of this took about ten seconds.

As I looked down to try and visually find an AAA gun to roll in on, I saw the Jolly Green, streaming snow-white smoke, slip away from his treetop hover position and slide down the side of the dark green jungle-covered hill to the right—fighting to regain control of his obviously badly damaged chopper.

"We're hit! WE'RE HIT! Get us out of here! Heading. GIVE ME A HEADING!"

Captain Chuck Kennedy, a highly experienced fighter pilot who was a member of my flight that day, had the best view at that moment of a relatively safe egress route and was the first man to respond.

"Right, Jolly! Come right to 260 degrees!"

One of our Sq Weapons Officers, Capt. Gerry Felix (L), and Capt. Chuck Kennedy in front of their Hooch. (Photo from Crow Wilson)

The crippled helicopter slowly came right through the hail of enemy fire to 260 degrees—almost due west to get away from the threat area and back into the sparsely populated countryside. After attacking all the 23mm, 37mm, 57mm AAA guns we could find, as well as that SA-2 complex, we and the other SEAD flight rejoined the crippled Jolly (easy to see now while still streaming white smoke and contrasted against the dark green jungle) and the five Sandys that were "sanitizing" the egress path out of North Vietnam (NVN) ahead of him with their 20mm strafe. Two more SA-2s were launched at the package during this period, but they too were detected early and out maneuvered.

What a mess. But we were all on the way out! The silence was broken by Sandy Low:

"Jolly, how're you doin'?"

His answer sent a cold chill through me:

"My co-pilot's wounded, PJ is wounded, and I've lost the right engine. I don't know how long this thing's gonna' fly."

Sandy Low's reassuring reply came right back: "Roger, Jolly, copied that. No sweat—you're lookin' good. Do you have the Survivor on board?"

Jolly's one-word reply was branded in my memory forever: "Negative."

We egressed the rest of the way out in silence as we all pondered the mission and what had gone wrong. It had been a flack trap. The North Vietnamese had brought in mobile AAA guns and the SA-2 overnight, and set them up around the survivor only a few hundred meters away—then waited for the SAR package to arrive. He never knew he was being used as bait.

When I finally got back to Korat and landed on runway 06, I had logged 10 hours and 15 minutes in A-7D number 71-0309, with mission symbol 01B: combat sortie—NVN. It had been one of the longest single-seat, single-engine jet fighter combat missions in history. It had included six in-flight refuelings—on-loading over 60,000 pounds of JP-4 fuel.

Looking northeast at the large dip in the approach end of runway 06
at Korat in December 1972

Many of the other details of the mission have been blurred with time, for nine days later on 19 December, Operation Linebacker II started—the last heavy bombing of NVN. The peace talks had stalled, so President Nixon ordered the renewed massive bombing of the North to get them back to the peace tables. It worked.

We flew interdiction bombing missions against key targets in NVN, and we continued with our SAR commitment "Up North." We also flew CAS missions in South Vietnam, Laos, and Cambodia. In one night during this "11-Day War" of Linebacker II (19-29 December), six B-52 bombers were shot down—each with a six-man crew. All of these thirty-six new "beepers" (personal locator beacons that activate automatically upon bailout or ejection) on the ground, along with those already plotted, blended together to make pinpoint locating of each almost impossible. How many of these men became POW's and were released, and how many are still carried as MIA, I don't know. Less than two months later, on 12 February 1973, Project Homecoming, the return of 591 POWs from North Vietnam, began.

And the survivor we went after on 10 December 1972? I don't know. Either POW, MIA—or killed on the spot after we left. I never found out, and we never went back after him. But I'll never forget Kansas 01 Bravo.

Prior to our deployment to Korat, I was the "A" Flight Commander as well as Squadron Scheduling Officer. Not only was I in charge of the seven pilots in my flight, but I also had the responsibility of the daily, weekly, and monthly flight schedule, as well as all the myriad prerequisites for upgrading and checkout sorties. These duties continued for the duration of our time at Korat.

One of our birds, with wings folded to save ramp space, gets a well-deserved rest.
The A-7 was an original Navy design; therefore, the wing-folding capability. For
the Air Force to delete that capability from their "D" models, it would have cost
tens of thousands of dollars extra per bird. The USAF said "Leave it in."
(Crow Wilson Photo)

Guys would hang around my desk, trying to get on the
flying schedule for the next day. It was never difficult to find
pilots to fly—the hard part was to try to make all flying equitable
and fair—about the same number of all the different types of
missions for each of our pilots. However, if some didn't want
certain types of missions, there were always others willing to step
in and get a "counter!" Scheduling really became an issue
beginning on 19 December as Linebacker II began. Everyone
wanted to "go North," but there were more pilots than missions.

Chapter 12
Linebacker II: 19 – 29 December 1972

*T*he on-again, off-again, on-again, off-again bombing of the North (what a wonderful way to fight a war) was about to heat up again. The last bombing of North Vietnam, known as Linebacker II, the 11-Day War, or The 11 Days of Christmas, began on 19 December 1972 and ended 29 December. A-7s from our Wing's three squadrons flew nine of the eleven days. I flew with my squadron on four of the nine. These missions, flown into the most heavily defended area in aerial history, are all memorable.

Although the SLUF was making a name for itself in CAS missions all over SEA and SAR missions up North, we never had the opportunity to "go North." This was left to the F-105s and F-4s that had done this during past missions when the air strikes up North were on. Now, with the beginning of this new bombing campaign, we were allowed to go, but only on the wing of F-4s.

The F-4 was the dominant fighter in the Air Force at this time, and the generals were thoroughly convinced of its unequalled status. It was truly an F-4 Air Force. They were not about to let these new-fangled A-7Ds, which were relatively slow and no match for MiGs and easy prey for SAMs and large AAA, venture into this domain and be wiped out.

Due to adverse weather, the majority of the missions were LORAN (Long-Range Navigation) drops initiated by F-4 lead aircraft. Along with our MiG Cap to protect us from MiGs and

Wild Weasel aircraft to jam the enemy air defenses, a flight of three F-4s would lead us to the target at 20,000 feet straight and level. We would be in close formation with the F-4s, and would all drop our bombs as the F-4s dropped theirs. This looked like a B-17 raid over Germany during World War II—and it had about the same results: poor.

LORAN was 1950s technology and left a lot to be desired—especially accuracy for dropping bombs. Our A-7D inertial navigation system and computerized weapons delivery computers were pretty much state-of-the-art 1970s technology. Our systems were vastly superior to the mighty F-4—consistently demonstrated, but never accepted by the powers that be.

Flying on the wing of F-4s straight and level at 20,000 feet and "puking off" our bombs when the lead F-4 dropped theirs was totally unproductive, and to us, a tremendous waste of time and resources. Even when we got to the target area and found the weather suitable for us to go in visually to drop, we

were not allowed. Our Wing Commander, Col. Tommy Knoles, asked numerous times to let us plan our own missions and do our own thing. Every time he was turned down. After another "bomb puking mission" when the weather over the target was almost clear, Col. Knoles told the generals to either let his Wing plan and fly their own missions, or they could relieve him of command right there and then—he was not going to send his planes and people on another worthless LORAN drop in good weather.

Our 354th TFW commander,
Col. Thomas M. Knoles, III

That certainly raised some high-level eyebrows. Col. Knoles was highly respected, so they reluctantly agreed. They would give us the target, and we would plan how and with what ordnance to hit it with. During marginal weather, we would still go with the F-4s; however, when we got to the target area and our A-7 mission commander determined the weather to be suitable for our visual attack, we would leave the F-4s and roll in for our pre-planned strikes. We were all ecstatic! We still had our MiG Cap and enemy air defenses jamming support, but it was up to us to attack the target anyway we wanted.

Taxiing out for takeoff from Korat AB, Thailand for a *Linebacker II* strike in December 1972.

And so it was for my first Linebacker II mission North on 22 December. Our assigned target was the Viet Tri Transshipment Point Song Lo. It was a transshipment complex located on water route segment W37A 28.5 miles northwest of Hanoi. The target was being used to unload supplies coming from

China, and destined for the Viet Tri and Hanoi area. Destruction of this target could result in the loss of a shipping facility with damage to supplies and valuable material.

We were "fragged" (scheduled based on a very detailed Fragmentary Order that went out to every wing in Theater—the "sheet of music" that everyone sang from) for our entire squadron of twenty-four birds; each carrying 2 MK-84s (2,000-lb slick bombs) each. We would be six four-ship flights: Lt. Col. Davis would be our A-7 leader of the first four-ship, Goose Flight; Maj. Layne (with no thumbtack required!) led Cardinal; Maj. Hoskins had Parrot; Maj. Wood was next leading Canary Flight; Capt. Crow Wilson led Sparrow; and I brought up the rear, leading the four birds of Dodo Flight. Of all the names of birds those higher headquarters staff weenies who made up the Frag each day could have come up with, I had to get Dodo. But no one noticed—we were all too busy.

Unfortunately, the weather was forecast to be marginal. Sure enough, as we approached the target area, the weather was a solid undercast below us. There was no way to attack visually. It was my first LORAN drop on the wing of the F-4 Phantom, and the results reflected it. All forty-eight of our bombs, and those of the F-4s, went about 3,000 feet long—into the water. The bomb damage assessment (BDA) for the entire strike package: zip, nada, zero. A complete waste.

Another of the scheduling decisions I had made was the flight schedule for the day before Christmas—24 December. Many of us were flying Linebacker II missions up north that day, but Capt. Chuck Riess was scheduled for a Barrel Roll strike mission on the southern edge of the Plaines des Jarres (PDJ) in northern Laos—also a very hostile place. He was working with a Raven FAC who was flying an O-1 Bird Dog, which was a small, light prop bird built by Cessna.

226

Chuck, in aircraft #71-0310, had been cleared "hot" to attack a target, and as he rolled in, he collided with the FAC. The other pilots in the flight only saw Chuck's good chute and talked with him after he landed when he came up on his survival radio. He confirmed no injuries, but he talked for only a few minutes.

There were many enemy troops in his area closing in on him, and his radio promptly went off the air. Chuck was officially listed as MIA. The pilot of the Bird Dog, Capt. Paul Vernon

O-1 *Bird Dog* used by Raven FACs in Laos with a small can of napalm. Note very small aircraft markings. (Photo from Raven FAC web site)

"Skip" Jackson, was killed in the midair. The A-7 had sliced through the O-1's wing.

Incredibly, word was received less than six weeks later on 2 February 1973 that Chuck had been taken prisoner. This was even more extraordinary, as only ten POWs were ever taken in Laos. Most were executed on the spot. Capt. Riess was released after ninety-four days from Ha Lo Prison, Hanoi, on 28 March 73. Here is the account quoted from the Official History of the 354th TFW:

> Captain Riess was originally captured by either the Pathet Lao or North Vietnamese forces on 24 December 1972 in the center of the Plaines Des Jarres (PDJ) in northern Laos. Capt. Riess

was flying as Slam 04. His flight was returning from a search and rescue mission when they rendezvoused with a FAC in the center of the PDJ. The target was a known enemy location (KEL). The FAC first briefed all four aircraft [of Slam Flight] on the target information. He then cleared all aircraft to attack the target using random roll-in headings. Capt. Riess lined up on the target and started in. Then he saw the FAC start a hard climbing turn into his attack heading. Capt. Riess saw the possibility of a head-on mid-air so he tried to dive under the FAC. The A-7's canopy did not clear the FAC and the next thing Capt. Riess saw was the flames on the right side of his aircraft. The right wing had flames coming up over the leading edge flap. The dive had thrown the aircraft out of control and the "G" forces prevented Capt. Riess from reaching the ejection handles. At approximately 3,000' he was finally able to reach the handles and eject.

He landed in the middle of the PDJ very near the aircraft crash site. He took a few steps and realized that his right foot was injured. It was later determined that his Achilles tendon was injured. He then heard automatic weapons fire from the west. He immediately dove into the 25-inch grass in which he had landed. He proceeded to crawl 100 feet to clear his parachute and the immediate crash site. Then he used his survival radio to notify his flight of his location, his injury, and the hostile fire that he heard.

The first wave of Pathet Lao or North Vietnamese ran past him toward the parachute and crash site. The second wave was offset from the first wave. One member of the second wave stepped on Capt. Riess' foot as he searched the grass. The searcher raised his M-16 [American automatic rifle] and pointed it at Capt. Riess. Capt. Riess slowly raised his hands out of the grass and then raised them over his head.

The searchers knocked Capt. Riess to the ground and then proceeded to strip him of everything except his flight suit. His hands were bound behind his back, and then they led him off to a nearby gully. Capt. Riess then saw his A-7 flight, along with other aircraft, in the area searching for him.

In an underground bunker in a nearby gully he was again searched by another soldier. When the soldier found nothing, he became irritated and slapped Capt. Riess several times. He then placed a bayonet at Capt. Riess' throat. An apparently higher ranking individual (possibly an officer) then entered and proceeded to "chew out" the soldier.

That night (24 December 1972) Capt. Riess was marched by moonlight to a small compound near the Laotian/North Vietnamese border. During the march he met several other Pathet Lao/NVA soldiers on the trail. Once one of the soldiers placed a small submachine gun to his head. A superior NCO or officer immediately reprimanded this individual. After a march of several days, Capt. Riess was loaded on a truck and sent to Hanoi.

Capt. Riess recounted how the Communists always dress their prisoners in red-stripped uniforms, which are easily identifiable in the jungle and clearly mark an escaping prisoner.

He also related how his truck convoy was attacked twice by American aircraft. During the first attack the truck in front of him and the one behind his truck were destroyed by American planes. Later another bombing attack by American planes struck his convoy. Bombs exploded within lethal range of Capt. Riess, but he was not injured.

Once in Hanoi Capt. Riess was placed in Ho Lo Prison with the nine other Laotian prisoners. He was immediately placed in solitary confinement by prison authorities. While in prison, he was repeatedly asked to sign a number of statements on the morality of the B-52 bombing of Hanoi. Throughout his capture period he was given much propaganda. In the block where all ten Lao prisoners were held, a radio speaker broadcast the NVA propaganda program. Capt. Riess has mentioned numerous communication systems used by the prisoners to communicate with one another. He mentioned the tap system, the written note drops, and various other variations.

Capt. Riess was informed by the radio propaganda speaker of the 27 January cease-fire in Vietnam. The Vietnamese-held American POW's received a copy of the agreement on the evening of the 30th of January. The Lao prisoners received a copy through the communication net. Upon the signing of the cease-fire agreement in Laos on 22 February the Lao prisoners received a copy of the peace agreement. He and nine other POWs captured in Laos had been told that their release was not a part of the Paris Agreement—that while others would go, they would be left behind. As group by group, the others left, the remaining ten grew more apprehensive. Then a North Vietnamese photographer brought the news that President Nixon had interrupted the timetable for the entire prisoner exchange until he was assured that the Laotian prisoners would also be released.

After ninety-four days as a POW, Capt. Riess was released on 28 March at Gia Lam Airfield, North Vietnam. The POWs were medevaced by C-141 to Clark AB, PI. Upon deplaning at Clark, Capt. Riess heard Lt. Col. Scott Harpe (353rd Asst Ops Officer) call "Welcome home, Chuck!"

After several days in the Clark hospital, Capt. Riess was flown to Andrews AFB, Maryland. On 6 April he was flown back home to Myrtle Beach AFB.

I had been tasked to put together his welcome home ceremony, and I was there to also welcome him home. He was a *very* lucky individual—to survive a midair collision with another aircraft; the ejection; and being taken alive as one of only ten POWs ever to be released from Laos.

Capt. Chuck Riess at his welcome home ceremony at Myrtle Beach AFB on 6 April 1973. (Official USAF photo)

My next Linebacker mission was on 27 December. This time we had a strike package of thirty-two A-7s; carrying twelve MK-82 500-lb bombs each, for a total of 312 bombs. Our targets, only 4.1 nautical miles southwest of Hanoi, were the Hanoi International RADCOM (Radar & Communications) Transmitter #1 and Hanoi RADCOM Transmitter #2—better known as Radio Hanoi.

Target No. 1 was the largest and best-equipped radio transmission facility in North Vietnam. Destruction of this facility would disrupt radio communications in the North and would cause overloading of other transmitting facilities in the Hanoi area.

Target No. 2 was capable of being linked to the Hanoi Defense Communication Network and could supplement early warning electronic facilities. Destruction of this target could hamper the air defense effort in the Hanoi area and would result in the loss of valuable communication equipment. It was also the home of "Hanoi Hannah" who constantly broadcast propaganda to the Americans in English. She was about to get her eyes watered.

This load of twelve bombs on an A-7 is, what we called, a "dirty" load—it wasn't aerodynamically "clean" or "slick." In addition, our two fuel drop tanks were not on this time to make room for the two multiple ejector racks (MERs) with the six bombs on each. We also carried an electronic counter- measures (ECM) pod under one wing to jam enemy air defenses. In other words, hauling this load through the air caused a lot of drag—and very high fuel consumption—sort of like holding your hand out the window of a car at 70 mph with your palm flat to the wind instead of with your palm down, fingertips pointed forward in the low-drag slick configuration.

One of our birds loaded with 12 x 500-lb "slick" bombs—six bombs on each MER hung on each middle wing station. Note the 354th TFW patch on the side of the aircraft just aft of the cockpit and the "Welcome to Korat" sign in the background.

Consequently, our entire force required pre-strike in-flight refueling. We took off, joined up, and met the tankers over northern Laos, west of the PDJ, on our way to the targets. I couldn't help thinking I was here over eight years ago in 1964 doing this same thing—but from the other end. It was a long war—and not over yet.

Our TOTs (time on target) were five minutes apart for the two targets, so we basically went in two waves. The first wave of four four-ship flights was led by our squadron commander, Lt. Col. Brown Howard in Trigger Flight. Maj. Hedgepeth led Saddle Flight; Capt. Dwight "Crow" Wilson was next with Pistol; and Capt. Welde had the fourth flight with four Sixguns.

Lt. Col. Scott Harpe led the second wave as Carbine Flight; Capt. Chuck Kennedy had Rifle Flight; Capt. Allison was next with Cactus Flight; and I brought up the rear again leading the four SLUF's of Rattler Flight. This time I had a respectable callsign, but again, we were too busy to notice. Unfortunately, six of our aircraft had to air abort because their assigned tanker had to abort, and the other tankers didn't have enough fuel for them. They returned to base with their seventy-two bombs. The rest of us continued on.

As a side note, Lt. Col. Scott Harpe was promoted very rapidly over the next few years, until he was killed in an F-16 accident in Spain as a Maj. General. He was a fine officer and a great individual.

As we approached the targets, we could see in the distance that weather in the target area was good with just a few scattered clouds. The decision was made—we would go in for a visual strike.

The two targets were 1.5 NM apart. As we approached from the south, Lt. Col. Howard would take his wave in on Target #1, the western-most transmitter complex, and egress to the west—away from our target #2. We in Lt. Col. Harpe's wave would attack target #2 and come off the target to the right, or to the east. This would deconflict all of us being in the same piece of sky at the same time. The call was made over our secure radio strike frequency to arm our weapons—*"Green 'em up."* Our bombs were selected to come off in six pairs with fifty-foot spacing between pairs. Our M61 cannon was armed, as well as our two air-to-air heat-seeking AIM-9 Sidewinder missiles mounted on our two fuselage rails under each wing—our protection from MiGs. We were ready.

As our MiG Cap of Phantoms stayed above us on the lookout for enemy aircraft, our two attack waves slowly descended to 17,000 feet and drifted apart slightly as we concentrated on our individual targets.

There it was. Just as we studied in mission planning with the intelligence maps and reconnaissance photos provided to us, we were approaching Radio Hanoi. We watched as Col. Harpe and his Carbine Flight rolled into their 45-degree dives. By this time Col. Howard and his wave were attacking their target a mile and a half to our left. However, our strike that day would not go unchallenged.

As they rolled into their dive bomb passes, our RHAW scopes came alive with multiple SAM and AAA threats. Our MiG Cap also called out multiple SAM launches, as well as the AAA guns. That unmistakable rattlesnake sound of the SA-2 SAM launch in my headset was enough to test my concentration. There was only a split second to glance at the scope as I watched the eight birds of Rifle and Cactus Flights roll into their dive bomb passes in sequence just ahead of me. We were there to knock out Radio Hanoi that day—not to study RHAW scopes! Sure enough, our beloved propaganda-spewer, Hanoi Hannah, promptly went off the air in mid-sentence.

At the right point with the target in sight, I rolled into my 45-degree dive with my three flight members peeling off close behind. My SLUF, loaded with three tons of bombs, accelerated rapidly as I pointed the nose down and picked up the transmitter under my aiming symbol. 15,000 feet... 14,000... 13,000... 11,000. The altimeter was unwinding faster and faster as I accelerated in the dive. I had time to make final adjustments to my aim as my trusty mount hurtled toward the ground! When my computerized aiming symbol was exactly on target, I pressed and held the red consent button on the top left of the control stick underneath my thumb. With this button held down, it gave consent to the weapons computer to release the bombs in the preselected sequence when it calculated the proper point in space to do so to hit the target. Therefore, exact dive angle, airspeed, and altitude were not critical, because the computer compensated for each in conjunction with the others.

With the "pickle" button still mashed, I started my 4-G pull for recovery from the 600-mph, 45-degree dive, at 8,000 feet. With the smooth pull, I felt the distinctive *ka-chunk, ka-chunk, ka-chunk* six times as pairs of bombs were released. I knew it was a good run. But now to add to our fun came the call on Guard frequency in our headsets, "White bandits—270 at 6 from Bull's-eye!"

There was a code set up by our intelligence community. Red Crown was a Navy Intel ship just off the coast of North Vietnam in international waters. Five other agencies also transmitted MiG warnings: Disco, Big Eye, College Eye, T-Ball, and Deep Sea. Enemy aircraft were labeled Red, White and Blue

Bandits, which translated to the MiG-17 Fresco, MiG-19 Farmer, and MiG-21 Fishbed, respectively. There were also two other types of bandits: Black (any one of the prior too low on gas to pose a

Mig-17 *Fresco*

threat), and Green. Green Bandits were individual pilots known to our Intel community who had, we were told, a fifty percent shoot-down percentage—their top guns batting .500—their top pilots. As we suspected and found out for a fact later, most were Soviet pilots.

Hanoi was known as "Bull's-eye." This call could have come from one of the other five facilities that tracked these birds, but when it came from Red Crown, we all knew

Mig-19 *Farmer*

there were some very dangerous MiG-19s six miles due west of Hanoi.

It was now time to forget about the target and concentrate on "Gettin' outa Dodge" as I bottomed out of my dive at 4,000 feet. This was 2,000 feet lower than I wanted, because I was now in prime AAA country. I started jinking left, right, up, down in random patterns to make me an unpredictable target to the visual and radar-controlled gunners on the ground. My Radar Homing And Warning scope was still alive with active threats as I pulled off to the right and started climbing back to 17,000 feet. Even with the three tons of bombs gone, that takes quite a while in the SLUF with those aerodynamically dirty multiple-ejector racks (MERs), which the bombs were mounted on, still under the wings.

Downtown Hanoi was straight ahead three miles as I continued around to the east, then south. It was also time to start "checking 6"—looking behind you to make sure MiGs weren't sneaking up on you. This also required a quick roll-up on a wing every minute or two to check for bandits coming up from behind and low—in your blind spot.

This was the one and only time I wished the A-7D had an afterburner. That climb out coming off the target downtown Hanoi with SAMs in the air and AAA guns shooting at you was unbelievably slow. It felt like I had the throttle in my left hand bent in half as I pushed it all the way to the firewall, but the acceleration and climb seemed in slow motion. Total elapsed time since I rolled in for my attack until I was heading back south and climbing through 6,000 feet had only been a little over one minute.

Without the concentration needed to hit the target, it was at this point I truly became conscious of the extreme danger I was in. I looked around for the other three guys in my flight. They were nowhere to be seen. We had become separated and I was now on my own. Being alone in that environment was about as healthy as swimming in a tank full of sharks. With a quick glance at all my instruments to confirm all was okay with the bird, I had my head on a swivel, not only looking for MiGs, but also looking for a friendly bird to join up with for mutual protection and preservation.

And there, off my left wing about 3,000 feet, was one of the most beautiful sights I had ever seen—a flight of two F-4s in close route formation (about 100 feet apart) heading south on a parallel course with me at about the same altitude! I was sure happy to see them, but I wondered why they were in route formation and not spread out further for better mutual protection and support. I don't know if they saw me or not. I never got a chance to ask them.

"Blue bandits—180 at 3 from Bull's-eye—southbound!" came another call from Red Crown over Guard frequency.

"Oh SHIT!" I said to myself, *"I'm at 185 at 5! Those are MiG-21s coming up from behind me to my left!"* I snapped my head back to the left, and there he was—a sight branded in my mind forever. A bright silver delta-wing MiG-21J "JayBird," the best fighter the North had, and one of the best in the world at that time, gleaming in the sunlight against the dark green vegetation as he came streaking south out of the Hanoi area at very low altitude "down in the weeds" and already near supersonic speed, was coming our way. He was really movin', or as we said in the business, haulin' ass! I stopped jinking and tried to become as invisible as possible as this predator came out to play. I didn't want to risk sunlight flashes off my bird that would signal a very easy prey was available to this quite formidable enemy.

MiG-21 *Fishbed* down in the weeds—the most prolific fighter ever built in the world. At least 10,000 were made—some estimate 13,000

Our A-7s were camouflaged greens and tans on top to blend into the jungle when seen from above, and grayish white underneath to blend with the sky from below. I sure hoped it would work now. My finger was on the jettison button to blow off the empty MERs if I was about to get "bounced." With a clean aircraft, I could maneuver a lot better—like being able to swim slightly faster away from the sharks in the fish tank. I rechecked to make sure my 20mm cannon and two AIM-9 Sidewinders were armed. They were.

Another stroke of luck I had going for me that day was that our A-7Ds didn't smoke—they had clean exhausts. Unfortunately, F-4s smoked like a chimney. You could see one from ten miles away—not the bird... just the black smoke from its two engines.

AA-2 Atoll
Air-to-air missile

F-4 *Phantom II*

As I watched in awe, the single MiG-21 popped up behind the two F-4s, closed to within a thousand feet, fired an Atoll air-to-air heat-seeking missile, and broke down and to the left away from me as the trailing F-4 wingman exploded from the missile's direct hit. The F-4 leader immediately broke down to the left, as he went to full afterburner back towards downtown Hanoi in hot pursuit of the MiG. They both disappeared at supersonic speeds into the ground smoke and haze drifting up from multiple bomb strikes.

I don't know if the Phantom ever caught the MiG or not—I didn't wait around to find out. I looked for two 'chutes from the F-4 wingman. I saw none. I don't know if they got out or not. This entire sequence—from hearing the Bandit call to seeing no chutes—took approximately fifteen seconds. I had no time to make a radio transmission to warn the Phantoms. I assumed they had heard the same Bandit call on Guard frequency as I had, but evidently, not, as they never reacted to the MiG until the number 2 Phantom disappeared in a ball of flame. There was normally always a lot of chatter on Guard frequency, so many pilots turned it off and didn't monitor it, as it could be very distracting. It overpowered all other frequencies in your headset. Unfortunately, all the warning calls were made on Guard, so if you didn't have it turned on, you were really missing out on an important part of the show.

I was back on my own again. Evidently there had been only one MiG, and he didn't see me—but I had to make sure. Maybe he *did* have a wingman! I rolled up on my left wing to take a quick look behind at my 6 and 7 o'clock high and low positions, then back and up on my right wing to check my 4 and 5 o'clock positions. No birds in sight—good guys or bad.

I made my turn to 250 degrees to head southwest out of North Vietnam into Laos, and then back south over the PDJ to Korat. As I got nearer to Korat, other SLUFs were coming back, too. I joined up with a flight of two, and we came in, pitched out over runway 06, and landed. I only logged 3.0 hours on that mission, but it was so chock-full of adventures, it felt like I was up there a day and a half. We taxied in and shut down in our revetments. We met each other walking into the intelligence and maintenance debriefing. We were all soaked with sweat. It was a very busy three hours.

All thirty-two of our birds returned safely that day. Our bomb damage assessment (BDA) from photos from a reconnaissance run over the target after our strike confirmed our gut feelings—we had wiped out Radio Hanoi. The official BDA from our Wing History reads as follows:

Target #1: Several direct hits resulted in 1 confirmed transmitter and control building destroyed, 2 medium sized probable support buildings destroyed, 2 probable support buildings heavily damaged, and 2 buildings with medium damage.

Target #2: Target received several direct hits resulting in the destruction of 1 transmitter and 4 buildings, heavy damage to 1 multi-story control building, moderate damage to 2 probable administration/support buildings, and light damage to 1 cooling tower and southeast section of security fence.

These were very tense times. Most of us were flying every day, and the missions were quite demanding and extremely life threatening. Needless to say, many of us acquired the attitude of living life to the fullest each day, for tomorrow may never come. In keeping with that outlook on life, a bunch of us, under the very competent leadership of our Operations Officer, Lt. Col. Wayne Davis, decided to have a Squadron party one Friday night—one of many! However, this one sticks out in my mind as especially noteworthy, as we decided a few hours into the party that we needed to borrow the jukebox from the Officers' Club so we could dance with some nurses that had ventured into our party area.

Our Ops Officer, Lt. Col. Wayne Davis, sitting next to Capt. Mike Hembrough. Mike received the Silver Star for his part in the Bobbin 05 SAR. Col. Davis became Commander of the 353rd TFS on 19 March 1973. (Crow Wilson photo)

Of course, every great military operation has to have a thorough detailed plan in order to be successful. Our plan was for about eight to ten of us, all dressed up in our red Squadron party suits and already feeling no pain, to pile into Wayne's orange Datsun pickup truck and head for the KABOOM (Korat Air Base Officers' Open Mess). When we arrived, we nonchalantly walked into the crowded club, unplugged the jukebox, wheeled it out to the truck, and loaded it in the back. All went very smoothly, but for some reason, the Club Officer, a young, non-flying lieutenant, came running out to see what was happening. Wayne explained to him, in the best slightly slurred speech he could muster at the time, that we were just borrowing the jukebox for a party, and we'd bring it back when we were done with it.

"No, no, no—you can't do that!" the young officer told him. Well, that sounded like a challenge to the rest of us, and we all decided that we could.

By this time the Air Police arrived to see what was going on. The Club Officer told them we were stealing his jukebox, and Wayne told them we were just going to borrow it for a few hours, then bring it back. The two junior enlisted Air Police were not dummies. They knew what was going on, and there was no way they were going to tell a dozen fighter pilots led by a colonel, "No." And besides, how do you go about arresting half a fighter squadron during a war?

The two young Air Policemen asked Col. Davis again what we were going to do with the jukebox. Col. Davis reiterated to the APs what was going to happen, and they politely said that, if we promised to bring it back when we were done with it, we could borrow it. There was a big roar of applause from the rest of us, and many slaps on the backs of the relieved APs who had defused the tense situation. We even invited them up to the party for a drink, and they happily accepted—they came over and had Cokes, as they were on duty.

However, this episode must have sent the innocent young Club Officer over the edge. The last we saw of him, he was sitting cross-legged by the edge of the Club pool rocking back and forth and mumbling to himself. I think he was sent back to the States shortly afterwards. As for the jukebox? We had a great time with it, and our Squadron party that night was the talk of the town! We took the jukebox back the next morning, and things returned to "normal."

The famous Korat O'Club—the KABOOM (Korat Air Base Officers' Open Mess). It had an old western-type bar about 30 feet long—which got a lot of use each night. The pool is to the left in these photos. (Photos from Crow Wilson)

The day before Christmas, 24 December 1972, I was on another SAR looking for Jackal 33 — an F-111 crewmember

from the 474 TFW that had gone down in the PDJ of Laos. It was a long, involved SAR over a period of several days. When we finally reached him and the PJ in the Jolly Green chopper could see him,

Our Sq Commander & Ops Officer quarters. Note the orange Datsun pickup truck on the right of jukebox fame! (Photo from Crow Wilson)

he had been propped up against the wreckage of his aircraft to look like he was alive. He wasn't. He had been executed and propped there to draw in the SAR forces. After we all egressed the area through a hail of AAA fire, we finally returned to our bases without any further losses. We were all lucky that day— except for Jackal 33. It had been another flack trap. This mission again drove home the fact that being taken prisoner in Laos was rare indeed. It was a sad Christmas that year.

Three of us in the Squadron, Barry Barrineau, Dwight "Crow" Wilson, and I, came out on the Majors' Promotion List while we were at Korat. It was nice to be promoted while flying combat! I was also selected at the same time for Air Command and Staff College (ACSC) at Maxwell AFB in Montgomery, Alabama. The class would start in July of 1973.

My last, and the last Linebacker II mission flown by the A-7Ds, was, unfortunately, another sky-puke mission off the wing of F-4 LORAN birds on 29 December —the last day of the bombing of North Vietnam. The target was a

A-7D dropping a pair of MK-82 500# "Snake eye" high drag bombs. The large metal fins pop open upon release to immediately start slowing the ordnance. This allows a safe, low altitude delivery with the aircraft well out of the way before detonation.

SAM storage area thirty-four nautical miles north of Hanoi. The area had no permanent buildings or structures. Although over 200 rounds of large radar-controlled 85mm AAA (about 3.5 inches in diameter) were fired at us and numerous MiG calls were made, all thirty-two SLUFs, led by Lt. Col. Davis, returned safely. I was number four bird in the 4-ship Sixgun Flight. And the BDA from that uneventful mission? "None reported." Wonderful—just wonderful.

After we came back and landed, we walked into Intel and maintenance debriefing. Word had just come in that a cease fire had been declared for north of 18° north latitude in Vietnam. Three days later on 1 January 1973, the U.S. broadened the bombing halt to include all of North Vietnam. I flew another seven CAS missions in South Vietnam, Laos and Cambodia after that before our 353rd TFS redeployed to Myrtle Beach on 14 January. Our Wing was setting up our squadrons to begin a leapfrog schedule for staggering our redeployments back to Korat if the War continued.

However, on the 15th of January 1973, President Nixon suspended all bombing, shelling, and mining of North Vietnam. Our 354th Tactical Fighter Wing was awarded the Air Force Outstanding Unit Award for the period 15 June 1970 to 31 May 1972 on the 17th of January, and on 24 January, President Nixon announced a Vietnam Agreement was initiated. The Vietnam War ended 27 January 1973.

The other Squadrons in our Wing flew other sorties in Laos and Cambodia, but I had flown my last combat sortie and never knew it.

Chapter 13
More Great A-7D Time – 1973 - 1978

*A*fter returning from Korat in January 1973, I was the Chief of Wing Training for the six months before leaving Myrtle Beach for Air Command and Staff College (ACSC) in Montgomery. All of the flying now was very anticlimactic compared to the heart-pounding rigors of combat flying. We all felt like fish out of water. This was a very ho-hum six months, and although I would miss the flying, I wanted to get to school, get out, and get another good job. I was ready for something new.

In June, about a month before I left Myrtle Beach for Maxwell AFB, Paula and I had Mom and Dad to our house for a spaghetti dinner. After dinner, Paula went off to play Bingo, while the three of us stayed home to fix a TV that wasn't working. After looking at it for a few minutes, Dad and I decided to take it up to a TV repair place in town. We carried it out and loaded it in our car. It was a heavy table model, and we both were huffing and puffing to get it in the back seat—and it was hot outside. We shouldn't have done that on a full stomach. After we went in and sat down, Dad became light-headed, sweaty, clammy and faint. Mom and I managed to get him in the car and raced him to the hospital. Dad had had a heart attack. He recovered quickly, and he was released five days later.

All during this period my marriage to Paula was deteriorating. Details do not belong in this book, but one episode needs listing, as it stands out in my mind to this day. I was sitting at my desk in the squadron one afternoon when the phone rang. It was Paula.

"When will you be home?" she asked.

"I should be home by about five," I answered. We lived twenty-one miles away through moderate traffic, towns and red lights. I walked in the door at 5:10 that afternoon, and incredibly she said, "Where have you been?"

I replied, "What do you mean?"

Her next remark still rings in my ear, "You told me you were going to be home at five—you're late. Where have you been?" The yelling and screaming that followed went on for three days. Her irrational temper that I had witnessed before we were married was alive and well. Many other incidences occurred, but I'll pass them over in this work. I was not changing her as I thought I could prior to getting married. Conversely, my temper was being systematically destroyed.

ACSC was a twelve-month mid-level Professional Military Education (PME) school for senior captains and majors. In conjunction with the PME, Auburn University had a great opportunity for us at the school. We could take night courses and complete a Masters Degree in that one year. I decided to do that, as I was already in a full-time school, so this would be the perfect chance to get my Masters. I decided on Business Management.

Mom and Dad drove over to see us in Montgomery in September, and then headed south to Florida for a visit with his mother and sister—Grandma and Edna. We had a great visit and had a superb dinner in the Officers' Club there at Maxwell. We shook hands, gave each other hugs, and off they went.

Just after arriving in Florida, Dad said he wasn't feeling very well, so they decided to return home to Myrtle Beach. As Mom didn't drive at that time, Dad had to do all the driving.

They arrived home okay, but on 25 October Dad had another heart attack and was in the hospital. While I was sitting at my desk studying on Saturday night, two days later, I suddenly thought of Dad and decided to call him in the hospital. I got through to him in his room, and he sounded quite tired and had slightly slurred speech. We only talked for a couple of minutes, as he needed to rest. That was the last time I talked with my father.

Mom called the next morning, Sunday, 28 October 1973. A nurse had gone into Dad's room to take his blood pressure, pulse, and temperature. Dad sat up on the side of his bed, and while the nurse was taking his blood pressure, he slumped to the floor. They tried for thirty minutes to revive him, but he was gone before he hit the floor. He was twenty-six days shy of his seventy-first birthday—too young. Unfortunately, he had been a heavy smoker since he was sixteen, and had smoked two packs a day of unfiltered Camel cigarettes for most of that time. He was too young. What made me suddenly think of Dad that Saturday night? That's an interesting question...

As he wished, Dad was cremated and his ashes were scattered at sea in Myrtle Beach. He loved the ocean and surf fishing. He was a good man, and the best father any one could hope for. Rest in peace, Dad—you've earned it.

These remaining nine months of the schools were equally as busy. With ACSC classes during the day and the Masters classes at night, homework for both was accomplished after school into the wee hours of the morning each day and weekends.

I finally graduated from ACSC in July 1974, and received my MBA from Auburn University at the same time. It had been a very busy year, but quite productive. My next assignment was

Chief of A-7D Operational Test & Evaluation (OT&E) at Nellis AFB, Las Vegas, Nevada. What a great job!

After a trip back to Myrtle Beach to say goodbye to Mom, Paula, Mary Jane, and I headed west to Las Vegas. I was quite fortunate to return to flying in the bird I loved instead of being sent to a "grooming" staff job in the Pentagon or other high-level staff job. For those who aspired to one day become Chief of Staff, that was the desired course. I didn't want to be Chief of Staff—I wanted to fly. I was lucky.

We got to Las Vegas, bought a house, and after a couple of months of living in a small trailer off the end of the runway while waiting for it to become available, finally got to move in. Not any too soon, as the little trailer shook every time aircraft took off from the base—and that was often! Paula and I really enjoyed playing Blackjack, and she decided she wanted to go to dealers' school and get a job in town as a 21 dealer. She did that and had a few jobs in small casinos downtown, out on the Strip, and in nearby Henderson.

My job as Chief of A-7D OT&E in the 422nd Fighter Weapons Squadron at Nellis was simply outstanding. The Squadron had three sections: the F-4 OT&E; F-111 OT&E; and our A-7 section. Our Squadron was responsible for testing new hardware for our respective aircraft. After thorough testing, we would evaluate the different pieces of equipment, write a report on them, and come up with a recommendation to the Air Force on which to buy as a retrofit to all the aircraft of that kind and which to scrub. Very interesting work, and very interesting flying.

One of the tests we had was on new metals for our 20mm cannon ammunition. This cannon was used by just about every fighter in our inventory. We loaded up our gun with each of three different test loads of new ammo, and went out to the tactical ranges in the vast military area in the desert north of Las Vegas to shoot it. One of the metals was

Another "hero" photo of me as Chief of A-7D Operational Test & Evaluation in the 422nd Fighter Weapons Squadron, Nellis AFB, NV from 1974-1975. Notice the checkered helmet visor and scarf of the 57th Fighter Weapons Wing (patch on left shoulder) at Nellis—*"Home of the Fighter Pilot."* Notice the pop-out internal steps and ladder that fold up and snap closed.

way too hard, and the rounds jammed every time we fired the gun. Another was rejected because the extractor couldn't grab the shells. And yet another overheated too rapidly, and rounds went off before they were in the chambers. I came back from one of those missions with a hole in the side of the nose where a round had "cooked off" prematurely and blew the front left side of the bird out. Not good.

Other tests involved new and proposed instrumentation for the SLUF. These tests took me to places in the desert north of Las Vegas where these items could be tested. On one such flight, I had finished my testing for that day, and the people on the ground that worked out there asked if I could put on a little air show for them. We were a couple hundred miles from nowhere—what better place to do some hot doggin' than there? I said, "Sure!" They spread the word and everybody came out to see the show.

I started with some rolls and "wifferdills" as I turned my fuel dump switch on and off briefly during each to simulate the smoke on the Thunderbirds' jets. It looked real good, they told me! After a few minutes they asked if I could come down and make a low pass by the crowd. Why certainly! I love buzzing.

I started down from about 4,000 feet in an accelerating curvilinear approach in full power. I planned the pass as low as possible to really give them a show. I picked up speed rapidly with the clean bird, and I rolled out at about twenty feet above the ground and over 600 mph as I waived to the crowd off my left wing with my left hand. They were all waiving back! Great pass! I brought my eyes back forward, and there directly in front of me was a slight hill with a small shed.

I snatched the stick back, and as my heart pounded, cleared the shed by not more than a couple of feet. They told me the shed and I had disappeared in a cloud of dust I had kicked up from the desert floor from my exhaust and wingtip vortices. I told them it was time for me to go home. They said thanks for the show. I returned to Nellis straight and level at 10,000 feet and a slow cruise speed and landed after I had stopped shaking. That was the closest I ever came to killing myself—and I had no help from anyone else that time. However, I would try again ten years later.

One of the pilots in my A-7 section was Capt. Jim Bafus. He was a good pilot, and had been in the section before I arrived. He was the Project Manager for quite a few different tests. On one of his missions, he was to drop twelve practice bombs one at a time on a tactical range north of Nellis. His flight went well, and he made eleven very fine passes on his assigned target before coming around for his twelfth and final pass. He rolled in, dropped his last bomb, but for some unknown reason, never pulled out. He crashed into the target without any attempt to eject.

The accident board didn't find anything wrong with the jet, nor did they find any drugs or alcohol in Jim's body. The cause was a mystery. Although the cause was never agreed on 100%, it was speculated he may have had a heart attack, stroke, or some other incapacitating attack which prevented him from flying the bird and recovering from the 30-degree dive bomb pass. Other theories suggested he may have committed suicide, but a thorough investigation into his and his wife's backgrounds ruled that out. In any case, it was up to me, as his boss, to go out to his house with the chaplain and flight surgeon to tell his young wife, Beverly, and children that her husband had just been killed. It was one of the hardest things I ever had to do in my life, and the most regrettable. That was not a good day.

Only a few months later it was decided at pay grades way above mine that the A-7D OT&E would close down, and our few SLUF's would be moved down to Davis-Monthan AFB in Tucson, Arizona. This came to pass in August 1975. We closed up shop, completed most of our tests and reports, sold our homes and moved ourselves and our birds down to DM. Jim and Beverly Bafus had a small camper that Bev wanted to take to Tucson. She asked me if I would drive it down for her. I said sure. We were all happy to see Bev move to Tucson with the rest of us, and use us as family until the shock of Jim's death wore off, and she could decide with a clear mind what she wanted to do after that.

I was initially assigned to the Wing Weapons and Tactics shop at DM. It was here that I met Capt. Barry Johnson. We got along great and loved to talk about our Chief of that section—a guy that had been passed over for promotion a few times and was just waiting out his time for retirement. In a few short weeks I was reassigned as the Assistant Operations Officer in the 354th Tactical Fighter Squadron there at DM. And, although I had been an instructor in the SLUF since 1971, I was also checked out as a Formal Course A-7 Instructor Pilot after checking into the 354th.

Unfortunately, soon after my checkout, I was tasked for a special project from the commander of the base, Brig. Gen. Curry, whom I had known when he was vice wing commander back at Myrtle Beach. This project consumed the next thirty days, and about a week after that, I received another project. My flying and duties in the squadron were taking a back seat. I was reassigned as Assistant Operations Officer in the 357th TFS down the street, but the special projects kept coming.

When the Lieutenant Colonel Promotion List came out, I was on it. Promotions in the military, as in any profession, get harder with each successive step up. The promotion rate for this rank was about fifty percent of all eligible officers. Along with the promotion, I was again reassigned as Ops Officer to the 358th TFS further down the street Regrettably, the special projects kept coming, and I couldn't do what I really wanted—be the Ops Officer in the squadron.

Another of my car accidents happened in 1976. I had picked up a Chevy Monza in a "good deal." I was driving home from the Base one afternoon, and as I approached an intersection, another car coming at me swerved abruptly to make his left turn right in front of me. I don't know if he didn't see me, or he thought he could make it without having to wait for me to go past. Anyway, he didn't make it, and I hit him in his right rear fender even as I tried to stop and swerve to the left. The Monza had substantial damage to the front end, so it was a good excuse to get rid of that vehicle. I was uninjured, and the guy received a ticket for reckless driving.

In 1977, I was mesmerized with the TV program *Roots*. The twelve-hour mini-series aired on ABC from 23-30 January 1977. For eight consecutive nights it riveted the country. Based on Alex Haley's best-selling novel about his African ancestors, *Roots* followed several generations in the lives of a slave family. I had always been interested in my family's ancestors, but had never taken the time to research any of its history. About all I knew was that my Dad's family came from Germany, and my Mother's came from Sweden. My brother Paul was my only sibling, my Dad had two sisters—aunt Edna and aunt Helen, and my Mom had one brother—uncle Edward. None of the aunts or uncle had any children, so I had no cousins. Paul and his wife Mae had a son, Jack, and a daughter Ellen. The only other living relative I knew of was my paternal grandmother. Dad's father and both of Mom's parents had died before I was born.

That was the extent of my knowledge and involvement until watching this TV show. *Roots* remains one of television's landmark programs, wining over thirty Emmy awards, and it had truly sparked my desire to trace my family ancestors. One of these days I was definitely going to do it. Unfortunately, it would be another eleven years before I began my project of family genealogy.

My mother, Paul, Mae and I began the project in October 1989 at Mom's home in Garden City, South Carolina, by talking and taking notes. Mae mentioned that she had a document given to them by Aunt Edna, which was the thirty-two-page "Recollections of Grandpa John Riedel" written in 1909 for his children. She mailed a copy to me, and my project leaped into high gear. What a fantastic treasure this hand-written document was! The names, dates, places, and other priceless details of my family mentioned in it by Johan (John) Riedel, my great-grandfather, dated back to the 1700s! I meticulously went through the pages, gleaning each piece of information to enter into the genealogy computer program called Brother's Keeper. What fantastic luck to have such a document to begin my project. Without it, I would be, at best, years behind in my research.

A major branch of the Riedel family tree was brought to my attention in a July 18, 1990, letter from Felix "Danny" Riedel of South Australia. He had been in Altenplos, Germany, visiting close relatives, and was given a letter from me that had been sent to the little village of Neudrossenfeld asking for family information—it was in English, and they couldn't read it. On 14 August 1990, Felix sent a package of approximately 200-210 names of Riedels in Australia who are descendants of one of my great-uncles, Konrad Riedel, and until this time, were unknown to any of the Riedels in the United States. We had a family reunion in 1990 out in Washington state; I met Danny there. He had flown all the way from Australia for the occasion, and what a wonderful person he was!

The project grew as more information was gathered. The Mormon Church has always been the major keeper of genealogy histories, and their vast repository of family files was recently made available to the public. Now, with the aid of the personal computer to keep track of the data and compute complex relationships, genealogy is not only fun and a great project, but much easier than it was before the PC with pen and paper.

At least fifteen of my ancestors were Lutheran ministers. Another fact that stands out is that many families in the 1600s and 1700s had twelve to eighteen children—many dying in infancy and early childhood from today's common sicknesses. Hard times.

Today I have over 5,000 names on three continents in my family history dating back to the little Bavarian village of Zell in 1615. Are there more? Absolutely—but I'll pass the data and computer program on to the next generations to continue the hunt and update the information. Keep it going!

In early 1977 I went on an exercise to Roosevelt Roads Naval Air Station in eastern Puerto Rico. On one of our off days, another friend, who was also in the exercise from Davis-Monthan, and I caught a ride on a C-130 over to St. Thomas in the United States Virgin Islands. It is a beautiful island, and we had heard snorkeling in the crystal clear water was an absolute must. We took a taxi out to one of their primary snorkeling areas, rented some gear, and headed out into the bay. What a beautiful experience! The warm tropical water was as clear as a swimming pool, and underwater visibility was close to 100 feet in the eight to ten foot deep water. As we slowly paddled along enjoying all the beautiful multicolored tropical fish and shells contrasted over the white sandy bottom, my friend tapped me on the shoulder and pointed straight ahead. I looked up, and there, about fifty feet away, was a barracuda about three to four feet long. He had also stopped, and was looking directly at us. We were the intruders in his domain. His mouth was full of razor-sharp teeth, and it looked about a foot long! My buddy and I decided to slowly turn to the left in a non-threatening move, and luckily, this very formidable adversary decided to also turn to his left and continue on his way. We kept an eye on each other as we retreated, and my buddy and I were more vigilant for the rest of our outing to any other underwater potential enemies. Luckily, that lone barracuda was the only one encountered that day.

My last job at DM was Chief of Safety, Tactical Training—the head of both Ground and Flying Safety for the entire DM complex. However, as fate would have it, I was about to get another assignment. I had now been at Davis-Monthan for three years, and it was time to move on.

In December 1978 I received orders to the 8th TFW "Wolf Pack" at Kunsan Air Base, South Korea with TDY en route to McDill AFB, Florida. I was to receive a quick checkout in the F-4 Phantom II at the F-4 school there.

On the 22nd of November 1978, three days after my thirty-ninth birthday, I took my last ride in the A-7D. It was time to bid farewell to the SLUF—the bird that I had also taken to war and flown for over 1,400 hours in eight years. When I landed from my mission, I again sat in the cockpit of my trusty chariot one last time, and reflected on all those very enjoyable years—including those missions "up North" during the Vietnam War where we went "downtown" to Hanoi together as one to try to change the world. But we didn't—no fault of our own. It was a very sad goodbye as I climbed down the built-in steps that last time. But now it was time once more to move on to another fighter!

Chapter 14
80th TFS "Headhunters" – 1979 - 1980

I had been really sweating out this next assignment after Davis-Monthan, because now, as a lieutenant colonel, active flying positions were becoming quite scarce. Lieutenants, captains, and majors do about ninety percent of the active flying in the Air Force. Getting promoted is great, but with each promotion, you get closer to that day all pilots dread— the day you take your last flight and become a paper pusher strapped to a desk. It is not a pleasant time in your career, and many of us tried our best to maneuver ourselves so as to pass up those key staff positions needed for advanced promotions in order to keep flying. Flying jobs for lieutenant colonels were quite limited. Squadron commanders; operations officers, which is the number two person in the squadron; and a very few staff jobs were about all there were. But now I was on my way to a one-year remote tour in Korea, without family, with no specific job spelled out in the orders. However, getting a new checkout in another fighter before going over was quite promising—they wouldn't waste the time or money if I wouldn't be flying. Would they?

Sure enough, when I arrived at Kunsan on 4 February 1979 after completing my short F-4 checkout, I was assigned as Operations Officer in the 80th Tactical Fighter Squadron "Headhunters"—a flying job! The other squadron in the wing was the 35th TFS. I had no idea which one was better, or the most desirable to try to get into—I had not done my homework. However, the 80th, which I had been assigned to pretty much by

Aerial view of Kunsan AB looking north. The Yellow Sea borders the base on the west and south as seen here. North Korea is fifteen minutes away.

chance, would become another life-altering experience for me— still in my life full time to this day more than thirty years later.

Kunsan Air Base is located on the shores of the Yellow Sea, on South Korea's west coast, some eight miles from Kunsan City. The city has about 280,000 residents. It's some 100 miles southwest of the country's capital, Seoul. Kunsan AB is often referred to as the last of the "warrior bases." As an unaccompanied remote tour, servicemen and women spend a quick twelve months at the "tip of the spear" fulfilling the wing's mission, "To deliver lethal airpower when and where directed by the Air Component Commander."

Kunsan sits 109 miles south of the DMZ—only about a fifteen-minute jet flight from North Korea. The base is within easy reach of North Korean weapons capable of delivering chemical munitions. Hence, the need for chemical warfare classes for everyone immediately upon arrival. And, if anyone dares to forget, Army Patriot missile sites and machine-gun bunkers around the Base serve as constant reminders that the front lines of battle could be as close as the front door.

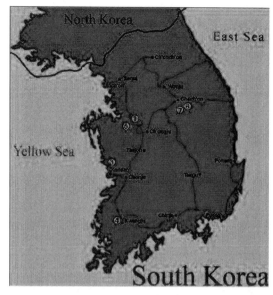

Kunsan AB is located on the west coast of South Korea at the "3" on this map.

I had been in nine different operational fighter squadrons at this point, but it soon became very apparent that this squadron was as good as the 353rd TFS back at Myrtle Beach, and head & shoulders above all the rest. Not only were the people in the squadron very highly competent in their jobs, but also the one-year remote tour at Kunsan allowed another big factor in this equation. In the States, we would all come to work in the morning and go home to our families each night. That's really great; however, at Kunsan there was no going home to the family each night. Your family was the Squadron, and we all became a very close-knit group of people.

Another benefit was that many of the guys worked and studied their jobs well into the night and on weekends. This produced people who were extremely knowledgeable in their duties. I had a saying about them—"You ask them what time it was, and they tell you how to build a clock." One such

80th Tactical Fighter Squadron patch from the 1979-80 time period.

individual was Capt. Mike "Speed" Brake, our Weapons Officer. He and Capt. Barry Barrineau, the Weapons Officer from the A-7D 353rd TFS back in 1970-1972, were the two most knowledgeable individuals I ever had the pleasure to work with in the Air Force. They both would go on to be promoted well "below the zone" many years before their peers and retire as colonels.

Everyone in the 80th at that time, except for a small handful who volunteered for an extension, was on a one-year tour. Therefore, there was a constant turnover of pilots in the Squadron—one or two arriving and leaving about every week. We always had "Hail and Farewell" Parties to hand out Squadron plaques and say goodbye to the guys leaving, as well as making the new people feel welcome. As in Vietnam, we all had our Party Suits, tailor-measured and ordered the day we arrived, and for the 80th TFS, our Squadron colors were black and yellow. Our suits were black with yellow trim—quite nice to see, especially in a group.

Within a few days after five or six new pilots arrived in the Squadron, we would take them for a "sweep" of A-Town (American Town)—a small hamlet a few miles off base. The uniform for these sweeps was, of course, sweep shirts, blue jeans, and flight boots. Our custom-made shirts, from the same tailor that made our party suits, were yellow with a wide black band—

our Squadron colors. Twenty or so of us on any given sweep was quite a sight. It was on these sweeps, over a few local beers and many fighter pilot songs, that a new pilot was given his callsign by the rest of the other pilots. I was christened with "JayBird" which reminded me of that mission "Up North" during Linebacker II in 1972 when I met with the MiG-21J *"JayBird."* It has stuck with me ever since, and I use it to this day.

Most "normal" assignments in a fighter squadron in the States are anywhere from two to three years. During that time, there are a number of different inspections, exercises, deployments, and visits from the powers that be. Our tours there in Korea, although being only one year in length, had just about the same number of these types of activities. Therefore, the pace was quite hectic. It seemed like we were constantly going from one exercise, to getting ready for another inspection, to planning for a deployment. It made the time pass quite rapidly.

(L-R) Brian "Mac" McDonald, Tom Blaikie, Richard "Rookie" Rook, Denny "Lonestar" Rea, and Jim "Pacman" Pack on a sweep of A-Town in early summer of 1979.
(Photo by Rookie Rook)

Our Squadron Commander at the time was Lt. Col. Mike Quinlan. When it was time for him to rotate back to the States in June 1979, a successor needed to be named. I was called into the Wing Director of Operations office. Col. Skip Rutherford was Mike's boss, and it was up to him to find the replacement.

This was a very special time. Not only was the 80th TFS "opening up," but the other squadron on base, the 35th TFS, needed a new commander—as well as our satellite squadron over at Taigu. All three squadrons had to be assigned new commanders within a few weeks—very rare. Col. Rutherford pointed this out to me, and told me that I was first in line to "move up" to a command position. He asked me if I had any preference as to the squadron I'd like to have. This was early June 1979. I had been in the 80th since February, so I knew the people well and knew their operation. The 80th was also, I truly believed, the best of the three squadrons. I told Col. Rutherford that I'd like to move up and stay in the 80th.

"We don't usually do that. It's normally best to move in a commander from another squadron," was his reply. "However," he continued, "if you want to stay with the 80th, that's fine."

I couldn't believe it! Not only did I have a choice of three different squadrons, but I was granted my first choice—the Headhunters! The change of command ceremony took place in June when Mike rotated back to his next assignment in the States. These next eight months, the rest of my one-year tour as Commander of the 80th Tactical Fighter Squadron, was the culmination of my Air Force career. Whether the Squadron excelled or faltered was now my responsibility. I had plenty of opportunities to have it do both.

The inspections and exercises kept coming at a steady pace. It seemed like we were just finishing up one exercise or inspection when it was time to get ready for another. But we did well on each, and when it was time for the two squadrons to have a "Turkey Shoot" gunnery competition, our Squadron, almost consistently, brought home the vast majority of the awards. It was a gratifying feeling to be part of another great squadron.

The major deployment we had was taking the entire Squadron down to Clark Air Base in the Philippines for Cope Thunder in June 1979. Cope Thunder was a chance to fly as close to actual combat as possible during peacetime—an outstanding way to introduce a near-combat experience to the younger troops who had never seen the real thing. Not only were we there, but other units of various other types of aircraft were also there doing their thing. Our targets were very realistic setups in very hard to get to locations. Radar, "smoky SAMs," and "enemy" aircraft protected the targets. Smoky SAMs were similar to flares shot up towards us when we were detected to simulate actual surface-to-air missiles. "Enemy aircraft" were USAF F-5 Aggressors that were trained in enemy tactics and simulated MiGs in the target area.

We had to plan strike packages consisting of other types of aircraft as well as our F-4s. The routes in and out were mostly up to us, as the targets were in very remote areas of almost uninhabited corners of the island. These remote areas were also the sanctuary of anti-government rebels that didn't have a lot of love for Americans, either. It was a very dangerous area to fly over, as, unfortunately, one of our American Missionary couples found out in the spring of 2002.

I remember one mission from this deployment in particular. We had taken off in a strike package flying low level while ingressing to the target a couple hundred miles away. About halfway there, I had complete hydraulic failure. We immediately declared an emergency, pulled up and out of the low level away from the other strikers, and headed back to Clark. With no hydraulics, the bird flew sluggishly, and there would be no brakes or steering for landing. The emergency procedure for this was to make an approach-end engagement of the barrier cable on the runway—in other words like a landing on an aircraft carrier at sea. All well and good, but I am no Navy pilot checked out in carrier landings. We are trained to land about 300-500 feet down the runway.

I received vectors to a straight-in landing and made sure the approach-end barrier cable was up and ready for the emergency. The crash vehicles and ambulance were also there waiting for us—the "meat wagons" we called them. After I lowered the gear with the emergency system, I dropped the tail hook—that large, heavy steel hook used to catch the cable as on carrier landings—the same type hook I used back in 1970 in the F-100 with battle damage at Pleiku.

As we approached and slowly reduced speed, the aircraft became more and more sluggish. As I came over the runway threshold, I was high and fast. The trick was to get the bird on the ground well before the cable so the hook can engage and bring you to a sudden stop within a couple of hundred feet. Unfortunately, I didn't get it on the ground soon enough—I was still about two feet in the air as I snagged the two-inch diameter steel cable with the hook. *Wham!* The cable slammed us to the runway and brought us to a very sudden stop. We were literally snagged out of midair and slammed to the ground. I had just made my first and last carrier landing! My very sharp back-seater, Maj. John "Smiley" Deloney, probably straightened his helmet and muttered under his breath, "Well, that was fun!"

I remember sitting in the snack bar in the Cope Thunder lounge getting a quick bite to eat before going out to fly on one of the missions. The TV was on and the announcer broke in to the regular scheduled programming—John Wayne had died. It was 11 June 1979. Our country lost a great patriot that day.

In July of that year I met a local Korean girl, Sun Ye Kim. Although I was still married, I was in the process of divorcing my second wife. I'll spare you all the details, but it'll suffice to say that I could no longer live with that woman. Her yelling and screaming for days on end over insignificant trivial things could no longer be tolerated. Sun Ye and I started seeing a lot of each other, and it pointed out to me what a relationship was supposed to be like. I had forgotten over the past eight years being married to Paula.

Kunsan Air Base is situated only minutes from North Korea, so everyone took the continuous stream of exercises quite seriously—especially after South Korean President Park Chung Hee was assassinated on 26 October 1979. We immediately went to a high state of alert, for we weren't sure what was going to happen next. The loss of President Park left a huge void in the South's government, so things were quite tense for months afterwards.

Another great memory I have of this period is about twenty of us dressing up in our sweep shirts, blue jeans, and flight boots and riding over to a Korean orphanage about twenty miles from the base on our motorcycles. We helped this orphanage a lot, and we had just gotten them a refrigerator they had requested.

We were quite a sight to see as we all headed down the highway through the Korean countryside and turned into their driveway. We looked like a swarm of bumblebees, and when we passed local Korean people on the road, they all smiled and waved to us. When we got there, all the little children were out playing, and when they saw us and heard the motorcycles, they ran towards us and screamed with delight—what a wonderful sight! We stayed most of the afternoon playing with them and giving short little motorcycle rides around their large two-acre play yard for all who wanted to go. When it was time for us to leave, most of the kids gave us hugs, and in their best English, told us, "You come again fast, okay Juvat?" "Juvat" is the nickname for our 80th people; it was a great experience, and one of my fondest memories of that time in Korea.

John Deloney (L) & Dick Swope meet and congratulate me after I landed from the mission that took me over the 4,000 hours of total flying time mark.
It was 2 November 1979.

Our main gunnery range, where we practiced with our little twenty-five-pound smoke spotter bombs and strafing, was Koon-ni Range on the west coast. Koon-ni Range is located about twenty-five miles northwest of Osan Air Base. One mission I remember up there involved low-angle strafe on their strafe target. I rolled in, lined up, put the pipper on the target, and squeezed the trigger on the control stick. It was a short, half-second burst—about fifty rounds. As I pulled back on the stick to recover from the shallow 15-degree dive, I felt a thump and my right engine started to vibrate. I had picked up a half-pound 20mm ricochet and ingested it in the right engine.

I had to shut it down, declare an emergency, and air abort into Kimpo Airport. It was the closest base with the best facilities for the emergency. We left the bird there for a maintenance team to fix, and my back-seater and I grabbed a commercial flight back to Kunsan. I had literally shot myself down! It was a good thing the F-4 had two engines. An investigation and statement from the range officer that day concluded that it was a freak accident, and that I didn't press in too close, foul, and pick up the ricochet as a result. Very good for me!

As the time grew near for me to get a new assignment, it was again time for the Wing ORI—our Operational Readiness Inspection. I was supposed to rotate back to the States on February 4th, but the ORI hit and Col. Rutherford asked if I would consider staying an extra seven days until the ORI was over. It would not be fair to put a new commander in the job a day before the major inspection—which I had, or had not, prepared the Squadron for. I agreed to extend without hesitation.

We flew the required missions and had all of our other Squadron areas inspected along with the rest of the Wing. We received an overall "Excellent" on the ORI, and our Squadron received many "Outstanding" Ratings in our areas. It was a real source of pride for all of us. I had flown my last mission on 31 January, but I didn't know it. I was also unaware that I had flown my last mission in the Air Force as pilot-in-command.

This photo of two F-4's at sunset signifies the end of my flying career. Not realized at the time, but my last fighter mission as pilot in command, an F-4D flight as Commander of the 80th Tactical Fighter Squadron *Headhunters,* was on 31 Jan 1980.

It was now time to turn over the Squadron to my successor. Lt. Col. Dick Swope, who had been my Operations Officer since July 1979, was to be the new commander. We had our change of command ceremony in early February 1980. The photo on the next page shows Dick receiving the 80th Guidon from the Wing Commander, Col. Richard Beyer (second from right). I had just relinquished command by giving up the Guidon to Col. Beyer. Dick Swope went on to retire 1 October 1998 as the Inspector General of the Air Force as a Lieutenant General— a very sharp individual.

I had received orders to Headquarters Pacific Air Forces in Hickam AFB, Hawaii, as Chief of Requirements. Three years in Hawaii! It was a tough job, but someone had to do it. Hawaii was a beautiful place, but it was the beginning of the worst period of my life.

Lt Col Dick Swope assumes command of the 80th TFS as he receives the Squadron
Guidon after I relinquished command in early February 1980.

Chapter 15
The Turbulent Years – 1980 - 1988

*T*hat spring, summer, and fall of 1980 was a nightmare of promises and stalls by Paula, as she knew I wanted out of the marriage at just about any cost. She made sure that was going to happen. She demanded everything—the house in Tucson, for which I was to keep up the mortgage payments; furniture; car; support; pay all her bills; and of course, my personal stamp and coin collections from when I was a little boy—all, or she wouldn't sign the papers. The only thing my lawyer at the time knew how to do was to collect regular payments from me for the legal proceedings—in advance. Needless to say, this woman, whom I despise more than anyone else in my life, walked away with everything—and *I* was the one that filed for divorce!

I finally got my divorce from Paula on 7 November 1980, and Sun Ye and I were married four days later. It was here that I made up my mind that no relationship is better than a bad one. Unfortunately, I wasted nine years of my life with Paula before I figured it out. It also gave me a new and refreshing look at our legal system...

I lost the extensive stamp collection to that second ex-wife. Although she had nothing to do with the collection, our wonderful legal system awarded it to her, along with a fine coin collection I started in sixth grade, in the divorce decree. There is only one person in my life I can truly say I loathe—it is this second wife. I despise her to this day for taking these irreplaceable and memorable treasures from me.

I filed appeals to get my stamp and coin collections back, but after many thousands of dollars in more legal costs, with a lawyer more adept in collecting advanced fees and less competent in legal outcomes than the first, nothing happened. My stamps and coins that Dad and I had started and worked on together, and with which Paula had no input whatsoever, were gone. 1980 was the worst year of my life. My hair turned gray that year.

Things slowly returned to "normal," and our wonderful daughter, Angela, was born on 19 March 1982. As with Kris and Mark, she was beautiful, too.

There was no operational flying in my position, but I could go fly in a T-33 to get some flying. This was the same T-33 T-Bird that I had flown in pilot training back in 1962. It was, to me, a giant step backward, and I wasn't much interested. I also found out after over 250 total hours in the T-Bird, that my legs, between the knees and hips, were too long. If I had to eject out of that small, cramped cockpit, it was determined my knees would have struck the canopy rail on the way out. That made my decision easy—that was the end of my T-Bird flying.

All was going fairly well until the Colonel Promotion Board met and the promotion list came out in October of 1982. I was confident I would be on it. But I was not. The last Officer Effectiveness Report (OER) I had received prior to the Board meeting was, I thought, pretty good, but when I went to the Personnel Office to see what had happened with my promotion, they told me it was not. It had stopped my promotion. On the surface the OER sounded good, but it was damning with faint praise, as the saying goes. The ho-hum words sounded good, but said nothing. There was also no mention of promotion potential—critical for this stage.

I was crushed. I couldn't believe it. I had always been promoted to every rank until now—and I had just completed the best and most successful service of my career. To be selected above my peers to be a squadron commander, and then to be highly successful in that extremely important position in the forward area of Korea, was almost a sure road to promotion. There was nothing in my records except the best of reports. What was going on?

I started checking around, and found that Paula, while she was in Hawaii for that summer of 1980, was regularly calling my boss, and telling him how bad I was, and that I wasn't supporting her. She even asked him if she could borrow five dollars so she could eat! This wonderful boss never called me in to get my side of the story. The key break came when Paula boasted to me that he had told her, "I'll fix that son-of-a-bitch so he'll never get promoted."

I went to the Personnel Office and asked how to get an Officer Efficiency Report (OER) thrown out and to be looked at again for promotion. They showed me the regulations, but told me I was wasting my time. To get an OER removed from your records is very difficult, but *then* to have your records looked at again for promotion as a first-time eligible was extremely rare. I decided to try. I certainly had nothing to lose. I was dead in the water, and I was shuffled off the front burner and put in the rear as Deputy Director of Support Operations. For the first time in my life, I was a pass-over.

The main thrust of my rebuttal to the pass-over was the fact that I had just completed my assignment as a fighter Squadron Commander in a critical forward area, and had received outstanding OERs for that duty. The Squadron had received some of the highest grades ever given by inspectors on our ORI.

The regulations said to get signed statements by every supervisor in my chain of command. Each was to spell out my job performance and fitness for promotion with an "If I had known..." statement relating to these special circumstances. All of these statements were then to be put in a report and forwarded, with a cover letter as to why this happened, to a special board for the correction of military records in Washington, D.C.

It took months to get all the statements, and I was constantly told by the Personnel people, "Good luck, but don't hold your breath."

When I finally got all the documents together, I added my cover letter and mailed the package off. All I could do now was wait. It was already August 1983, and time again to move on to my next assignment.

Sun Ye and I had decided we wanted to go to Nellis AFB in Las Vegas, so I had put that assignment at the top of my preference list. The assignment came down—Chief of Plans in the 474th Tactical Fighter Wing at Nellis. Although the 474th was an F-16 wing with three squadrons, the Chief of Plans position was a non-flying position. I was definitely on the back burner, but at least we were at Nellis—"Home of the Fighter Pilot."

Soon after arriving in Las Vegas, we decided to drive down to Tucson to find out what was going on with Paula and the house that I was still paying for from the settlement. When we got there, there it was, empty, with a large "For Sale" sign in the front yard—and a "Sold" sign on top of it! I found out from a neighbor that she had remarried, sold the house, and moved to Boca Raton, Florida a month or two earlier. And I was still paying the mortgage on that house, alimony, and support. I found out the guy she married worked for a large international company there in Tucson and had been transferred to Florida. I called his boss in Florida and let him know what type of individual—and his wife—was working for him. I don't know what happened to them, but his boss sure sounded interested. Probably gave him a raise. Needless to say, that was the immediate end of all money pouring out of my pocket to that woman each month. It's a good thing we decided to drive down that day to check it out, or I'd probably still be paying.

In 1984 while I was Chief of Plans in the 474th TFW, I was sent over to Bentwaters Air Base in England for about a week to investigate a security breach. One early morning while I was there, I was supposed to meet a helicopter, before dawn, to go on one of their missions. The helicopter landing area was at a different location from the air base, and I thought I knew exactly where it was. However, that morning was quite foggy, and after driving my staff car to where I thought I was to meet the chopper, I knew I was in the wrong place. By this time I was behind schedule, and panic was beginning to set in—it was still dark, very foggy, I was on a back country two lane road, and I didn't have a clue where I was.

I picked up the speed, and as I was traveling along a straight segment of road at close to 60 mph, I saw a set of headlights coming toward me. I didn't think anything of it, as I was concentrating on trying to determine where I was, and if I would get to the chopper in time. However, all of a sudden the headlights swerved to the right while the car, with horn blaring, whizzed by me barely missing me on my left side! What on earth was he trying to do to me? Then it dawned on me—in England they drive on the left side of the road, and I was on the right side—HIS side! In my haste and preoccupation with trying to think where I was, being late, etc., I had reverted to my normal habit of driving on the right. Luckily, that car veered at the last minute to avoid me and a head-on collision at over 120 mph, as he was also going at least 60 mph. I was very lucky that foggy morning, because I could have realized my error at the last minute and swerved directly into him as he was trying to get out of my way. After I stopped shaking, I was very conscious of my driving responsibilities for the rest of my time in England. This was the second time I almost killed myself—along with someone else this time.

Sun Ye decided she wanted to be a 21 dealer as Paula had, so she, too, went to dealer's school, graduated, and went to work as a blackjack dealer out on the Strip in the El Rancho and the Riviera casinos. She also wanted to become a U.S. Citizen, so she went to night school for her Naturalization studies. She was very proud to receive an overall "Excellent" on her Naturalization exams, and she became a U.S. Citizen in 1984.

On the 12th of October 1984, I received a call from the Nellis Personnel Office. I went over, and they showed me a message that had just come in. I had been promoted to the grade of Colonel by a special board on 11 October 1984, with retroactive date of rank to 1 December 1982—my original date of rank if I had been promoted on time with my contemporaries.

All the time and effort had paid off. However, although I had won the battle to get that OER removed and then promoted, I had lost the war. In those two years it took to go through that entire process, I had been put aside, and the good jobs had passed me by. It was too late to get back into the running for general officer promotion.

I was also very fortunate to get a few backseat rides in the two-seat F-16s in the Wing. The F-16 didn't have a conventional control stick in front of you as other fighters had.

It had a side-stick controller—only the grip—located above the right instrument panel. It didn't have the travel that a conventional stick had, either. I remember about all I had to do was *think* about moving the grip, as it only needed slight pressures to move the jet. The bird is capable of nine Gs, so your arm must have an armrest to be able to maneuver at those high G-forces without slipping off the grip. I thought it would be very hard to get used to this new grip way over on the right, but I found it a quite easy transition.

These were my last flights in Air Force planes, and I enjoyed every minute. The pilots in the front let me fly most of the missions from the rear seat. It was a great end to my flying career to be "flying" this beautiful state-of-the-art frontline fighter, which is still the backbone of the Air Force today.

In the early summer of 1985, four of us from the Wing were on a TDY and had to spend overnight in Lake Tahoe, Nevada. That night we were lucky enough to get front row seats at the Sammy Davis, Jr. show. What an incredible talent he was, and that memory will stay with me for the rest of my life.

Once more it was time for a new assignment. It was August 1985. Sun Ye had found a home in the glitter of the Las Vegas Strip and its lifestyle. One of her friends told me in confidence that when I left Las Vegas for my next assignment, Sun Ye wouldn't be going with me. I had heard this all before, and the reasons were the same. Although it was still very hard to accept, I did this time easier than the first.

My assignment was Senior Air Force Representative to the U.S. Army Infantry School at Ft. Benning, Georgia. I left Las Vegas and my third family, house, a car, and furnishings, and headed east alone in late August 1985.

After I got settled in the new job, I became interested in tennis. I had never played before, but I had always wanted to take up this great sport. Now was the time. Benning had nice soft clay courts that were much easier on your legs and knees than the hard concrete courts. I started out by taking a couple of lessons to find out which end of the racket to hold, and started playing. It is a great sport, and I really enjoyed it. I met a few people on the courts and became good friends with them. Sidney Hines, a retired Army Special Forces colonel was one; and Fred Young, the Director of Safety for Ft. Benning, was another. Fred was a great player and gave me many pointers on the game. Sidney was a happy-go-lucky guy who enjoyed his can of Pabst Blue Ribbon beer. Unfortunately he liked about a case of them a day, and they finally killed him in late 1993. What a waste of a good life.

Another friend that I played tennis with was the German Army's Representative to our Infantry at Ft. Benning, Lt. Col. Fred Shultz. Fred was a good player, and we had many great games together. One day in October 1986, Fred asked me if I had ever been to Yellowstone National Park. I had not, but always wanted to go. He had a plan that we could fly out with the Army Rangers later that month, spend some time with them at their training area near Salt Lake City, then leave from there. That came to fruition. After spending a few days with the Rangers, we signed out  on leave, rented a car, and headed northeast to Jackson Hole, Wyoming, Grand Teton National Park, then up into Yellowstone. We had a great time, as it was new to both of us.

The two memories that stand out on this exceptional trip are stopping at a roadside stand to buy a pint of raspberries each and eating them by the handful as we drove, and standing on a hilltop in Yellowstone Park and toasting each other with a flask that Fred had in his pocket. We had a great time, and were very fortunate to be there at that time, as the great fire of July through September 1988 that burned over 793,000 acres (36% of the park) was less than a year later. It won't be the same for decades.

I was sitting in my office at Fort Benning one day in 1988 when a call came in from a guy up in Maine. He asked if I ever had a purple party suit? My mind immediately flashed back to 1969 and the 510th TFS at Bien Hoa. I said yes, and he asked if it was from the 510th TFS? Again my answer was yes—"The Buzzards of Bien Hoa." I asked how he knew this. It turns out, he was a military memorabilia collector and had recently acquired my party suit at auction from a military memorabilia sale in St Louis, Missouri. He asked what had happened to the right leg of the suit, and I told him the story of the Wheelie-Popping Contest.

"Oh, by the way," he said, "I have your 4 December 1969 Distinguished Flying Cross medal and Air Medal—and the citations, too. You're welcome to have them back for what I paid for them--$100 for the party suit and $250 for the engraved medals and citations."

"No thanks," I said, and hung up.

How did my personal items end up at an auction in St Louis? After some checking with the neighbors back in Tucson, I found out that Paula had stuffed all my personal memorabilia—clothes; models of the planes I had flown that had been engraved and presented to me from the various aircraft companies; all my records, maps, photos, mission logs, gun camera film, and other items from my three times in Vietnam; medals;

A photo of my 510th TFS purple party suit sent to me by Will Schaefer. Pilot wings and my name are embroidered over the left breast pocket; BUZZARDS over the right pocket; our squadron patch on the right pocket; captain bars on the shoulders; and a party patch on the right arm. Note the chewed up and repaired right leg from the infamous "wheelie-poppin' contest!

citations; trophies; plus other keepsakes—in cardboard boxes and left them out in the empty garage when she sold the house and moved away. What happened after that is unknown, but obviously some items reached collector's hands at that auction in St Louis. I was less than six hours away in Las Vegas at that time, but she never let me know. That woman was so nice...

As a side note, I was at home recently, working on the computer with Steve, when the phone rang. It was Sunday night, 9 February 2003. The man introduced himself as Will Schaefer from Massachusetts. He explained that he had acquired my purple party suit and two medals from the individual a few years back, had packed them away, and had just found them again while repacking for a pending move. He told me he had been in the Army and knew what these medals must mean to me, so he wanted to return them to me! However, he said he wanted to keep the party suit. It was the best of the five he has, because it has my letter of explanation as to what happened to it along with a little history of those bygone events.

I gave him my address, and he sent the medals to me Priority Mail. I received them on 14 February, and they're finally back home after twenty-three years! I sent a reward back to Will for his thoughtfulness. It's a great comfort to know there are still people out there who understand right from wrong. He also sent a picture of my party suit on 2 January 2004 that he has as a centerpiece of numerous displays he sets up. It is shown here, and it was also the first time in over twenty-four years that I had seen it. Thank you again, Will Schaefer.

As another side note, Will and I continued to correspond, and in 2007, he told me that he was planning on donating the party suit to the USAF Museum at Wright-Patterson AFB, Ohio if they wanted it. That sounded like a great idea to me. They came back with a positive reply, and that's where the famous purple party suit is today—an important part of our Air Force history and those bygone days preserved and displayed for all to see.

By now, as we used to say in our business, my "fun meter" was pegged. My tolerance for pouring money into a relationship that wasn't had reached a new low. Reality set in. I remembered my conclusion from a few years back: "No relationship is better than a bad one." I filed for divorce, and Sun Ye and I went our separate ways in January 1987. She remarried shortly thereafter. I decided to finish out my Air Force career and become a bush pilot up in Alaska—far away from people. But it was not to be. I was about to have another life-altering experience.

The phone rang in my office one day in late 1987. "JayBird?" the caller asked.

"Yes?" I replied.

"This is Kirby from the Headhunter Squadron," the caller said. "I was in the Squadron during WWII, and we are having a reunion in Williamsburg, Virginia on May 19-22. We're inviting all the Juvats, and wanted to know if you would like to come?"

What a great opportunity! This Squadron that I had been the commander of had a great history, and here was a chance to meet some of those people who were legends from its early days.

"I sure would!" was my reply. It turned out that Marion Franklin "Kirby" Kirby was an Ace from the 80th Fighter Squadron in WWII, and was now in the process of building a master roster of as many of the people from the Squadron as possible—from its beginning in January 1942 to the present day. I gave him my mailing address, and we started corresponding back and forth on different Squadron matters, including adding names of the guys in the Squadron with me in 1979 - 1980 to the Roster.

In 1969 Kirby had received a phone call from two of his Squadron buddies, Lt. Gen. Jay T. Robbins, another Ace with twenty-two aerial victories, and Norb Ruff. Both were feeling no pain, from what Kirby tells me. Anyway, they just wanted to call Kirby and say hello and talk over old times from WWII in the 80th. They said, "Why don't we all get together and have a reunion?"

Kirby replied, "I'll do it!"

80th Ace M.F. "Kirby" Kirby in his WWII leather flight jacket with an original 80th Fighter Squadron patch of Donald Duck dumping a chamber pot on the Japanese Rising Sun. After this photo was taken, Kirby took his jacket off and presented it to me as a gift for our Association. (Photo by Bob Kan taken at the Washington, DC reunion 6 April 2001)

That was how the reunion group got started. Kirby began tracking people down by old rosters, Squadron orders, telephone information service, and so on. Remember, this was before the days of the computer! One year later in 1970, the WWII members had their first reunion in Jackson Hole, Wyoming—a fantastic get-together! They decided to have reunions every two years after that; changing to every eighteen months after a few. In a few years the Korean and Vietnam-era people were included and added to the roster and reunions. Now, in 1987, they were adding the "Juvats" to the group—the newest Headhunters starting in 1971.

On 15 February 1971, the 80th had moved from Yokota AB to Kunsan AB, Republic of Korea. After a few months, the 80th was in the process of being deactivated. Fortunately, former "Headhunter" Lt. Gen. Jay T. Robbins, who was Vice Commander of Tactical Air Command at the time, caught the action and rescued us at the last minute. Instead, we were re-staffed with new personnel, primarily from the 391st Tactical Fighter Squadron. The 391st Tactical Fighter Squadron's insignia was a tiger's head on an inverted triangular green background. Below the patch, on a rocker, was the 391st motto "AUDENTES FORTUNA JUVAT" which translates from the Latin: "Fortune Favors the Bold." As the new Headhunters removed their old 391st patches, they grasped the triangular patch by the upper left hand corner to tear them off. All tore off except the word "JUVAT." It caught on immediately. The harder the higher echelons attempted to stamp it out, the more entrenched it became—even to the point of covering the Wing Commander's flight suit with "JUVAT" patches each time he hung a flight suit on the line to dry! The motto has also been adopted by the Squadron, with very common usage.

My next encounter with poor drivers happened in early 1988 with my brand new 1988 Toyota Camry. I was on Ft. Benning stopped at a red light in front of Martin Army Hospital heading east. I needed to make a left turn at that light, but there was no turn lane. When the light turned green, I started to move to the center of the intersection to wait for a chance to make my left turn. The car behind me started to move also, but didn't see me stop. He rear-ended me, and at only about five or six mph, it was enough to knock my sunglasses into the back seat! Luckily, I had my headrest up and adjusted correctly—these are extremely important. We got out and checked damage. The front of his car had a lot of damage, but the rear of my Camry had *none.* Toyota advertized back then that their Camrys had five mph bumpers—they could withstand a hit at up to five mph without damage—front and back! Incredible. It was true, but I would test it again.

I went to that reunion 19-22 May 1988 in Williamsburg, and had a great time. I finally got to meet Kirby, Gen. Robbins, Norb Ruff, Paul Murphey, Lou Schriber, Yale Saffro (who drew our original Headhunter logo in April 1943) and a host of other greats from our WWII, Korean, and Vietnam era people. I was sold! Those terrible years of the early 1980s were over.

Chapter 16
Happiness at Twilight – 1988 - Present

*K*irby and I kept corresponding by mail and over the phone, and we again renewed our friendship in person at the next reunion in Phoenix, Arizona, 7-10 September 1989. It was here he asked me if I would take over for him and keep the group going. I agreed.

Kirby held the reins for twenty years, lining up hosts for the reunions, and keeping the organization together— before we had dues. He would pass the hat at each reunion to get donations to pay for postage, printing, etc. until the next reunion. It would cost thousands—he collected a couple of hundred from only a few of the same people over and over.

Current patch of the
80th Fighter Squadron "Headhunters"

I was now the "Head Headhunter." We started dues of ten dollars a year. We publish quarterly newsletters (usually twelve pages in length), a 1,960-person Master Roster, a 675-person master email list, have reunions every eighteen months around the country, have a Headhunter Store with different Squadron goodies, etc. We have over 1,000 members from WWII, Korea, between the wars (BTW), Vietnam, and up to the present-day Juvats. We also incorporated as a non-profit

Veterans' Association—the 80th Fighter Squadron Headhunters Association, Inc,—and started our own web site on the Internet. It is a great organization, and we continue to this day with our reunions every eighteen months. The Association is still my full-time job, and Kirby has kept his promise to double my salary every year since I took over!

In early 1990 I was out playing tennis and ran into a guy that was on our same tennis team. He was with a very attractive lady, and I thought how pretty she was. Unfortunately, she had a wedding ring on, so she must have been married. Bad luck. Her name was Bonnie Rose—like the flower.

But now, for the second time in three years, I was about to encounter another major fork in my life—another life-altering experience. I played more and more tennis on different men's teams, and started winning some matches in doubles with Sidney and others. These were good times.

One day in the summer of 1990, Sidney asked if I wanted to go play golf. Although I didn't play much, I knew he didn't, either, and I enjoyed the game whenever I did play. I told him, "Sure!" He asked if he could bring a lady friend along to ride around with us—someone that he played tennis with a lot. "Sure—okay with me," I said. We decided on a date and time.

I met Sidney at the Ft. Benning golf course that day, and the lady friend who came to ride around with us? Bonnie Rose— like the flower. I couldn't believe it! I was very happy to see her again. She had a wedding ring on, but she told me she was a widow of an Army officer.

The three of us had a great time that day playing golf, and the way Sidney and I played, we kept Bonnie laughing all afternoon with our "automatic ball returns" from bouncing back off a tree or maintenance building after teeing off. Neither Sidney nor I had ever made the PGA Tour, nor the Masters, if you know what I mean…

When we were back in the clubhouse after the game, I asked Bonnie for her phone number. The rest is history. When I wanted to marry her, her five grown children, Jim, Kathy, Steve, Donna, and Bill asked me to submit a résumé for consideration! That bio is included at the end of this book. I guess it was approved, as Bonnie and I have been together ever since. Even my first wife Carol told me after meeting her at a family reunion in July 1993, "You finally got it right." A nicer complement could not have been given. My plans to be a bush pilot in Alaska had evaporated. Bonnie and I would stay here in Columbus, Georgia.

I remember the first time I met Kathy. It was September of 1990. She is a Flight Attendant for Delta Air Lines stationed in Atlanta. She had flown in to Columbus from a trip to see us and to meet me. Bonnie and I drove over to the airport to pick her up and bring her back to the house for a couple of days. I was so nervous at the airport that I left the keys in the ignition and locked us out of the car! She must have thought, *"You got yourself a real winner here, Mom!"*

The first time I met Steve was equally embarrassing. It had rained quite heavily one fall afternoon, and I drove through a flooded street on Ft. Benning a little too fast. My 1988 Toyota Camry coughed, sputtered, and just before it quit, I was able to urge it into a parking lot. I called Bonnie, and she said Steve was there visiting, and he would come out and fix it for me. Sure enough, Steve came out, we met, and he proceeded to unsnap my distributor cap, dump the water out, dry it out, and put it back on. As with everything he does, it worked fine after that. He was probably thinking to himself, *"This great fighter pilot can't even dry out his own distributor!"* I must have made quite a first impression with everyone.

On my way to the office at Ft. Benning on my last active duty day—31 March 1992

Bonnie and I hosted the 80th Fighter Squadron Headhunters' Reunion in Myrtle Beach, South Carolina, 21-24 April 1991. Mom was still living in Garden City just south of Myrtle Beach, so we went to see her every couple of months. It gave us the chance to have the reunion there. It was a good one.

I retired from the Air Force on 1 April 1992 after thirty years of active service. The Army had a retirement ceremony for me at Ft. Benning, and the Air Force supplied a guest speaker and a four-ship fly-over of F-16s. It was a happy day, but it was also a sad day. Never again would I climb into the cockpit of an Air Force fighter. Many of my friends have asked me why I'm not flying anymore. I tell them I want to remember flying the way it was. Anything else, to me, would be a very significant step backwards...except maybe an ultralight! I've been very interested in these beautiful little birds for years.

Maybe one day I'll try one. I've heard from many people they are as much fun as a fighter. We'll see.

Mom flew down to Columbus for my retirement. She had been living alone in her doublewide mobile home in South Carolina since Dad passed away in 1973. It was her first trip to Columbus. We all had been talking for a year or two about Mom needing to move closer to my brother, Paul, or me. She was now eighty-eight, and she wasn't as independent as she was a few years earlier. Paul and his family were retired and on their way to Idaho, so she was leaning more towards staying in the East by us.

Prior to Mom coming in for the retirement, Bonnie had shopped around, and found a beautiful one-bedroom apartment in a great retirement home here in Columbus. We took Mom over to see it, and much to our surprise, she liked it, and decided to move here. Bonnie and I met Paul and Mae at Mom's home two weeks later on 15 April, rented a U-Haul truck, loaded all her belongings, and moved Mom to Columbus. We all unloaded and moved her in. She was here to stay.

When we were first together, Bonnie and I lived in her beautiful old brick home in Columbus. It was only a block away from the Country Club and its tennis courts. Regrettably, the house was just a little too small for us and any company we had. We needed to find a new home. Bonnie started looking, and we went to see a few houses that we heard were available. None really caught our eyes.

One day in early August 1992, Bonnie told me she had found a house that she wanted to show me. She had seen the ad in the newspaper and had gone to see it that afternoon while I was at Benning. The next day we drove out to the two-and-a-half-acre property to take a look. It was a house on a lake in a wooded subdivision on the north side of town. Although there were other homes in the area, none could be seen from this lot because of all the trees—just beautiful. As with Bonnie, I fell in love with it as soon as we drove up the 100-yard long driveway from the short little dead-end street. We bought the house, and moved into our new home that September just prior to the Headhunter Reunion in San Antonio later that month.

One of our greatest joys is having coffee on our back porch, and we enjoy watching different kinds of animals and birds as they come around our feeders and birdbaths. It's always a thrill to see a new bird or animal for the first time in our yard. If you told me thirty years ago that I'd be watching birds on my back lawn in my retirement, I would've laughed in your face. I never thought I'd be a bird-watcher, but as we grow older, our priorities change. It's a great way to unwind, and sometimes as I watch these different birds, I remember that little sparrow as it lay bleeding on the clean white snow back in 1948. That was not a good day for me, but it taught me a lesson.

With this new home, it is the first time I have ever had a dedicated room as an office, and now that I spend full time on our Headhunters' Association, I put it to good use ten to twelve hours a day. Bonnie keeps telling me that the top of my desk is dark brown wood—not eight inches of white paper. I guess I need to scrape it off once in a while—it does get pretty bad.

In 1993, I still had my '88 Toyota Camry and was driving home one afternoon from the store. As I was coming north on Whitesville Road at about 45 mph, a deer suddenly jumped out in front of me from woods on the right. There was no time to react as he slammed into the front of the car. Unfortunately, the deer was killed, but incredibly, no damage again to that Camry! That was going to change a few years later in its ultimate test.

In the Fall of 1993, Kirby called me one day and said that he and five other WWII Squadron pilots were going up fishing at a camp in northern Minnesota for five days. He said they would like to invite me to go with them. What an honor! I immediately thanked him and said I would be truly honored to go. It was set for a couple of weeks later in September. We were all to meet in the Minneapolis-St. Paul airline terminal, and then drive up to the camp together. The camp was owned by one of the guys, Harrison "Sad Sack" Freeman.

Kirby had set up the whole trip, and wanted them to get to know me better, and vice-versa. He had also asked another WWII Ace, "Corky" Smith from Brooklyn, to go with us, but Corky had to cancel at the last minute due to sickness. That was too bad, as I had never met Corky, as I had the others at the last reunion in San Antonio in October 1992. I had talked with him on the phone, and, as it turned out, that was as close to meeting as we would get. I remember his thick Brooklyn accent. Corky passed away only a couple of months later.

The six of us at Freeman's camp on a large lake in northern MN. (L-R) Norb Ruff, Paul Murphey, Kirby, Mark Kasper, & Harrison Freeman. I took the photo. What a fantastic honor it was for me to be invited to go with them.

As it turned out, we didn't do any fishing, but we didn't care. We all had a great time playing golf and just being together telling "war stories" at each other.

On one of the nights, Kirby said that he would cook dinner for all of us. We could hardly wait. As it turned out, Kirby went to the store and bought a couple of frozen pizzas to warm up in the microwave. All went well, until he took them out of the oven—he had forgotten to take the plastic wrap off the top of the pizzas, and the heat had melted the plastic and fuzzed it to the top of the pies...what a mess! He joked and said that was the way they were supposed to be—gift-wrapped!

Freeman had arranged a pheasant hunt for us with a friend of his on the friend's property. Lots of fun, and the beautiful birds were fast frozen so they could be taken home. (L-R) Paul Murphey, Freeman's friend, Freeman, Norb Ruff, JayBird, & Kirby. Mark Kasper took the photo. I held a bird, but didn't shoot any.

Jay E. Riedel

We all had a good laugh, and managed to scrape off most of the melted plastic before devouring both pizzas in record time. It was also decided, by unanimous vote, that Kirby would no longer do any cooking. Kirby and I joke about his "gift wrapped" pizzas to this day. What memories. As I write this addendum today, 21 August 2009, all of those WWII heroes on that trip in the photos are gone except Kirby. He was 90 on 14 July of this year.

In February 1994 we had a lot of rain here. So much that our lake rose to its maximum of four feet above normal and flooded its banks as the excess water poured over the earthen dam spillway. While we were walking along our bank looking at the flooding, Bonnie and I found about thirty mallard eggs that had been washed out of their ground nests. We weren't sure what to do with them, so we decided to try and hatch them. We knew we had to keep them warm, but that was the extent of our knowledge. We carefully put the thirty eggs in an old suitcase and placed a heating blanket on top of them. Nothing ever happened, and we finally decided the heating blanket was way too warm.

A few weeks later we found some more eggs, and we decided to do it right this time. We purchased an incubator from a local feed store, read the directions, and put the eggs in for the thirty days to hatch at exactly the right humidity and temperature of 99.5 degrees. Sure enough, thirty days later, six baby mallards hatched! What a sight to watch the process of hatching from an egg—it's a true miracle. This was the beginning of our extremely gratifying hobby of raising ducks.

The first thing the baby ducks see that moves is usually "Mommy!" They imprint on it and become quite attached. We made sure it was Bonnie as we each peered through the small incubator window to see our new hatchlings. After they fluffed

295

out and became strong enough to walk around normally in about twelve to eighteen hours, we took them out and put them in a small area in our back sunroom. We put down old towels we called "diapers" over a waterproof plastic sheet and placed a carton box on its side with a forty-watt red bulb through the top for constant heat. We also put in a small dish of water and some special waterfowl starter feed. They were set for the next eight weeks.

Baby ducks are quite easy to raise. After they have been removed from the 99.5-degree incubator and are about twenty-four hours old, they are about ninety-five percent self-reliant. At that age they can walk, run, eat, drink, swim, swim under water, and generally enjoy life on their own. The only things they need and require at that age is warmth and protection. However, even without being taught by their real mother, they can spot a hawk high in the sky and make a low whistle to warn the others. Of course, they are a little afraid of butterflies at first, too, but they readily learn the difference.

When they were a few days old, we took them outside and introduced them to a child's plastic five-foot-diameter wading pool full of water. As the saying goes, they took to it "like ducks to water!" They loved it—jumping in and out, diving under water, and running around the outside of the pool like little kids! What a joy to see as Bonnie and I sat there with our coffees and watched the kids play.

We now found out these little ducks would follow us wherever we would go. So instead of picking them up and carrying them outside, we would just open their closed-in area on the porch, and they would line up and follow us through the house, jump down the one step into the enclosed carport, and out to their pool. We had a little ramp arranged for them to go up and down for ease of getting in and out of the twelve-inch-deep pool, so as soon as they saw the pool, they would run to it, run up the ramp, and jump in. The first few minutes of their arrival would be their exuberant running, jumping, splashing, and swimming under water to celebrate their joy—getting us soaked in the process. What a sight!

After a few weeks, we walked down the back lawn to the lake about 200 feet from our back porch. Of course, these six little ducks followed us without hesitation. When we got to the water's edge, they stopped momentarily to check out this new experience. Depending on the conditions and their age, Bonnie or I would have to put on our waders and walk in before they would venture out into this vast unknown. However, after a few minutes, they were again at home foraging for food along the bank and playing with weeds.

Bonnie and I even got our small rowboat out, and, using our quiet electric trolling motor, headed out into the fifteen-acre lake. Right on cue, the six mallards started swimming in tight formation after us. We took them around and showed them the little inlets all around the small lake before bringing them back to our bank of our back lawn. They quickly became quite confident in their abilities to do all that on their own, so they started venturing out by themselves in another day or so. They were growing up.

At about eight-weeks of age, after practicing flapping their wings to build up their muscles, or as I referred to it as "revving their engines," for two weeks prior, we could tell they were ready to fly. We walked them around back and then started running down the back lawn toward the lake. Again, right on cue, they started running after us, then lifted off and flew past us the

200 feet and landed in the lake! They were quite impressed with their new capability—they could *fly!*

It was at this stage that they became very independent. After another day, when it was time to go back to the house, they would slowly come up the bank and start following us up the

Family picnic in July 1994 in our backyard by the lake. (L-R) Daughter Donna; son Bill's wife, Gayle with their daughter Stephanie; Bill; son Jim's daughter, Nina; son Steve; Gayle's daughter, Tiffany; Bonnie, Mom, Jim; daughter Angie visiting from Las Vegas; Jim's other daughter, Lisa (in front); and daughter Kathy. Photo taken by me.

lawn, but after about fifty feet or so, we could see "the call of the wild" was pulling them back. They slowed down, stopped, turned around, and, looking back over their shoulders to us, ran back to the lake. They were ready to spend their first night outside on their own.

Their first night out was a learning experience for all of us. They didn't pay any attention to us when we were trying to bring them in for the night a few hours later. They were too busy doing their own thing out on the lake, and they put us both on "ignore."

About nine o'clock that night we decided to go back out to see where they were. It was very dark. We walked down to the lake with a flashlight and started calling them.

"Peep! Peep! Peep!" They immediately answered us from an inlet about a hundred feet to the left around the bend from our bank. We started walking toward the sound, and so did they! *"Peep! Peep! Peep!"* they cried in their young duck, high-pitched cry. As we walked along the bank toward them, we could hear them getting closer and closer. We finally saw them swimming around the bend to meet us. They were scared to death! *Now* they didn't hesitate a bit to come to us, climb up the bank, and follow us all the way back to the house, into the carport, up the one step into the house, through the house out to the sunroom, and into their blocked-off area and cardboard box home of the past eight weeks—all at "fast forward!" We could tell they were relieved to be safe at home. They settled down, walked up on their pillow under their heat lamp, and were sound asleep within ten minutes. Those big, tough, brave teenyboppers weren't quite ready to leave home—yet!

However, they did a couple of days later, and although they would answer us from across the lake when we called them for a few months after that, they became more and more wild and distant from us.

We were addicted! Our experience with our six little mallards in 1993 was so much fun and rewarding that we wanted to do it again—but this time with some other kinds of ducks—

namely, wood ducks. Bonnie and I had read in our book on North American waterfowl that these beautiful ducks were native to our area, but we had never seen any on our lake. We decided to try to raise some of these, and ultimately release them to build up a significant presence of these beautiful ducks in our area.

We found an ad in a newspaper for wood duck eggs from a lady about a hundred miles from us. We ordered six eggs from her, and when we received them in the mail, we placed them in

Our first Woodies raised to full maturity. (L-R) Bitey-Baby, Cuddles, and Rocky visiting with us on our deck on 15 August 1995.

our incubator and waited the thirty days. Unfortunately, wood duck eggs are quite sensitive, and being bounced around in the mail was not the best thing for them. Only one of the six eggs hatched—it was 17 May 1994. We named this beautiful little wood duck—our first—Woody.

Woody was quite different from the mallards we had raised the year before. This little guy bonded with us quicker and came running to us when we approached his box. When we took him outside when he was only a day old, he ran around so happily, and then jumped on one of our shoes to get a free ride as

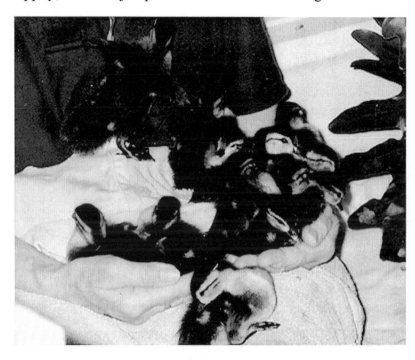

Twelve 4-day old Wood Ducks that we called the "The Wild Bunch." When they saw us coming, they would be so happy, they would run around almost in a frenzy! However, now it's nap time with Mommy.

we walked—as they do in the wild on their mother's back. We were so proud of him! We even took him up to Atlanta to show Kathy when he was only a couple of days old. Unfortunately, Bonnie and I still had a lot to learn about raising ducks.

When we checked on him the next morning after spending the night, he was near death in his box. We didn't know why. I picked him up and held him. He felt cool. I tried to warm him in my hands, but he didn't respond. He managed to get out one little peep before he died in my hands. This combat-hardened fighter pilot broke down and cried uncontrollably. It was 21 May. We had forgotten that newborn ducklings need to be kept warm—and wood ducks more so than mallards. We had left him in his box without a heat light all night. He had died from our neglect.

We still have little Woody preserved on top of our piano with a wood-burned sign next to him: "Woody—Our first Wood Duck— May 17-21, 1994—Our Little Friend who touched our

Our largest group—fifteen Woodies (one on outside of pool) enjoying their pool. They are about four weeks old here.

hearts in his brief 92 hours." We had learned a very simple lesson with very difficult consequences. Unfortunately we still had a lot to learn.

We checked around and found a lady up in Atlanta that had many different kinds of ducks for sale. We contacted her and found out she not only had Wood Ducks, but Mandarins, Blue Wing Teals, Green Wing Teals, Hooded Mergansers, and Ringed

Teals. Bonnie and I decided to get some more Wood Duck eggs, and we also bought two pairs of Mandarins, a pair of Hooded Mergansers, a pair of both the Blue and Green Wing Teals, two pairs of Ringed Teals, and three pairs of Wood Ducks. We rented a trailer and brought them all to our home in a large cage. After a few weeks for them to get adjusted to their new surroundings, we left the door open on their cage so they could venture out into freedom and swim in our fifteen-foot-diameter goldfish pond that was right in front of their cage. After a few days of enjoying the pond, they slowly made their way to the lake another hundred feet away and stayed around all summer. We walked down to the lake three to four times a day to feed them with waterfowl food in large clay dishes.

They all came over to our bank when they saw us walking down the back lawn. Food time! Murphy, our male Hooded Merganser, ran up the lawn to meet us halfway. He wanted to get fed first! He gobbled down the pellets as fast as he could before the others came up. He was a true clown. Although he has left as the others have, Murphy still comes back every November around my birthday for a few days. What a thrill for us to see our Murphy for a couple of days each year!

As I write this, on 25 November 2002, I was sitting on the porch with a cup of coffee, and sure enough—Murphy flew in and landed in the lake right in front of our house! He was back this year, too. He missed my birthday, the 19th, by only six days.

We named our pair of Green Winged Teals, Rusty and Dusty. Rusty, the male, had a beautiful rust-colored head, while his paranoid girl, Dusty, was smaller and, like most female waterfowl, quite plain brownish colored to blend into her surroundings while sitting on a nest. However, little Dusty took it upon herself to be the keeper of all eight food dishes, each spaced about two feet apart. She ran back and forth from one to the next, chasing all the other ducks from "her" dishes. This went on for at least half an hour until the others finally got in enough times to eat their fill—while Dusty ended up exhausted and not eating at all. Rusty would just look at her running back and forth, and you could immediately read his mind—*"What is the* matter *with you, girl?"* Bonnie and I sat on the lawn within three feet of these escapades, and we were kept constantly entertained by the show!

Bonnie with our twelve Ringed Teals in the summer of 1996. Notice the round white "ring" on the top and bottom of their wings. When they fly, their wings make a sound similar to a dove, and these rings are quite visible. What a sight as all twelve flew around the lake together. They are native to South America.

We also put up twenty-three Wood Duck nesting boxes around our property, as well as in another inlet a couple of hundred yards away. They look like giant bluebird boxes—about twelve by twelve by thirty inches. We have them mounted on four-by-four-inch poles, wrapped with aluminum sheeting to help prevent predators from climbing up, in the lake about six feet above the normal water level. There is a small ladder of wire mesh inside the box leading up to the entrance hole. This, along with the poles and boxes being set slightly tipped forward, allow the one-day-old chicks to climb up and jump out to their waiting mother swimming below them.

All of these new ducks use these nest boxes instead of nesting on the ground as Mallards do. Bonnie and I were out checking these nesting boxes one day in the early winter of 1997. We were cleaning them out and replacing the old wood chips used for bedding material with new in each of the twenty-three boxes to be ready for spring. The ducks use the boxes, but have no way of building nests as birds do. They depend on natural chips already being in woodpecker holes in trees, or in this case, man-made chips placed in the boxes for them.

When we opened one of our boxes in our inlet, we had the surprise of our lives. There, all by himself, was a one-day-old Ringed Teal! Ringed Teals, native to South America, lay eggs all year round because of the mild climate they're used to in their native land. Why was this cute little duckling all by himself in the box? Where was his mother and siblings? We had the answer as we reached in to pick up the little guy. He didn't see my hand as it slowly closed in on him. He was blind. His other brothers and sisters had hatched, and had left the box when their mother called them out. He had been left behind and abandoned. It was 9 November 1997.

This was the beginning of one of the most enjoyable times in our raising of ducks. This lone little duck, although totally blind from birth, was quite spunky—hence his name…Spunky. He looked completely normal. His eyes were clear and bright, but he never responded to any movement. There was no way he could survive in the wild on his own. We, of course, decided to keep him as a pet and raise him.

We set up his box with a warm light in our small hall bathroom that got little use—a perfect place for him. We lay old towels on the floor that we could change every day, along with his food and water. As he grew, he became aware of us and learned our sounds. He would stand still as we approached him and bent down with our hand. When our fingers were in front of him, we told him to "step up," and he would step up for us to carry him around. He loved it! As he got older his coloring confirmed our suspicions—he was a male. When he reached

"Spunky," our blind full grown male Ringed Teal by our goldfish pond in the summer of 1998. Ringed Teals are about a third the size of a Mallard.

maturity, Spunky was as beautiful and normal looking as any other Ringed Teal.

We took him to a bird ophthalmologist at Auburn University to have his eyes examined. After a close examination, they confirmed his eyes seemed normal, but concluded the optic nerve between the eyes and brain was not working—the images picked up by the eyes were not being transmitted to the brain. Many people asked us when they saw him, "How do you know he's blind?" Our answer was quite simple, "Because he *can't see!*"

Spunky rarely flew, as he didn't know where he was going. Therefore, we left him out in our enclosed carport with a two-foot-high fence to keep him from wandering off. Once in a while, neighbors' dogs or cats came by, but Spunky was never out at those times. There were also hawks, owls, coyotes, foxes, raccoons, and opossums, but we decided he was safe inside the carport.

Spunky getting ready to dive in our garden tub—one of his favorite pastimes!

Spunky was a great pet. Each night, as he sensed darkness falling, he stood by the door to come in the house. We would lie on our bed each night watching TV, and he would sit on the bed with us—happily listening to the TV. He also fixed his feathers, and then tucked his bill under his wing and went to sleep standing on one leg as ducks do. If we wanted to take him back to his room, and he didn't want to go, he would lunge blindly at us, trying to pinch us with his bill. Sometimes we would have to pick him up with both hands around his body to move him, as he would defy us by not stepping up on our hand when we tapped the front of his legs. He was truly "spunky" with a mind of his own.

He also knew where our shower and garden tub were, and he would walk into our bathroom, stand there in front of one or the other, and make his call to let us know which one he wanted to get into. He loved the water, and especially the shower! He would stand in the cool shower for as long as we would let him.

All of our ducks that we raise required one very important commodity — protection — until they can fly and be on their own. Spunky required it for his entire life, as he was one hundred percent dependent on us. We were about to learn this the hard way once again.

We went out one afternoon to visit our son Bill and his family here in town with Kathy and her family that had come in to

Spunky taking his daily shower! He loved to stand in the cool spray of our shower for as long as we would let him.

spend a few days with us. We left Spunky in the carport as we always did when we wouldn't be gone too long. Unfortunately, we stayed out much longer than we had planned—way after dark. We're not sure what had happened. Either Spunky decided to go "look" for us when we weren't there to let him in when it got dark and was caught by a predator, or some predator went over the two-foot-high fence and got him as he waited for us by the door. In any case, when we finally got home at 10:30 that night, Spunky was gone without a trace. We spent hours looking for him, hoping to find him hiding under a shrub, but with no luck—we only found two small feathers on our back lawn. Our beloved Spunky—an extremely unique pet—was gone. It was 23 June 1999. We were once again devastated by our ignorance and carelessness for allowing ourselves to let this happen. We didn't have dry eyes for many weeks.

In 1998, I was driving south on Whitesville Road heading into town. About a mile from our house, I saw some utility workers on the left side of the two-lane road clearing trees and undergrowth from under power lines. I stopped to ask them a question, and as we were talking, I received the hardest jolt I've ever felt in my life. A car had come up behind and rear-ended me at about fifty mph! I ended up prone in the driver's seat, as its back had been snapped. The rear of the car was smashed, and the trunk was now in the back seat. Luckily, I had my headrest up, as my neck would have been surely snapped.

I was quite dazed, and it took a few minutes for me to be able to unbuckle my seatbelt and sit up in the broken seat. The workers had to pry open the door, as it was jammed. When the ambulance and police arrived, I was out of the car, but sitting still trying to recover from that horrific shock. Luckily, the teenage boy who hit me wasn't hurt, only shook up. I asked him what happened, as there was at least a half mile clear visibility to see me. His reply? "I was changing my CD." Needless to say, my trustworthy 1988 Camry was totaled. This was my worst car accident in my life—and, I hope, my last.

In 2002, we took a year off from raising our Woodies. It just so happened this was a great year to miss, as our Woodies out on the lake were very successful in raising their own hatchlings. Twenty-four reached maturity that year—the most we have ever seen grow up on our lake. In 2001, only four Woodies survived to maturity on the lake. Although many more than that were hatched, they quickly disappeared due to hawks, large fish, turtles, and other predators picking them off one by one. It is very sad to watch a mother with fifteen newborns, then see her two hours later with twelve, the next morning with eight, and a couple of days later all by herself, but it's part of Nature. We always look forward to next spring and more eggs!

9/11 Remembered

*T*oday, as I'm writing this paragraph, is 11 September 2002—the first anniversary of the terrorist attacks on our country. As with the assassination of President Kennedy on 22 November 1963, I knew exactly where I was and what I was doing on 11 September 2001. I was home, still in my bathrobe, having my third cup of coffee in peaceful tranquility on our back porch when the phone rang. It was our daughter, Kathy.

"Do you have the TV on? Are you watching the news?" she said. I didn't have the TV on. Kathy said, "Turn the TV on, quick, a plane just flew into the World Trade Towers in New York!"

Bonnie had run to the store for a few minutes. I turned on our TV, and that first sight of the smoking tower was unforgettable. My first thought was, how could a pilot hit that tower in plain daylight on a clear day? But as I listened to the news, I knew it was no accident. Three other commercial airliners had been hijacked that morning, and this one, American Flight 11 with eighty-seven innocent men, women, and children on board, was deliberately flown into the North Tower. The Boeing 767 had struck at 0846. United Airlines Flight 175 with sixty non-combatants hit the South Tower six minutes later at 0852, and American Airlines Flight 77, carrying fifty-nine innocent people, rammed the Pentagon, while the forty very brave passengers and crew on board United Airlines Flight 93 fought with their hijackers and crashed in a rural Pennsylvania field instead of its most probable target, the Capitol or White

311

House in Washington, D.C. We also lost 125 people in the Pentagon that day, along with 2,647 in the World Trade Center Towers — 3,018 innocent people in all.

Some called this attack cowardly. I don't agree—no coward would hijack an airliner, kill the pilot and copilot, and fly it and himself into a building. No, these are not cowards—these are fanatics—people who march to a different drum—that have a different grasp of human life and decency than Americans. Our country and this world had been changed forever.

Epilogue

Well, that's about it. My seventy-plus years reduced to a couple of hundred pages—including pictures! It was quite a ride. I hope you all enjoyed reading this as much as I enjoyed recalling the memories and writing them down.

Bonnie & me in the fall of 2001—
Happiness at twilight!

I would also like to say that I am extremely proud of my three children, their families, grandchildren and great-grandchildren; and Bonnie's five children, families, grandchildren and great - grandchildren. We are both truly blessed to have such great and talented kids that we both love dearly. God bless you all, and may

God bless America.

MEMORIES OF A FIGHTER PILOT

I think I've known a million lads,
Who say they love the sky;
Who'd all be aviators,
And not afraid to fly!

For Duty, Honor, Country,
Their courage I admire!
But it takes more than courage, son,
To get to be a flyer.

When you are only twelve years old,
Of course you want to fly!
And tho' you know not what is Death,
You're not afraid to die.

But of the million, more or less,
All must have perfect eyes;
So only half a million now,
Can dream of future skies.

Then comes high school, science, math;
Some choose the easy way:
Football, cars, and dating girls;
Teen pleasures hold their sway.

And of the quarter million left,
One-half go on to schools;
The other half will dream and drift,
And never learn the rules.

Jay E. Riedel

Now comes the day of testing,
  Eight hours of Stanine Hell;
On every subject known to man,
  Four-fifths will not do well.

The one in five who pass this test,
  Apply for flying schools;
The Application Boards will now
  Eliminate the fools.

Then comes two days of nakedness,
  Flight Surgeons poke and prod;
To pass this Flying Physical
  One needs to be a God!

And now, five hundred lucky souls
  Will start their Pre-Flight days;
Endure demerits, hunger, cold,
  As upperclassmen haze.

One-half survive this mental game,
  And go to Primary schools,
But only half will hack the course,
  And move on to Basic rules.

Two hundred fifty now will try
  To pass those Basic tests;
Formation flight soon separates,
  The "tiger" from the rest.

MEMORIES OF A FIGHTER PILOT

One hundred twenty five will then
Pin on those pilot wings;
The best become hot fighter jocks;
The rest fly other things.

Some will die while learning those
Essential combat skills.
Some will die in combat;
Some will score their "kills."

But they have learned a lesson,
Sometimes lost on you and me;
We must always fight for Freedom,
Because Freedom's never free!

He's a knight in shining armor,
That the cruel tyrants fear;
He's that deadly drop of venom
On the tip of Freedom's spear.

Engaging him in battle is a course
That only fools would choose;
He's the world's fiercest warrior,
For he has the most to lose.

So when you see that fighter pilot
Standing at the bar;
Taking out the garbage,
Or tuning up his car,

You'd best walk up and offer him
Your thanks, extend your hand;
He's that rare "one in a million" who
Protects this sacred land.

(Author unknown)

Jay E. Riedel

This poem was originally dedicated to the memory of Brigadier General Donald R. Ross, USAF. He served in the 8th Air Force in Europe during WWII, flying seventy-two missions in P-47s and P-51s, prior to being downed and taken prisoner by the Luftwaffe. In 1953, he was a member of the 4th Fighter Wing flying F-86s in Korea, and was Commander of the 336th Fighter Squadron. He was Commander of Bartow AFB, Florida, 1960; Williams AFB, Arizona, 1961-1964, in Air Training Command, prior to being killed in action in an F-105 over Hanoi, North Vietnam, in 1967.

" *When once you have tasted flight, you will forever walk the Earth with your eyes turned skyward, for there you have been, and there you will always long to return.*"

---Leonardo da Vinci

Biography

Colonel Jay E. Riedel retired 1 April 1992 after thirty years of active service to his country. His last assignment was Senior Air Force Representative to the United States Army Infantry, Ft. Benning, Georgia.

Jay E. Riedel was born 19 November 1939 in Freeport, Long Island, New York, and graduated from Ithaca High School in June 1957. He received his Bachelor of Arts Degree in Mathematics from the University of Buffalo, Buffalo, New York, and his commission as a Second Lieutenant through AFROTC in July 1961. He also received a Masters Degree in Business Management from Auburn University, Montgomery, Alabama, in July 1974. His professional military education includes Squadron Officers' School in March 1968, and Air Command and Staff College in June 1974, both in residence.

Second Lieutenant Riedel entered the Air Force in March 1962 after spending eight months as a scientific computer programmer at Bell Aerosystems, Niagara Falls, New York, while waiting for his pilot training class to begin. He completed pilot training in March 1963 at Reese Air Force Base (AFB), Texas. He was assigned to KC-135 air refueling tankers in Strategic Air Command at Loring AFB, Maine, in August 1963 and served as co-pilot, Standardization/Evaluation co-pilot, and aircraft commander until October 1968.

After volunteering for "F-anything" (any fighter) in 1966, Captain Riedel received an assignment to F-100 school at Luke AFB, Arizona in October 1968 and was assigned to the 510th Tactical Fighter Squadron (TFS), Bien Hoa Air Base, Republic of

Vietnam in August 1969. When the 510th TFS deactivated in October 1969, Capt. Riedel was reassigned to the 615th TFS, Phan Rang Air Base, Vietnam, and served as an F-100 instructor pilot until July 1970.

Capt. Riedel returned from Vietnam in July 1970 and was assigned to the first United States Air Force A-7D squadron that was being activated at Myrtle Beach AFB, South Carolina—the 511th TFS that soon thereafter became the 353rd TFS. During this period, Capt. Riedel was an assistant flight commander, flight commander, squadron scheduling officer, mobility officer, and instructor pilot. In October 1972, Capt. Riedel deployed with the 354th Tactical Fighter Wing to Korat Royal Thai Air Base, Thailand, with the first Air Force A-7Ds in Southeast Asia, and he took part in the Eleven Day War of Linebacker II (19-29 December 1972) for the final bombing of North Vietnam.

During this period, Capt. Riedel also participated in the new Search and Rescue mission of the A-7D, and returned to Myrtle Beach in January 1973 to be Chief of Wing Training.

In July 1973, Maj. Riedel was assigned to the Air Command and Staff College, Maxwell AFB, Alabama, and graduated in July 1974. He was assigned as Chief, A-7D Operations Test and Evaluation in the 422nd Fighter Weapons Squadron, Nellis AFB, Nevada, until the A-7s were phased out of Nellis in August 1975.

Maj. Riedel was transferred to Davis-Monthan AFB, Arizona, in August 1975 and served as a formal course A-7D instructor pilot, and Assistant Operations Officer of the 354th and 357th TFSs; Operations Officer of the 358th TFS; and Chief of Safety, Tactical Training Davis-Monthan until October 1978.

Lt. Col. Riedel received an F-4D checkout at McDill AFB, Florida, from October 1978 to January 1979, and then was assigned to the 8th Tactical Fighter Wing "Wolf Pack", Kunsan

Air Base, Korea, in February 1979. He became the Operations Officer, then Commander, of the famed 80th TFS "Headhunters" until February 1980.

Upon leaving Korea, Lt. Col. Riedel was assigned as Chief, Operations Requirements Division at Headquarters Pacific Air Forces, Hawaii, in March 1980; and Deputy Director of Support Operations in March 1981.

In March 1983 he was assigned to the 474th Tactical Fighter Wing, Nellis AFB, Nevada, as Chief, Operations Plans Division and, upon promotion to colonel, Wing Chief of Staff. Col. Riedel was assigned to Ft. Benning, Georgia, as the Senior Air Force Representative to the U.S. Army Infantry in August 1985.

Col. Riedel's decorations include the Legion of Merit, Distinguished Flying Cross (V) with oak leaf cluster, Meritorious Service Medal with four oak leaf clusters, Air Medal with thirteen oak leaf clusters, Combat Readiness Medal with three oak leaf clusters, National Defense Service Medal, Armed Forces Expeditionary Medal, and the Vietnam Service Medal with seven service stars. A command pilot, he has logged more than 4,000 flying hours in the F-4D, A-7D, F-100, KC-135, AT-33, T-33, T-37 with stick time in the F-16. He has also logged more than 500 combat flying hours and 323 missions in three different aircraft in Southeast Asia between 1964 and 1973.

He was promoted to the grade of Colonel by a special board on 11 October 1984 with retroactive date of rank to 1 December 1982.

High Flight

By John Gillespie Magee, Jr.

Oh, I have slipped the surly bonds of earth
    And danced the skies on laughter-silvered
        wings;
Sunward I've climbed, and joined the
        tumbling mirth
    Of sun-split clouds—and done a hundred
        things
You have not dreamed of—wheeled and
      soared and swung
    High in the sunlit silence. Hov'ring there,
I've chased the shouting wind along, and flung
    My eager craft through footless halls of air.
Up, up the long, delirious, burning blue
    I've topped the windswept heights with
      easy grace
Where never lark, or even eagle flew.
    And, while with silent, lifting mind I've trod
The high untrespassed sanctity of space,
    Put out my hand, and touched the face of God.

Marge Bong Drucker, widow of America's "Ace of Aces" Maj. Dick Bong, summed up this beautiful poem best in her book, *MEMORIES The Story of Dick and Marge Bong,* with her words:

"Nothing ever written about a pilot's love of flying has been better expressed than the poem by John Gillespie Magee, Jr., 'High Flight.' Your mind soars with vivid imagination in the purity of his words.

This surely must be the drive for man to soar the skies, to unshackle himself from the binding forces of earth, to discover the vastness above the earth, unfettered, free and to realize the riches of that tremendous power.

The exhilaration of flying so eloquently expressed by Magee makes us understand more completely the love affair that pilots have had from the beginning as they 'danced the skies on laughter-silvered wings.'"

****

DISCLAIMER

Memories of a Fighter Pilot is a collection of as many of my personal recollections as I can remember that would be of a significant interest to most readers. They are as accurate as I remember them. However, due to the extended time lapse of many decades between now and the actual event, certain details may, in fact, be slightly different from my memory of the event. Any such differences are purely coincidental and not intentional.

Made in the USA
Las Vegas, NV
03 November 2024

11038757R10199